Th… Mu…ard Seed

Matthew, Chapter 13:31-36

"He presented another parable to them, saying, 'The kingdom of heaven is like a mustard seed, which a man took and sowed in his field; and this is smaller than all other seeds, but when it is full grown, it is larger than the garden plants and becomes a tree, so that the birds of the air come and nest in its branches.' He spoke another parable to them, 'The kingdom of heaven is like leaven, which a woman took and hid in three pecks of flour until it was all leavened.' All these things Jesus spoke to the crowds in parables, and He did not speak to them without a parable. This was to fulfill what was spoken through the prophet: 'I will open my mouth in parables; I will utter things hidden since the foundation of the world.'"

SEEDS of FAITH

An Inspirational Almanac

SEASONAL ESSAYS, RECIPES AND TIPS

Alaine Benard ✻ *Deb Anne Flynt*
Angie Ledbetter ✻ *Carol Schwartz*

Seeds of Faith - An Inspirational Almanac

ISBN 0-9723806-6-3

Published in the United States by

TurnKey Press
2525 W. Anderson Lane, Suite 540
Austin, Texas 78757
Tel: 512.407.8876
Fax: 512.478.2117
E-mail: info@turnkeypress.com
Web: www.turnkeypress.com

Cover Design and Layout by Gestalt Design Studio

First Edition: April 2003

10 9 8 7 6 5 4 3 2 1

We thank our husbands, children, parents, grandparents, siblings, and friends for their faithful prayers and support as we worked on this spiritual almanac.

Above all, we thank our project's patron–the Holy Spirit, with our guardian angels, and God for protecting, guiding, forgiving, and loving us all. We have been abundantly blessed.

Faith Through *the* Seasons

In the early spring of 2000, at the invitation of a mutual friend, Deb Anne Flynt joined Angie Ledbetter's faith based e-mail list, The Cajun Connection. Shortly after that, she joined a Christian women's health group. About this same time, Deb Anne noticed that several of the Cajuns were writers of one kind or another, and she began a Christian writers' group to which she also invited women writers from the health group. Angie and her twin sister, Alaine Benard, who was also in the Cajun Connection, accepted. A few months later, Angie and Alaine were persuaded to join the health group, and shortly thereafter, Carol Schwartz became a member. It sounds confusing now, but at the time it made perfect sense.

In this way, the Seeds of Faith writers originally met on the Internet. Several are also members of other groups together, but it was through these small groups that our bonds grew. We connected deeply through our common strength in the Father and our writing firmly took root from that seed.

The Louisiana twins met Deb Anne at the first annual Cajun Connection gathering in June of that year. In January 2001, the three finally met Carol in person. Through thousands of prayers and e-mails we already knew that the Lord was calling us to work together for him, and were fairly certain that it would be through inspirational writing-a gift that God gave us.

A working retreat left us with no doubt. Before we parted, our heads and hearts were brimming with ideas and hope. Our many prayers to know and do his will had been answered. That meeting at Lake Rosemound near

St. Francisville, Louisiana, gave birth to the beginnings of the book project that eventually became Seeds of Faith ~ An Inspirational Almanac.

Friendships begun in cyberspace were sealed with real hugs and parting tears upon leaving our gatherings. Ever linked through the wonders of e-mail, we have studiously planted, weeded, nurtured, watered, and harvested this work in the prayerful hope that readers will see themselves in these pages and benefit from our experiences.

We next met in May of 2001 in beautiful Lake Travis near Austin, Texas. The retreat was blessed with frequent prayer time, and especially with daily masses celebrated by friend and holy priest, Father Bob. Group friend, Dr. Betty Bosarge, encouraged our work by offering valuable editing suggestions and advice. We attribute our hurdling many roadblocks to her faithful prayers, along with those of friends and family.

We will count our work successful not by book sales, but in number of souls touched and brought closer to God. May this work plant seeds of faith, nurture saplings of inspiration within you, and help you sow to others. Our prayer is that you find fertile grounds and grow in faith, hope, and love. We will be with you in spirit throughout each season.

YOUR SISTERS IN CHRIST (YSIC),
THE SEEDS OF FAITH AUTHORS -

Alaine, Deb Anne, Angie, and Carol

Table *of* Contents

Spring

Summer

Autumn

Winter

For All Seasons

CALL *on the* HOLY SPIRIT

If you are having trouble finding balance in your life between the demands on your time and the desires of your heart, get help. In a world that seeks out easy answers, cure-all pills, and fast fixes, there are other, harder solutions which are much more satisfying in the long run, if you know where to look. There is a doctor who still makes house calls at any time of the day or night. He is the Holy Spirit, and you will get the best advice available from him. You may be directed to a certain person, program, Scripture passage, counselor, book, or situation.

Although the answer may not seem to fit the question you've asked, if you act in trust and faith, the power of the Holy Spirit will direct you in godly ways. Be open and be humble. Remember to always be thankful for your many blessings, and take care of those whom God puts before you to the best of your ability without completely running yourself down.

Pray for Christ to direct your way people who will benefit from your help, and if there seems to be no one coming, realize that perhaps Jesus is leaving you some time to take good care of yourself. If we want to serve others, we must first serve him and remember that he wants us to serve ourselves in ways that soothe our nerves, remove stresses, and recharge our batteries.

One way to put out the welcome mat for the Holy Spirit to enter your home and heart is to read or sing the beautiful hymn, "Come Holy Spirit." Pray from your heart and pay homage to the Lord. This encourages the Holy Spirit to dwell within us, and with that indwelling, we are given strength to accomplish much. What you do for others will be multiplied and returned to you.

Spring

MATTHEW, CHAPTER 13:23

"And the one on whom seed was sown on the good soil,
this is the man who hears the word and understands it;
who indeed bears fruit and brings forth, some a hundredfold,
some sixty, and some thirty."

Springtime Stroll with God

~ Carol Schwartz ~

When I begin my normal early morning walk through the park it is peaceful, quiet, and still dark in the Louisiana springtime. There is a warm windy mist falling on my face. I walk slowly at first and then pick up the pace as I start to breathe deeply. The walk gets comfortable and my mind wanders to my morning prayer and meditation. An old pastor at a retreat house in southern California once told me that prayer is talking to God and meditation is listening to God. I like those definitions.

My prayers are normally in the form of asking God to answer prayers for others, to heal sick friends and family, to help someone in need of a job, to ask for knowledge of his will for the day and his power to carry it out, and to thank him for his many blessings.

This particular morning my mind and heart wander back to the day I stood at 13,480 feet at the junction of the Mt. Whitney and John Muir trails in the California Sierra Nevada Mountains. It had just begun to snow and we could see the blizzard blowing in from the west. It seemed like just minutes ago we had stood on the crest at 13,777 feet, looking at the spectacular view in all directions.

I was only two miles from the summit of the highest mountain in the lower forty-eight states. There was still another 1,017 feet of elevation gain to reach the very top at 14,497 feet. Hiking goes ever so slowly at this elevation. It was decision time. My heart wanted so much to push on to the summit. This was my dream!

It had been my dream ever since friends-Marie and Bob, Jacque and Sid, and later Randy and others-inspired me to give up smoking and drinking and choose a better way of life. When I first started training I could barely walk, let alone run a block, without coughing and hacking from the cigarettes.

And here I was on top of the mountain, close enough to touch my dream. I stood with my aerobic shoes, sweats, an old wool scarf tied tightly around my neck, and a new Gore-Tex coat with gloves, weathering a storm on Mt. Whitney.

I looked up and smiled as my friend Mike took a picture. All of a sudden I got the strangest sensation, almost as if I could reach up and touch the face of God. It was such an extreme spiritual experience that tears streamed down my face. It reminded me of my friend Bob, who talks about his poster that says, "If I reach up as far as I can, God will reach down all the rest of the way." Gratitude overwhelmed me!

How can anyone look at such beauty and deny God? It was springtime in the Sierra Nevada Mountains. Flowers were blooming, birds were singing, and a light breeze was blowing soft snowflakes about my face, and yet I wasn't cold.

A Forest Service ranger chasing everyone off the mountain due to inclement weather interrupted my reverie. A bad storm was blowing in and they were expecting three feet of snow within a short period of time. Mike and I dejectedly picked up our packs and hiked the three miles back to our tents. We quickly pulled everything together and headed down the mountain. As we rounded the last corner on the mountain, after a record time of descending the last five miles, I looked up for one last view.

Her majesty, Mt. Whitney, was not to be seen! Black clouds crowded her peak, making us grateful that we had heeded the ranger's warning. As we drove back to Lone Pine in silence, my heart was heavy and light all at the same time. The gentleman at Whitney Portal Store who'd climbed this mountain many times relayed to me that he'd heard of other people having a similar experience to my own. He showed me a t-shirt, which hangs in my closet today, imprinted with the words "extreme experience." It mirrored my feelings perfectly.

I have yet to summit Mt. Whitney. However, maybe next year I will do so after I get settled in my new home in Boise, Idaho. This makes me recall how this new job all came about. Truly it is God's will. This job came to me as a gift of prayer and meditation.

In Matthew 7:7-8, God lets us know that if we "Ask, it shall be given you; seek, and ye shall find; knock, and it shall be opened unto you. For every one that asketh, receiveth; and he that seeketh findeth; and to him that knocketh it shall be opened."

These are God's promises. And oh, how many times I've experienced them in my own life and watched them come true for friends. Recently I wanted to move back to the West Coast to be closer to family and dear friends. I sent out thirty-plus resumes, wanting to transfer. I had a great interview with one department and was excited about it. I did not get that job, but I did receive a nice recommendation for another job.

I prayed about that job in my morning walks with God, asking only for his will to be done, dreaming of the beautiful mountains within thirty minutes of Boise. Oh, to be near the mountains, trek the trails, and train again for another attempt at making my dream come true to summit Mt. Whitney.

Now due to the new job, I have the chance, and you can be sure I will make that hike with God again.

The Sunshine of God's Great Love

The sun is shining bright today,
It warms my heart, mind, and soul,
To know He loves us all so much,
Never stops, as we grow whole.

The joy of spring is near,
All calm as I pray and walk,
The birds sing lovely this morn,
The Lord listens as I talk.

God's sunshine blesses us,
Red and blue sky greets the day,
In a walk outside in nature,
Ever listening to His way.

Let this day be mine to serve you well,
Your gifts I'd like to share,
With those who still don't know
Your love and endless care.

Thanks God for your great blessings,
I look skyward to above,
Abundant grace overwhelms me,
With the sunshine of your love.

Sunshine Salad

1 cup	Finely chopped walnuts
1 cup	Mandarin oranges
1 cup	Grated coconut
2 cups	Raisins
2 cups	Sunflower seeds
	Sweet poppy seed dressing
	Mixed salad greens

- Mix all ingredients except the salad greens in a small bowl. Lightly toss this mixture with your favorite salad greens. My preference is Italian lettuce blend.

- You may substitute finely chopped dates for raisins, or you can add sliced grilled chicken to make this salad a meal. Serve with warm homemade bread and butter for a spring delight.

This is one of my favorite springtime salads. All who've tried it really like it.

Nature's Bounty

~ Angie Ledbetter ~

Pulling into the dusty scout campgrounds, our nerves were frayed and still wired to the business of living, working, and schooling of the previous week. The hour-long drive hadn't helped us unwind, either. The three kids were overly rambunctious from keeping themselves in rigid quietness at school all week. Dad was still mentally going over the problems with the machines at work and the frustration of trying to get the children to help him pack and load all of the equipment needed for a weekend camp-out. Mom was tired from being the buffer between family members in the hours prior to leaving home.

As we drove over the graveled trail through the woods and around the huge lake to our assigned camping area, we all began to relax a little. The lush green of new growth enveloped us. The birds and squirrels scattered as we entered their territory. We rolled down the van's windows to inhale the deep, woodsy perfume and talked about all the exciting things we wanted to do over the next few days.

Cooking on an open fire, gathering wood for a huge bonfire after dark, hiking the nature trails, playing group games and races, whittling walking sticks, and enjoying scavenger hunts filled our heads. Now that we'd made it here, we were all more than happy to escape the confines and demands of city living.

We made camp in a nice area with woods at our back, not too close to the traffic that would dribble in through noon the next day. Our tent stood proud and tall, and our camping chairs, tables, and supplies made our site look homey. The kids ran off to find friends as we put on the first pot of coffee to brew. Drinking coffee made outdoors is one of life's simplest and most supreme pleasures.

"Yum! I smell something good cooking over there," called neighboring campers as they wandered over to join us. When do we ever take time out of our schedules at home to just sit among friends and visit?

Not nearly often enough. The peace was almost palpable as our small group happily chatted away. The kids ran wildly through the woods and trails with sticks, enjoying total freedom.

Our daughter came back to camp after a while with a sweaty, long face. She uncharacteristically came and sat on my lap, a pleasure that had become rare since she'd turned eleven. Drying her forehead with a napkin, I gave her a hug.

"What's wrong, Doodlebug? You don't look real happy," I questioned.

"The boys are being mean to me and calling me names. They are saying I'm too fat to keep up with them," she whispered as a tear slid down her red cheek.

"Baby, don't let them bother you. They're just boys." I tried to laugh it off, but inside, I was hurt for her. My attempts at advice sounded lame even to me.

"Some of the other girls will be here tomorrow with their families, and you'll have someone to play with then," I consoled. "Why don't you go see if you can find me something special in nature?" My diversionary tactics worked for the moment, and she shuffled away with her head down.

Lord, please give me the right words to help her, and please put a drop of your sweetness into the hearts of the kids who pick on my daughter, I silently breathed.

I'd gotten busy with supper and didn't see my girl return. In her little hands, she carefully held a small and perfect bird's nest. It held bits of straw, tiny pieces of litter, lint, and a swatch of yellow material woven into the small twigs and sticks.

"Mom, I guess birds are smarter than we give them credit for, huh?" she commented.

When I asked her what she meant, she said, "They are natural recyclers. They take the trash that we leave and make their homes from it. It would be neat if we did the same thing."

I took a moment to impress this little blessed moment upon my memory, and said a quick prayer of thanks for our sharing.

Before the "amen" silently escaped my lips, a boy ran by us and swerved over to bump into my daughter. "Watch out! You're so big you get in everybody's way!" he yelled out. I was too stunned to do anything but look at the bird nest now lying on the ground.

Taking a deep breath, I asked my girl to help me rescue our treasure. I tried to control the tears coming to my eyes by looking anywhere but at her crushed face.

Wrestling my emotions into control, I scooped up the nest and told her, "Hey, look, it's okay!" and gave silent thanks.

I hugged her to my side and asked her to come on a little walk with me down to the lake. We watched a beautiful orange and cotton candy-pink sunset finish off the day as we sat side by side. A light breeze lifted a small white feather from the nest and sent it out over the glassy lake.

"Baby, I know that others hurt you when they make ugly remarks, but you just have to try to forgive them and understand that if they weren't hurting inside, they wouldn't feel the need to be mean to others," I told my beautiful daughter.

"I know, Momma. I try to remember that, and that they are 'only boys' after all. It does hurt my feelings, though."

"I'm sure it does, but don't you ever forget that you are beautiful inside and out, and you have a lot of special gifts. They don't know that I had a disease when I was pregnant with you that made your body learn to absorb sugar in a strange way. But, we won't tell them, okay?" I continued our talk.

"And, Mom, it's a good way to help me learn who are good people and friends, because nice kids would never judge me by my weight," she hypothesized.

"You see how smart you are? How many kids your age could think like that? Not many, I guarantee." I smiled down at her.

"You know what else, Mom?"

"What's that, baby?"

"Cruel and mean people would not be able to see how pretty that bird's nest was with the sunset colors on it and the little feather flying away."

"Oh, baby, you are so right about that!" Thank you, Sweet Lord, for turning ugliness into beauty and for giving us these gifts that do not depend on the kindness of others.

"Come on, Momma. It's time to go back and get our song sheets out. I'm gonna sing that solo part you've been wanting me to after the campfire tonight!" my daughter announced with assurance.

"Girl, I know you will, and I can't wait to hear your angel voice!" Amen and amen.

Bird~Kid Feeder

4	Slices of bread
1 cup	Chunky peanut butter
1/2 cup	Honey
1/2 cup	Each: peanuts, pecans, almonds, sesame seeds, and sunflower seeds (shelled)

- Assemble ingredients in your kitchen workspace. Preheat oven to 400 degrees. Cut each piece of bread into four equal strips. Arrange on ungreased cookie sheet and toast until just brown, about three minutes in preheated oven. Turn oven to lowest setting and leave bread sticks in for two hours to dry. Leave longer if you like crunchier bread.

- Remove and let bread cool. Crush nuts and mix together in a bowl. In a separate bowl, blend peanut butter and honey well. With a small spatula, apply an even coating of the peanut butter/honey mixture to each bread strip. Dip sticky side down into the nut mix, and press down gently to cover the sticks thickly with nut mix.

- Place these delectable treats on your bird feeders, ledges, or your children's plates for a healthy after-school snack.

NOTE: Bird Feeder sticks can easily be hung from low branches. Make a hanger using needle and yarn or thick thread to form a loop in one end of the bread sticks.

YIELD: 16 snack sticks

FEATHERED FAITH

I wing across the azure sky
And soar beneath the clouds.
No need to ask the question, "Why?"
Nor ponder such aloud.

My Master sends me far afield.
He guides my every flight.
Body and soul to Him I yield
To be swept up on high.

I gather the seeds pointed out
Each day as duty calls.
And drop them carefully about,
With a prayer as they fall.

No need for frantic hurried pace
Or juggling of plans.
My seeds germinate with the grace
Extended from His hand.

I may not see the seedlings grow;
Fruition come to be.
It's not my destiny to know
If seed turns into tree.

Spring Fling

As budding flowers, plants, and saplings struggle to get their heads above ground, they are rewarded with the warmth of the sun's rays, a gentle watering from the heavens, and the sight of a whole new world. Dormancy is replaced by unfurling. We too can leave our winter hibernating behind and begin a new journey. One way to accomplish this is to notice things around us that we have taken for granted. There is no better place to see nature in all its glory than to abandon home and head for the camping grounds. When that's not possible, try one or more of these:

- Take note of a patch of wildflowers as you travel to work.
- Inhale the scent of budding trees, fresh-turned earth, or a fragrant candle.
- Fill your home with the aroma of gently bubbling soups, full of the treasures of the earth.
- Pray while you knead bread dough. Make your house work chores a time of prayer.
- Rejuvenate your senses and soul with a midday bubble bath.
- Treat your ears to a new tape or CD of uplifting music. Really listen to the words or notes.
- Start a new journal and note something fresh and new daily.
- Point new things out to your children and grandchildren.
- Begin a small crafting project such as a spring door wreath.
- Visit someone who does not have access to the touch, smell, sight, or sounds of the earth renewing itself because she or he is in a nursing home, prison, or hospital, or is shut in or just plain lonely. Bring to her or him a single colorful bulb or seedling planted in a small pot.

Gardener's Gift

To me You sent a simple gift
Filled with things so small.
Thanksgiving songs my voice did lift,
As my heart for help did call.

Your gift was seeds to plant and grow,
'Tho a gardener I'd never been.
But what You want and what I know
Are not always close as kin.

I soon forgot those tiny seeds
As life put them from my mind.
Years passed until I saw the need
And worth of Your gift so kind.

Those seeds I plant and help to raise,
Are flowers and fruit so sweet.
Your bounty brings from others praise
When You through my gifts they meet.

Small gardens bloom from that seed pack,
Yielding beauty and food too.
Lord, You're my garden's simple Host,
And I'm Your humble tool.

Bringing the Word into Nature

If you have a nature trail or park nearby, take a few close friends, maybe pack a lunch, and hit the trails for a day. Take along a Bible or book to stop and read once in a while, or a prayer book and rosary. Take your time, and enjoy the gifts of nature that God gives us. Listen to the birds, watch squirrels, and stop and smell the flowers-literally.

There's a real blessing in being alone with God, if there's somewhere safe to go alone; there is also a blessing in spending peaceful time with friends in communion with God. Either way, it's a special experience.

Quote to Ponder:

"Let us be grateful to people who make us happy;
they are the charming gardeners
who make our souls blossom."

~ *Marcel Proust*

He Sings to Me

~ Deb Anne Flynt ~

The Lord whispers to me quietly this early morning in the softness of violet-blue light that beckons me to join him in the hushed hours. I say my first prayers silently as I slowly get out of bed, careful not to disturb my sleeping husband.

As I dress in the half-light, the first birds begin their morning songs. I am grateful for the chance to hear them begin their daily chorus. This is our special time together-God's and mine. Too soon, I'll have to wake the children, and my day will become harried, but for now, all is peaceful. In the kitchen, I push aside the blinds and slide the back door open. Only the animals of the house join me. The air is fresh and woodsy and I inhale its fragrance as I walk into the woods.

The new leaves are still damp with dew. I walk further into the woods, allowing myself to be lost in the moment. A squirrel sees me as an intruder. He barks, chatters nervously, and throws an acorn at me, bringing me back to the present. It's time to turn homeward and begin the day.

Thank you, Lord, for this moment of peace with the birds to serenade my mind and your loving mercy to heal my soul of the scars from yesterday's battles. I am now ready to face this new day. Amen.

The Lord speaks to me vividly this midday, with the brightness of sunlight and the barking of dogs. The light streams through my kitchen window, warming a spot on the floor where my husband's kitten lies curled asleep. The butterflies beckon me to come out and play. I cannot resist. I step out the door and slide the screen closed behind me. Hopping down the steps, I wander into the woods. The sun plays hide-and-seek through the trees, the new spring growth tinges the light with green. My steps and my heart are light. Here and now, I am a child at one with nature. The birds are singing new songs, different than those heard early this morning. Now they sing brightly and happily. They seem to say, "Enjoy this day that God has made!"

Thank you, Lord, for this moment of joy, with the birds to cheer me and your loving face smiling upon me. I am ready to do your will. Amen.

Nature fusses at me this late afternoon, with the flashing and crashing of thunder and lightning. The cloud-darkened sky reminds me to listen to him. I neglected to do some things today, and if the electricity fails, I'll have more to do tomorrow. The wind-driven rain forces me to close the door and dry the puddle that came in and cooled the spot where the kitten had napped. The birds are now safely in their nests, sheltering eggs and young against the storm. I look out the door at the rain dripping from the trees. My children will soon be home from school, so I wait by the front door with an umbrella. I am grateful that the Lord has provided for my family, that we have shelter and that our needs are met.

Thank you, Lord, for this moment of darkness. Because of it, I appreciate the light all the more. I am ready to do my duty for my family, even if they don't seem to appreciate all my work. Amen.

The Lord hums to me gently tonight. I take one last walk of the day into the woods. Night birds are beginning to sing, low and bittersweet. Within minutes, my jacket and shoes are wet. I am drawn deeper into myself here, into my heart of hearts. There I find Jesus, waiting with open arms to dry my feet and my tears. The days are always filled with highs and lows, but everything is a blessing. I sit on a wet log and allow the dampness of the night air to wash away my petty concerns.

Thank you, Lord, for all you have given me this day. I am ready to rest, so I can start over tomorrow.

Now I lay me down to sleep,
I pray Thee, Lord, my soul to keep.
If I should die before I wake,
I pray Thee, Lord, my soul to take.

Amen.

EARTH SOUP

2-3	MEDIUM TO LARGE ONIONS
2-3	GREEN ONIONS
10-12	MUSHROOMS, CLEANED
1-2	CLOVES GARLIC (LESS IF PREFERRED)
16 OZ.	CAN BEEF BROTH PLUS ONE CAN OF WATER
1 POUCH	DRY ONION SOUP MIX
1 LB.	LEAN GROUND BEEF (OPTIONAL)
3-4	MEDIUM POTATOES, CLEANED AND UNPEELED (OPTIONAL)

- Roll the beef into meatballs about thumb-tip size. Chop potatoes, onions, and green onions (including tops) and slice garlic and mushrooms. Thoroughly brown the meat balls in a frying pan. Drain. (Keep the pan handy.)

- Bring beef broth, water, and soup mix to a boil in stockpot. Add meatballs, potatoes, and about one of the chopped onions. Cook at slow rolling boil for thirty minutes. In the frying pan, sauté the remaining onions, mushrooms, and garlic. Add them to the soup.

- Boil for another five minutes, just until flavors are well blended. Ladle soup into bowls, top generously with green onions, and serve hot with your favorite garlic bread. For an added treat, sprinkle soup and bread with shredded mozzarella (low-fat) cheese.

With Me Always

In places mystic
His presence I feel
While sunlight spills
Through windows artistic.

In everyday places
I hear His voice
In everyday noises
And feel His graces.

In church's splendor
He calls me from above
Asks for my love,
My will's surrender.

Here in this place, now
He calls me to action.
Ignoring distraction
I ask not "Why, Lord?" but "How?"

DEATH *of* THUNDERBIRD

~ *Alaine Benard* ~

Thunderbird lay mortally wounded, gasping for breath and surrounded by Tribunal members. Blood and tears soaked into the ground beneath his tormented body. Dust mixed with down still hung in the air above his struggles. His last request was to ask the Mighty One to forgive those whose beaks and talons had ripped him apart.

He tried to smile at them as confusion and pain swept him into the sweet light. "Oh, Mighty One, why do they hate me so? Please forgive them, I know they did not mean to hurt me."

"Close your ugly blue eye and die, misfit!" was the only comment accompanying T-Bird's passing. Spit and hateful curses bombarded his dead body. Thirteen perfectly formed, beautiful creatures admired their destruction. Several tribes were represented in the Tribunal, and none of them were of the same breed as the thunderbird. The Tribunal members' eyes were round and sepia, while T-Bird's had been almond-shaped and different colors, one azure blue and the other mossy green.

Tribunal members traded stories to justify their murder and convince one another that Thunderbird was a dissenter.

"The foolish bird refused to follow orders and caused troubles by his meddling!"

"Caw! Caw! Always trying to force us to listen to his plans!"

"He deserved his death, he tried to lead others away from the Wizen Ways-and always the liar he was!"

Jacor, the Tribunal member with an irritating conscience, spoke up. "With all the wrongs he did, should we not remember the good as well?"

The twelve turned in unison, staring menacingly at him.

"Hear me out!" Jacor stammered. "Remember how freely he gave when Foodgrowth ended? We were starving. He gave us his last hoard of seeds. Gave them all away!"

Tribunal members stepped in closer, hissing and clawing in the dust. "Watch your tongue, Jacor, your weakness is showing!"

He stood his ground and recalled the generous actions of T-Bird.

Others in the Tribunal brought up both true and false accusations to diminish Jacor's speech.

"Don't you remember the consummate lies he told?" They laughed and shoved each other and cackled gleefully at T-Bird's wild claims.

"The Mighty One talked to him!" "Caw! Talked to HIM!" they hooted uproariously. He had earned their fury when he swore The One had visited him to leave special instructions for the remnant tribes not succumbed to starvation.

Indeed, it was a gleeful remembrance shared when the Tribunal repeated T-Bird's wild stories to the Wizens. T-Bird's self-assuredness and refusal to conform to their authority was his downfall. The Wizens had never been ignored, nor would they abide it. This rebel had signed his own death warrant by speaking freely among his peers about such heretical subjects as visits from The Mighty One and his ancient teachings.

The hideous thunderbird perched grandly upon the platform mesa, hopping, whirling, and demanding total attention from the tribes. Without a shred of respect, he let out his shrill "SSSSssss Kkkkrrrrreeee!"

"I have been told by the One Mightier than All that he is displeased with our works. He ends our Foodgrowth season in warning so that we may change our ways and become a united tribe of faith and hope. The Mighty One would have us live in forgiveness and acceptance of each member, no matter our differences. We are equal, says he, and we are to disassemble our war councils and live in peace!"

The Wizens, being the leaders of all members, and also serving in various war councils, heckled the hungry youth without mercy. There was deep fear among them that T-Bird's warnings were truth. Slander soon turned into vicious fly-by pecking and pushing of the thunderbird. They finally succeeded in driving him from the mesa, where he flopped upon the parched ground, refusing to deny his claims.

His egg-mother prolonged his life by throwing herself over his sweating body. T-Bird's egg-father leapt forward to form a solid, silent barrier between the Tribunal and his family. Jacor, a secret believer in the Ancient Laws, diverted the attack by pointing out the changing features of the sky. Black, boiling clouds sped across the light of day.

In tears, the egg-mother held her wild one down. The egg-father pressed his weight into his son's wing, breaking it as he pinned him. With tears and no sound, the two exchanged a look that confirmed their worst sorrow: T-Bird would soon die. Despite the years of Ancient Teachings and love they had reared him with, his disobedience to the Wizens' law would bring his life to an end.

And so it came to pass. Three days later, out of fear and righteous indignation, the Wizens ordered the warrior put to death. The community, without the merest thought of thanksgiving or remorse, consumed T-Bird's body. It was their due.

His egg-family, along with Jacor, gave grateful homage for T-Bird's time among them. They placed one of his tail feathers upon the altar of The Mighty One. In mournful silence, they watched the sky signs as the malevolent thunderclouds gathered.

No-growth light and torrential storms held the tribes in deepening fear. All began to contemplate T-Bird's stories in their wet, empty coves. Unable to hunt for dried roots-all that remained of the earth's Foodgrowth-Tribunal and Wizen members begin to lose strength. For three days and nights they raged against the curse placed against them. In threes and fours, they tried in vain to plot against their neighbors-seen now as the next food source. The storms kept them from carrying out their missions, and so they each remained without rest, to keep from becoming the meal of those surrounding them.

In the glow of the last hallowed lamp, T-Bird's family and Jacor held vigil. They remembered the Ancient Teachings and gave proper homage to The Mighty One. In trust and belief, they praised with empty stomachs. They sacrificed their few treasures for the benefit of T-Bird's spirit as well as for the ones plotting murder. The three fell into peaceful rest when they placed the feather back onto the ledge.

This is the scene The One witnessed when he descended into their home. It touched his heart tenderly, and he was moved to tears. At the first tear, the sky burst into brilliant glory! The darkness gave way to light.

So startling was the New Day that all came out to witness it. Not stopping to glorify the gift, the tribes immediately looked about for their meal. Their neighbors did the same. Blood and tufts of flesh began to fly. The very air was filled with screeching and pain.

In his wrath, The Mighty One went among them with the Wing of Justice upraised. Upon seeing him, the Tribunal and Wizens fell to the ground in fright. They realized the truth was upon them and that this was their final due.

The three believers emerged from their place and bent, feather to beak, low to the ground. "Zhaaa, Zhuu. Zhaaa, Zhuu," the egg-mother cried her mournful song. At The One's feet, egg-father and Jacor joined their tearsong request to hers. They begged for his justice to spare the fighting members' lives. They offered their own in return.

The egg-mother lifted T-Bird's feather to the claw of The Mighty One. Seeing the faithful eyes upon his face, he could refuse her nothing. He accepted their gifts, both the feather and their faithfulness, into his palm. In great winds, his magnificence ascended into the golden sky.

As the blinding flash of The Mighty One's flight began to fade, the tribe witnessed a miraculous sight. Atop the mesa stood the warrior T-Bird, his feathers now pure silvery-white. The Wizens, the Tribunal, and the three joined their hearts in love. The Ancient Teachings now lived in their spirit, replacing the ways of war. In his perfect beak he held the gift of Foodgrowth seeds to share with all.

Humbled and trusting, they approached him in loving honor and thanks. He led them all in Praisesong as the seeds touched the newly fertile grounds.

"SSSSssss Kkkkrrrrreeee," they sang, while bright green seedlings burst forth from the efforts of loving hearts.

As Thunderbird turned to dance in the sun, the tribe admired his perfect feathers, all but one shining sterling. The longest, straightest quill supported one rumpled, dull gray feather.

And they gave thanks.

REFLECTIONS

Matthew 22:37-40

Mark 12:29

St. Thomas Aquinas, Summa Theologiae

Pope John Paul II,
Dives in Misericordia no. 14.2

The Face of God

Find His image, every creature,
Not only in perfection.
Turn thine eye toward each sight,
To see God's own reflection.

Praise the lonely winter tree,
Admire its branches broken.
In spring it blooms new purpose,
The Promise that's been spoken.

Taste the fruits of truth-filled life,
Abundant faith, hope, and love.
Share these gifts with the raven
As well as the white mourning dove.

Diversity Stew
(All the flavors of spring)

3 tbs	butter
3	leeks, white part only, thinly sliced
1	small onion minced
2-3	peeled potatoes, thinly sliced
2	carrots, thinly sliced
2 cups	water
1/4 cup	brown rice (Uncle Ben's 10-minute brown rice works well)
12	stalks fresh asparagus cut into 1-inch pieces
1/2 lb.	fresh spinach, finely chopped
1/2 lb.	cooked chicken, cubed (or seafood, beef, or pork)
4 tsp	salt
Dash	pepper
1 cup	half and half

- Sauté leeks and onions in butter until tender; add potatoes, carrots and water. Bring to a boil and simmer for thirty minutes. Stir in rice and asparagus and simmer for ten minutes. Add spinach and chicken, stir well, and simmer for five additional minutes. Add half and half and adjust seasonings to taste. Continue to heat on low for thirty minutes. Thicken with cornstarch if necessary. Makes four to six servings.

A WALK *with the* LEPERS

~ *Carol Schwartz* ~

"The political and journalistic world can boast of very few heroes who compare with Father Damien of Molokai- it is worthwhile to look for the sources of such heroism."

- GANDHI

It all started so long ago. Damien sailed for Hawaii in 1863, which is the time leprosy grew to epidemic proportions on the Islands. Damien, a lay brother, volunteered to join Sacred Hearts Mission in his ill brother's place, and he was ordained a Catholic priest the following year. In 1865 Kalawao, the north end of the rugged Kalaupapa Peninsula, was chosen as the site of the leper prison as it was surrounded on three sides by ocean and cut off from the rest of Molokai by steep cliffs, accessible at that time only by boat.

In 1873, when Father Damien turned thirty-three, he volunteered to live among the outcasts in the land of the living dead. When he first saw the lepers he was "frightened beyond belief." Within the week he wrote his superiors, "I am willing to devote my life to leprosy victims." In John 15:13, it is found that "no one has greater love than this, to lay down one's life for his friends."

The Church of St. Philomena's, which Father Damien built with his own hands before he died at the young age of forty-nine, was pretty much like it was back then. There were holes in the floors at the end of some pews, so those with open wounds could come, sit, and allow their wounds to weep into the ground and not ruin the wooden floors.

In 1888, when Father Damien became ill, Mother Maryanne Cope and other sisters of St. Francis of New York came to help. Her first response was similar to others, as she looked into the "face of horror that day," and stayed.

Mother Maryanne was responsible for bringing law, order, music, and hope to the place, primarily by separating young girls' living quarters from young boys', by scrubbing and keeping the quarters clean, and by giving care and love to the living and the dying. She introduced singing, dancing, and other games in the lives of the young girls so that they could have a semi-normal life in this "hell hole." She separated those without leprosy, hoping they wouldn't catch this dreaded disease. She planted trees, flowers, and gardens for fresh produce and beauty.

Among the many gifts delivered to her, Mother Maryanne received a piano and a poem from the famous poet Robert Louis Stevenson. The portion quoted below so typifies what I experienced when I visited Molokai:

To see the infinite pity of this place,
The mangled limb, the devastated face,
The innocent sufferers smiling at the rod,
A fool were tempted to deny his God.

He sees, and shrinks; but if he look again,
Lo, beauty springing from the breast of pain!
He marks the sisters on the painful shores,
And even a fool is silent and adores.

- Robert Louis Stevenson
"Songs of Travel and Other Verses - To Mother Maryanne"

It was not a normal day in Molokai. It was raining, windy, and cold. Of all days for me to have planned an airplane trip to the leper colony. I had serious thoughts about giving up my seat on the plane. I love to fly; however, those conditions made even me a little nervous. Of the month I was spending on this little Hawaiian island, I had less than a week left of vacation. So it was now or never to visit Kalaupapa.

The ride to the peninsula was rough, and I was grateful when we safely landed. I had arrived earlier than the rest of the bus tour folks, because I had flown down, so there was some extra time before the others arrived on mules via the steep trail.

Richard, the leper tour guide, local sheriff, and mayor, asked if I wanted to accompany him to gas up the bus. I was delighted. We got on a rickety old bus that sounded like it would fall apart any minute and drove to the gas pump a few blocks away. The peninsula is quite small.

As we drove up to the pump, I noticed there were two lepers sitting in front of the dilapidated building.

I jumped up quickly to take a picture. However, before I could even get the camera focused, Richard stopped me. No taking pictures of the lepers. Oh, what a disappointment. I got off the bus and proceeded to sit with them for the better part of an hour, until it was time to get back on the bus.

I sat with one of the lepers, whom I had guessed to be about my age. He told me his story of how he'd been captive on the island for forty-nine years. When he was brought to this forsaken land, he did not have leprosy, but both of his parents had it. He was only a young boy, about the age of my grandsons, when he was dropped off several hundred yards from the shoreline onto large slippery rocks and jagged lava boulders. They were required to swim ashore or drown in rough seas. He remembered several of his family members drowning, especially his grandmother, whom he tried to save.

Most of his family had died from this disease, except his three children, who were taken from him and his wife when they were born as they were not inflicted with the disease. They were taken to Molokai to be raised by strangers.

He told about how it eventually became known that the federal government had a cure for this dreadful body-destroying Hansen's Disease forty-nine years before they gave it to the Hawaiian lepers. He shared his thoughts about Fr. Damien and Mother Maryanne and all they had done for the lepers.

The leper was Catholic, and he touched my soul as few ever have. It was an experience I'll always remember.

Other than the time I was on the Mt. Whitney trail and felt like I could reach up and touch the face of God, I'd never had quite as extreme an experience. When I looked into the leper's eyes, it felt as if I was looking into the eyes of Jesus. It was as if his eyes could see everything within me, straight through to my soul. There was always a twinkle in his eyes as if he was inspired by God to share with me. He told his story with a contented smile on his face, joy in his voice, and laughter coming from deep within his heart. It was a most incredible and spiritual experience.

For nearly a month prior to visiting the leper colony, I spent many hours each day on the beach doing a lot of praying and meditating. It was a time of peaceful, contemplative solitude. The remainder of each day I spent either reading scriptural and inspirational materials, writing, or getting to know the Molokai locals.

My experience with the lepers can best be explained from research on contemplation and mysticism.

Mysticism implies a relation to mystery. It is a religious tendency and desire of the human soul to unite intimately with the Almighty. It is attained through contemplation and love; it is a direct and immediate intuition of the Infinite. "According to its tendency it may be either speculative or practical, as it limits itself to mere knowledge or traces duties for action and life; contemplative or affective, according as it emphasizes the part of intelligence or the part of the will." (From Holy Man: Father Damien of Molokai, Gavan Daws, New York: Harper & Row, 1973, 1984).

This type of vision of God is the work of grace and the reward of eternal life; thus, in the present life, few souls reach it but by a special grace. It contains a more perfect knowledge of God than is possible for most in this life, beyond the attainments of reason even enlightened by faith, through which the soul contemplates directly the mysteries of divine light.

It is a natural desire of the human soul to aspire and seek the highest truth, the absolute truth, and the infinite good. The knowledge and enjoyment of created things cannot give fullness of truth to completely satisfy our desires. The capacity of our soul needs more. It is with God that we can reach satisfaction of our aspirations, but the rational effort of our intelligence and positive goals of our will find their limits.

What man cannot know by natural reason, he can know through revelation and faith. As the Bible teaches in Hebrews 11:1, "Faith is the realization of what is hoped for and evidence of things not seen." What man cannot attain by his natural power he can reach by the grace of God. At that point, God has elevated human nature to a supernatural state. In this condition, God has given a very special grace, which enabled them to feel his presence; this is the true mystical contemplation. God becomes intimately present to the created mind, enlightened by special illuminations, and reflects with indescribable joy the divine essence.

I had one such experience in 1998 when I walked and talked with the lepers of Kalaupapa in Molokai, Hawaii.

A Walk in Nature

A walk in nature,
Not a cloud in the sky,
The sun is rising,
Now scarlet to my eye.

The soft white sand,
A glistening shore to walk,
And God is with me,
For our early morning talk.

It is ever so peaceful,
In my heart, mind, and soul,
To Him this day I follow,
When He shows me my role.

Palm trees gently sway,
As the winds softly blow.
With Him I choose to be,
His lift makes me to glow.

He forgives and forgets,
Always loves us so dear;
Just as the sea flows,
God's love is ever near.

HAWAIIAN PUMPKIN BREAD

1/2 CUP	VEGETABLE OIL
1/2 TSP	NUTMEG
2	EGGS
1/4 TSP	SALT
1 1/2 CUPS	PUMPKIN**
1/2 CUP	FRESH PINEAPPLE
1 2/3 CUPS	FLOUR
1/2 CUP	CHOPPED NUTS
1 1/4CUPS	SUGAR
1/2 CUP	COCONUT
1 TSP	BAKING SODA
1/4 CUP	WATER
1/2 TSP	CINNAMON

- Mix oil, eggs, and sugar. Mix in remaining ingredients. Add a little water for mixing if dough is too stiff. Place in greased glass baking pan and bake one hour at 350 degrees.

** You may substitute sweet potatoes for pumpkin. Sweet potatoes were a plentiful crop on Molokai.

Our Rock~a~Chaw Tree

~ Alaine Benard ~

Dear Coach Shelly and Oren May:

Just wanted to let you know that I am keeping most careful watch over the little tree we've been growing for five years now. This morning I had the opportunity to admire all its fresh, chartreuse buds reaching toward the spring sky. I sent a silent thank-you heavenward for you both.

I must confess that I had little hope of it surviving or thriving with such stressful beginnings. You two were instrumental in getting it to shoot up to its current height of five feet. Amazing! Who would have thought that such a small, cantankerous little pariah could have grown into such an extraordinary gift? Not me, for sure. I am so very relieved that you two had the foresight to see past the doubts and envision its strength and heartiness.

I must also confess, when God gave me that sapling, I was overwhelmed-sometimes a bit sad that he choose to send it to such an unworthy gardener. I don't have much of a green thumb. I was most blessed when the Lord saw fit to send such talented landscape architects to my aid.

And to think, I almost decided to try to grow this tree alone. At the time it seemed like the best way to make sure it got all the TLC it needed to flourish. I guess I was worried about the fact that you had so many other trees and plants to take care of. Thank goodness, you saw through my dilemma and offered your help! Did you see how hesitant and unsure I was? Already having tons of perfect little pines seeded, I didn't think my sweet gum would fit in. Sometimes we novice horticulturists are filled with too much pride and mistrust when it comes to our treasures. How very little faith I had in myself and in the good Lord to provide for my tree's every need.

With summer only one season away, I assure you that we will continue watering, pruning, and tenderly nurturing our sweet gum when we care for him at home. With the healthy root system and fertile soil you've provided, I know it will continue to grow strong branches and put out new shoots. Funny, those porcupine-like pods can be such a pain when they lodge in the bottom of some unaware, barefooted arch. Never thought of the positive things they contribute. When used for target practice and children's games, the sticky balls (rock-a-chaws, to us Southerners) are prized ammunition. They are also used in perfumes and adhesives. What wonderful gifts the tree produces!

Looks sure are deceiving, as the old cliché attests. You advised me to see the good attributes of the tree and to overlook its differences. I spent countless months comparing my crooked sweet gum to your other trees. Thanks for showing me that pines have their own unique challenges like burrs, dropping needles, and the tendency to dry out and rot over time. Most thankfully, your gardening skills showed me that prejudices and preconceived ideas are not reality. Looking beyond outward appearances, you pointed out that every tree is worthy and deserving of the same tender and constant attention.

Coach Shelly, this letter probably seems odd to you, as we have never met. I wouldn't know you if you walked through my door. All the same, I do know your heart. You are the one teacher who has encouraged my sweet gum, my son, to look beyond his own self-image, his past reputation, and labels. You encouraged his strength of body and mind.

Oren, as our boy's scout leader, you have been a continual sower of God's loving seeds. You devoted five years of your time to his weekly meetings, camp-outs, and spiritual growth. You trained our son in the ways necessary to become a better scout, a better person-a better Christian. When we felt pinned down and surrounded by the enemy, you were always there to offer us rays of hope, acceptance, and the firm hand of unwavering equanimity.

Coach, the words of encouragement you offered him this school year will mean more than you'll ever know. Seeing himself as a chunky, clumsy loner, you told him he should try out for the football team next year. What a difference that made. He came home so full of positive self-esteem and a new, non-defeatist attitude. All the cool kids play football, you know, and to have the team coach pat you on the back is a priceless gift.

Oren, the freedom he enjoyed in the wilds of nature showed him how to spread his wings and fly. His flight brought tears of happiness and relief to us, his parents. Coach Shelly and Oren and your wife Cathie, you have looked at him through the eyes of the Lord. You found ways to spark his personal growth. Since your involvement, he has transformed from a moping, disgruntled preteen into a young man who is willing to change his diet and exercise to get in shape for next year. Planning his future Eagle Scout activities, he is now energized and excited, not dreading life's challenges and trials.

I spent much time agonizing and worrying over his social skills. Years of being told he is a square peg took a toll on my emotional strength that undermined our family unity. When I should have relied on trust in God's will, others' thoughts and opinions consumed me. This lapse in faith caused so much grief that I was in a state of spiritual dryness. Shamefully, I ran away from God's grace by anticipating my soul's groaning. But the good Lord sent you into our lives. My silent moaning and separation from his merciful gifts quickly ended.

Your willingness to share your time and heart with my son has shown us that the face of God is indeed available. We witnessed it through your loving, Spirit-filled actions. The stormy seas of chaos engulfing us became calmer because of your compliance to the Word. Truly you never faltered to administer the Golden Rule. When I became overwhelmed with negative emotions, the Lord reminded me that you were there to guide and encourage our rock-a-chaw son.

To honor your being true lights of Christ, our family has planted a special tree in your names. The Arbor Day Foundation will send you the details. You will continue to be in our daily prayers, and we hope one day you will see the multitude of ways you have blessed all of the trees you so tenderly planted and tended.

Our own special tree will one day stand tall, straight, and gloriously sturdy in the Sonlight of God's graces. This, in part, will be a credit to your faith in action. We bless you for being a monumental part of our family life.

May the Holy Spirit continue to guide your works.

Prayers,

Pete, Alaine, and Turner Benard

Psalm 42

As the deer longs for streams of water,
so my soul longs for you, O God.
My being thirsts for God, the living God.
When can I go and see the face of God?
My tears have been my food day and night,
as they ask daily, "Where is your God?"

Those times I recall as I pour out my soul,
When I went in procession with the crowd,
I went with them to the house of God,
amid loud cries of thanksgiving,
with the multitude keeping festival.

Why are you downcast, my soul;
why do you groan within me?
Wait for God, whom I shall praise again,
my savior and my God.

My soul is downcast within me;
therefore I will remember you
from the land of the Jordan and Hermon,
from the land of Mount Mizar.
Here deep calls to deep in the roar of your torrents.
All your waves and breakers sweep over me.

At dawn may the Lord bestow faithful love
that I may sing praise through the night,
praise to the God of my life.

I say to God, "my rock, why do you forget me?
Why must I go about mourning
with the enemy oppressing me?"
It shatters my bones, when my adversaries reproach me.
They say to me daily: "Where is your God?"

Porcupine Meatballs

1 lb.	Hamburger
1/2 cup	uncooked rice
1/2 cup	water or beef broth
1/2 cup	chopped onion
1 tsp	salt
1/2 tsp	pepper
1/2 tsp	celery salt
1/8 tsp	garlic powder

Sauce:

1 can	(5-oz) tomato sauce
	or
	small can tomato paste
1 cup	water
2 tsp	Worcestershire sauce
2 tbs	ketchup

- Mix the hamburger, rice, 1/2 cup water, onion, salt, celery salt, garlic powder, and pepper in a small bowl. Shape into small balls. Place on an ungreased baking dish.

- Combine the tomato sauce, one cup water, and Worcestershire sauce and drizzle over the meatballs. Cover with foil and bake at 400 degrees for forty-five minutes. Remove foil and bake for fifteen more minutes.

Makes 15-20 meatballs.

THE STRANGER *in the* GARDEN

~ Deb Anne Flynt ~

It was a neat little flower garden, not too small, but not so large that she couldn't tend it herself. It was lined all around with wooden beams, which did a poor job of keeping out the crabgrass but added to the charm of the spot. A pretty, sweet-looking older lady sat in the middle of the garden in a lawn chair, pulling up weeds. I pulled over to the curb in front of her, got out, and introduced myself.

She wore latex gloves like doctors and nurses use. They were dirty from her work, so she was reluctant to shake my hand. We talked while she weeded and I watched and learned. She leaned down and tugged on a vine. She extracted it skillfully, roots and all, much as a surgeon removes a damaged organ.

She told me about her brother, as if she had read my thoughts about surgery. She explained that he had cancer and was scheduled for an operation soon and that he was undergoing chemotherapy in hopes that the tumor would shrink before the operation. I asked how far she would have to travel for that visit.

"Oh, he's in Florida," she informed me. She would drive herself there, which surprised me, since she had already said she spent most of each day in a wheelchair. I looked in the driveway to see if there were vehicles belonging to someone who might live with her and drive her around. I found nothing that so indicated. I sat on the ground just outside the wooden barrier to be sure I didn't damage anything that might be planted beneath the soil.

"You want to move inside?" she offered.

When I declined, she warned me, "Your bottom's gonna get wet there."

"I'm not worried about it," I answered truthfully. "These are old jeans."

It would not have surprised me at all to think of this lady either keeping house alone or taking care of someone else. I knew as soon as I saw her sitting in her little garden that she had a nurturing spirit. This dear lady would probably be the first to volunteer at church, even if standing for that long meant discomfort for her. I felt like I was in the presence of a future saint, but not one who would back down if she knew she was right. The sparkle in her eye told me that she would fight if she believed in her cause.

She confirmed my suspicions, seeming to read my mind again. She explained that she didn't have any problem driving, since her reason for having to sit most of the time was due to poor circulation in one leg. It didn't bother her to drive for several hours at a time, and in fact she drove to her doctor in a town about ninety miles from her home. This dear lady intrigued me more and more.

She pulled another weed, untangling the vine from the first green shoots of her daylilies. As she did so, she commented that she needed to break up those bulbs. She looked up suddenly and asked me if I wanted some of them for my garden.

She showed me where she had planted blue-violet coneflowers between the daylilies. I pictured them blooming and contrasting beautifully with the pale orange lilies.

Weeds were a cancer in her garden. She told me that she was a cancer survivor herself, and that she was diabetic. I wondered if she was younger than she looked, since she was obviously a veteran fighter.

"I came up during the Depression," she informed me. Her family had once had a large cotton farm, and she had spent many hours in the fields. It takes a long time to get good at picking cotton, and she had become quite proficient. She'd started picking when she was four years old.

"Mamma made me a sack from half of a flour sack," she said.

I could imagine her tiny finger getting pricked the first few times, and wondered if she quit, or kept picking. I decided that it was probably the latter, with some encouragement from her mamma. I was shocked when she told me that she was ten years older than she looked. As lovely as she was at eighty, I marveled at what a beauty she must have been at twenty, and how many beaus must have vied for her hand. Whether she had ever been married, I didn't know. If she had been, asking her about him might have been painful for her, so I kept my curiosity to myself.

Pulling another weed, she said, "I have a nice garden in the back." She explained that it was her vegetable garden, and that it was much larger.

"Last year, I had turnips that were knee-high."

The daylilies in the front she described as having been "solid blooms," and the daisies in the flowerbed had been shoulder-high.

"I don't know what it was about last year. It must have been a good season."

A cloud passed overhead, its shadow making me think of rain and baptism. Maybe God blesses rain before sending it to her gardens. By the time the sun came back out, I had been thoroughly inspired.

When I said my good-bye, I again extended my hand, and she drew back, pointing out that I would get dirty. I reached out again anyway, wishing in my heart that I could hug her, wanting her to know what an honor and joy it had been to meet her. Besides, I'm not afraid of a little fertile soil in my hand.

Flower in Her Garden

Lovely among her lovelies
Beauty beyond skin-deep
She sat alone in her garden
A flower in her own garden
Tending her tiny keep.

Each precious sprouting bulb
Every tiny springing seed
Nurtured with loving kindness
Yet she showed no kindness
To the invading weed.

Time after time she bent down
Examined each little sprout
But if it was a weed
If 'twas a sorry weed
She mercilessly tossed it out.

The lady in the garden
Made me ask of my heart
Am I a flower or weed?
For if I am a weed
Of Heaven I'll see no part.

My life is not my own
I'm grown from the Father's seed
He planted me among roses
A thorn among sweet roses
But He did not make me a weed.

FLOWERPOTS

1 PKG.	CHOCOLATE SANDWICH COOKIES
	SHREDDED COCONUT
	GUMMY WORMS
	CANDY BUGS
	CANDY FLOWERS
	ICE-CREAM CONES
	GREEN FOOD COLORING

- Crumble the cookies into a bowl until you have what resembles loose soil. It's okay if it's not perfectly consistent – neither is dirt.

- Spoon the "potting soil" (cookie crumbs) into ice-cream cones, adding a (gummy) worm to each one as you go, until they're about three-quarters full. Plant some "grass" (coconut with green food coloring) on top and a candy flower. Decorate with candy bugs, and serve.

THRIFTY TIPS: Use generic cookies, dye your own coconut by putting it in a zipper bag with a few drops of green food coloring and shaking it together, and use cake icing to make your own flowers and bugs. This is an inexpensive treat to make for parties, and kids love them.

Learning from the Experienced

I thought of people in my community who love having gardens but let them go in the past few years because they could no longer tend them properly, due to illness or infirmity. My own grandparents had done the same thing in another town, and weeds took over their lovely roses for a year.

When you have gardening questions, consult an older gardener or farmer and ask for their expertise. You never know what a little time spent chatting with them will mean to either of you, and it helps them realize they are still important to this world. You might learn a gardening secret or two that might otherwise have been lost.

Today, plant a small garden for someone, or help neighbors tend theirs. If you have a flower garden, add some color to the lives of those who don't. Take a basket of flowers to a nursing home or hospice, and let a child hand them out to everyone; or take a potted plant for them to tend. Besides making you feel good, you are teaching a child the importance and the pleasure of sharing blessings.

Sally's Dream

~ *Angie Ledbetter* ~

I met a woman, whom I'll call Sally, not too long ago. The circumstances that brought us two strangers together are part of the mystery of God's divine directing, inspiring, and planning which we humans seldom see. But when we do get a tiny peek behind the curtain, it can be a blessing.

Sally has a vision. She knows how she wants her life to be, and she has put her total trust into Jesus' lap to make her vision come true.

On the very first day of spring, I was sent on a job by one of my employers to a small town in my home state. It's a village really, with a population of less than 1,000. Because the journey would include a nice country drive, I invited my sister. We spent the trip talking about family business, future dreams for our own small families, and just enjoying the warm breezes that for once weren't accompanied by a blanket of humidity.

We laughingly called each other "Maw Maw D." after our grandmother who never missed an opportunity to point out pretty flowers, birds, and every road sign encountered on a trip. "Stuckey's, 3 Miles Ahead," "Snake Farm - Next Left!," and "We Sale Kerosne! (sic)" gave us miles of giggles.

Beginning my work of setting up the rented housewares was delayed, as the doors to the house at which we were working were locked tight. After tracking down the owner by cell phone, we were told that the doors weren't locked. Trying the handle again, it easily and amazingly swung open. I was aggravated with myself for the wasted twenty minutes we'd have to spend in this Podunk bayou town, but the work went smoothly and we enjoyed our extra time together.

Finishing up ahead of schedule, we began the return trip. Dee, being enamored with garage/estate sales, antiques, junk, and treasures of any kind, persuaded me to pull into the parking lot of a gray cinder block building. "Petticoat Junction Thrift Shop" was painted neatly on the building in huge, royal blue letters. I sat in the van as several other vehicles crowded in. The sign in the window clearly said, "Closed."

When Dee didn't return shortly, I went inside to find her. Workers already sweating in the morning heat were stocking the neat shelves of the interior. There was a feeling of camaraderie and excitement between them. Babies played happily with old dolls as mothers, grandmothers, friends, and sons-in-law went about their work. Dee was gathering items like a madwoman, so I perched at the huge storefront counter and chatted with the owner, Sally.

"Are you sure it's okay for us to be in here since you're not actually open for business yet?" I asked her.

Mopping her neck with a crumpled paper towel, she winked, "Cher, it's fine that y'all came early. We just got here a few minutes ago to do the last minute things before we open tomorrow."

Sally began telling me how her little business had come into being. Tough years, including her husband's bout with cancer, had taught her the important things in this life.

"When my husband caught that terrible cancer, I knew I just had to trust the Lord to fix him. We had so many, many people praying for him to recover since he can't work, and he is now doing fine," she said with relief etched into her smile.

"Gosh, it must be hard on you to work and take care of him too," I offered.

"Well, it has been hard at times, but I've always done work for my church and I knew God would heal him. That's how my dream came true for my business. I have the faith," Sally explained.

The story leisurely unraveled as Dee browsed among the rows and shelves. Sally shared the dream of how she'd never wanted anything but to help others. Daughters and friends filled in the pieces of Sally's story. She'd had another thrift shop on the main street in town, but the crime and violence there had made the location dangerous. Sally set to praying for a new and better location. At Christmas, she'd given away much of the clothing in her store to the poor, who were trying to buy gifts for their families. A beautiful cycle of giving and receiving began. To underscore this thought, a man drove up in a brown, rusty truck to bring Sally some huge carpet remnants.

"When this building came up empty and I got the call to see if I wanted it, I was so thankful. Now I'm in the middle of town and people can find me real easy. And my little church is right across the street!"

Driving home, Dee and I talked about what a great day it had been, and how much we'd enjoyed meeting Sally and her family. We thanked God for helping her dream come true and prayed for continued success with her mission to give to others. We also marveled at God's timing in holding us up at the job so that we wouldn't miss the pre-opening of Petticoat Junction and the fine folks who work there.

As Dee unloaded her treasures from the car trunk, we smiled at the little surprise gifts that Sally had put into her bags-an angel lapel pin, a little worn Bible, and two sterling spoons. Maybe God wanted to remind us through Sally's generosity to be mindful of our angels, to steep ourselves in Scripture, and to always try to feed others from his bounty.

Reflections from the Word

Isaiah 66:2-

"'Has not my hand made all these things, and so they came into being?' declares the Lord. 'This is the one I esteem: he who is humble and contrite in spirit, and trembles at my word.'"

2 Corinthians 8:7-

"But just as you excel in everything-in faith, in speech, in knowledge, in complete earnestness and in your love for us-see that you also excel in this grace of giving."

Sharing Our Abundance

When our closets and storage areas are overflowing, we should give some of our extras away to those less fortunate. God's generosity to us should be shared with others.

During your spring-cleaning this year, how about boxing up the items not really used or needed to share with others? If you live in a large city, your phone book is full of organizations wanting donations and organizations that will gladly come and get them. If you are in a rural area, you already know where to go!

Ask your children to clean out some of the toys, books, puzzles, and games they have outgrown. Bring your kids to a shelter such as the Salvation Army that has an on-site store, so that they may be part of this sharing ministry work.

In the world of excess today, children need to see that there are those truly in need. It will build up their giving natures.

Vision

How can I walk with head held high
Upon these broken streets?
My poor brothers' needs are denied
By my own self-deceit.

I close my eyes to their sad plight
When I am blessed with much.
I cannot bear the lowly sight
Of those who need my touch.

Loving Lord, make me a seeker.
Help me to find the ones.
Yes, I am my brother's keeper.
I am chosen by Your Son.

STONE SOUP

Most likely, if you have children you've read to them the wonderful story of Stone Soup at one time or another. An economical and fun way to spread its message of sharing and pulling together is to invite your friends and neighbors to a stone soup party.

- Make simple invitations out of small paper bags. Include a note about the message behind the famine-struck village that survived through the sharing of resources when they pooled their meager food items and made soup for all to share.

- Ask recipients to bring an item back in their sack to add to the pot. You do not have to specify the ingredients. Seeing what your guests bring is part of the fun.

- On the day of the gathering, have your work area set up and ready, and a huge pot or two available to be filled. This works especially well outside using Southern-style boiling/frying rigs. A makeshift table made out of lumber put across sawhorses is perfect.

- Chop up all fresh vegetables and meats. Brown meat chunks and save the drippings in which to sauté the veggie contributions.

- To the pot, add any canned mixes, soup starters, liquids, and enough water to cover the ingredients. One sterilized rock may be added. The person who gets the stone in their cup or bowl will receive a small prize from the host or hostess.

- While the soup cooks, backyard games and conversation will flow nicely.

- To follow through with the theme of sharing, make a second pot of stone soup to bring to one of your city's shelters or soup kitchens or a shut-in neighbor.

Run the Race

~ Carol Schwartz ~

"Go confidently in the direction of your dreams. Live the life you have imagined."

- Henry David Thoreau

I remember a particular event in my life to which I was totally committed to and asked God's help in completing the task. I had trained for months. Other than climbing in the high country, it would be the greatest physical challenge I had ever faced. I knew that God's strength was with me to achieve the goal. Little did I know how much and in what ways he would help me along the journey.

At fifty-four years of age I was about to run my very first marathon, a distance of 26.2 miles over the rolling hills of California coastal Highway 1. It's a beautiful coastline course stretching from Big Sur to Carmel.

It was April 3, 1997 at 3 a.m. in Monterey, California, and I was wide-awake before the alarm went off. I gulped down two cups of coffee and some water before getting on my knees to thank God for getting me this far. I asked him to help me just finish the race.

The national weather prediction was for warming trends over the next few days with lows in the 40's and highs in the 70's. I dressed for warmer weather with shorts and a t-shirt, taking gloves, an ear band, and a long-sleeved undershirt because it would be cool in the morning. I would have layers as the weather conditions changed.

At 4 a.m. I drove to the bus stop in Carmel where we loaded into buses for the one-hour drive to the race starting line in Big Sur. We arrived in Big Sur about 5 a.m., two hours before race starting time. It was cold that morning, so a lot of us were huddling together on the ground to keep warm while trying to catch a little rest before the big event.

I was anxiously standing at the side of the pack on a slight hill when the starting gun went off. The shot was fired and the crowd of thousands took off. Knowing it was best for me to start out walking the first couple of miles, to warm up for the endurance needed for such a long run, I walked and jogged for thirteen uneventful miles.

Passing Bixby Bridge at the mile 13.1 halfway mark, I noticed blisters forming on my feet. This was not a good sign. I trudged up to Hurricane Point. Its name describes it perfectly, because there's always a strong wind blowing off the Pacific Ocean. I'd take one step forward and be blown backward by the 55-mile-per-hour, bone-chilling head wind.

At mile 15 my feet were burning and the blisters were raw, so I decided to get on the bus and call it quits. I stood in line to do just that. Every person got on the bus except me, because it was full and there is a safety law that no one can stand in the aisle. The driver was kind enough to let me know that another bus or the runner pick-up van would be coming along shortly. Well, I'm not the patient type, so decided to walk until that happened.

At mile 18, I took a pit stop at the portable toilets and sat in the chair at the aid station for a few minutes waiting for the pick-up van. When it didn't come along right away, my pride wouldn't let me sit any longer, so I got up and started walking again after downing Gatorade and water. About that time a little lady in her seventies with whom I'd sat the night before at the great pasta feed came walking up, so I joined her. We were chatting away, and she encouraged me to keep going, so I passed up and didn't get into the pick-up van when it came along.

Mile 20 found me standing in line one last time to get on the bus, because by now my feet were killing me, and I'd been walking in the dirt along the road just to ease the pain in my feet. Yes, I was praying, as I had been throughout the entire race. About that time another runner, a good-looking Italian man about my age, came along and asked if I was going to quit now that we were almost home. With his encouragement to walk the final 6.2 miles, I didn't get on the bus, where there was room for me. He was feeling about as sick as I was, but he didn't tell me that until we had walked for a while.

We continued to encourage each other. About two miles from the finish line we were wondering if we'd receive our runner's medal, because we were past the five-hour time limit. The medal was an important reminder that we had finished this grueling task. Buses and cars containing finished racers drove by, honking, waving, and yelling words of encouragement. One last time the pick-up van came and offered us our final ride. Between the two of us, what little strength we had left, and a loving God with a weird sense of humor, we declined the ride.

About one-half mile from the finish line, one of the race directors drove out and handed each of us a medal for promising to complete the marathon. He had heard we were struggling to finish and had decided to kindly drive our medals to us. Tears of joy streamed down our faces all the way to the finish line. We didn't run anymore, but we did walk the last bit encouraging each other to keep on trudging.

It had taken six hours to complete my first marathon. When I started hurting and doubted my own abilities, although I had run a couple of twenty-mile-plus practice runs, I trusted and never doubted God's help. What a victory for God! God had encouraged me all along the race with his angels and Holy Spirit using my impatience, vanity, and pride.

I believed and had faith that God would help me. And when I lacked strength, he picked me up and carried me. Faith is referred to as a supernatural gift from God. I had received gifts from him to help me along the way with those cheering and those accompanying me on the journey; and with the Holy Spirit within, the will is very strong.

After the race, I ate a little food and took a long, hot bath. I decided to thank God by attending church. The holy Catholic Church means God's whole universal community of believers. It had been a great day to witness God's love shining forth through the Holy Spirit and God's angels.

When I feel weak, I know that God will send me strength in the form of friends, supporters, or even strangers to help turn my own inadequacies into winning characteristics. And through the workings of the Holy Spirit, I hope to be inspiring and instrumental to others on their walks through life's journey.

TIPS

The principles learned here can be applied to all areas of our lives. Set a goal that is in accordance with God's plan and a plan for reaching that goal. Plan, but don't plan the results. It is important to establish benchmarks along the journey to know whether we are reaching our goals in life. God helps us do that. Often he uses others to help us along the way. One of the most important factors in success is our set of beliefs.

Hebrews 12:1-

"Therefore, since we have so great a cloud of witnesses surrounding us, let us also lay aside every encumbrance and the sin which so easily entangles us, and let us run with endurance the race that is set before us."

Hebrews 10:36-

"For you have need of endurance, so that when you have done the will of God, you may receive what was promised."

Beliefs and Goals

Example of my beliefs and goals: friends and family are part of the treasures in my daily life. A healthy body is a fine temple of God. Pray and meditate, exercise five times a week for at least one-half to one hour each time, eat healthy, and drink plenty of water. Get enough rest for the body to recover. Keep life in balance emotionally, mentally, physically, spiritually, and socially. This results in a life that is filled with happiness, joy, freedom, and peace of heart and soul.

What are your beliefs and goals?

Italian Spaghetti

2	LARGE CANS CHOPPED TOMATOES WITH LIQUID
2	CANS TOMATO PASTE
1	PASTE CAN WATER
1 TBS	SALT
1/2 TSP	GARLIC POWDER
1 1/2 TSP	SUGAR (OPTIONAL)
1/2 TSP	PEPPER
1	QUARTERED ONION
1 TSP	DRIED BASIL
	COOKED SPAGHETTI

- Combine all ingredients except pasta. Simmer for two hours, stirring occasionally. Add additional water for thinner sauce. Serve the sauce over your favorite spaghetti pasta. Add fresh grated Italian cheese, meatballs, or cooked chicken for variety. Serves six.

This is my favorite feast for the pre-race banquet the big night before a long run or race, preferably served with a bowl of fresh green salad and garlic bread.

Sprinter's Spritzer

This thirst quencher is good any time you need bodily refreshment, but it makes an especially nice change from sports drinks when you are walking, running, or pursuing some other vigorous physical activity.

- Mix equal parts of the following to fill your sports bottles with:

  Lemon/lime flavored Pedialyte or sports drink

  Any brand of lemon/lime soda

  or

  sugar-free powdered mix

  Your favorite fruit juice

  (orange, pineapple, grapefruit, etc.)

- Add two tablespoons cherry juice or a dash of cranberry juice for a little color. The spritzer can also be poured into ice trays to make flavorful ice cubes to add to sports drinks, or frozen for a healthy popsicle.

The Drive Home

~ Deb Anne Flynt ~

I love the first warm days of the year in Mississippi! Even though most trees are still bare, they no longer seem barren. Everything looks almost the same as it did throughout most of the winter, but there is a difference. Buds so tiny I can't see them wait on the tips of the trees and bushes. It seems like each one is striving to be the first spring leaf of the year. The earth is waking from its long rest, and soon all this will be green.

Today on my drive home from town I put on a tape of one of my favorite Christian rock bands, turned it up a bit, and rolled down my window. The warm breeze felt fantastic! The smile in my heart made its way to my face. My hair tangled in the wind as I danced around in my seat, bobbing with the beat.

I sang along with the songs I know almost by heart, drawing stares from people along the highway working in their yards and gardens. I was singing loudly enough for them to hear me, but I didn't care! I was not singing to them, but I made no attempt to hide my faith. It's odd to think that God might use me in this way to introduce someone to the joy of loving Jesus, but I guess a jubilant drive-by singing could seem inviting.

Psalm 95:1-2 says, "O come, let us sing to the LORD; let us make a joyful noise to the rock of our salvation! Let us come into His presence with thanksgiving; let us make a joyful noise to Him with songs of praise!"

My noise was joyful; and I was just grateful that it isn't required to delight others, as long as it pleases God.

In the backseat was a bag with packets of vegetable and flower seeds I will plant soon, and many that I will send to my friends. I carefully chose each packet for myself or to match the personality or preferences of my dear friends. I know my small gifts will be appreciated, because they, like my friends, are also gifts from God; they are small offerings of love.

Occasionally between the near-naked trees along the road, I could see daffodils and buttercups. They are as much a part of the promise of spring as the first red-breasted robin. My heart leapt at each little yellow bunch, and I thanked God again for his merciful bounty. Each passing mile and every minute held more promise.

I was reminded of how this time of year reflects life so perfectly. We go through hard times, and when the world seems barren and cold, a breath of fresh warm love comes through; we know that God will sustain us, no matter what. Faith is a blessed gift for which I thanked God aloud as I switched on my turn signal.

On the final stretch, I drove slowly, watching for children and pets, and I turned the stereo back down. Still in the same frame of mind, I continued singing, just not quite as stridently as before.

Yesterday, I saw a fawn crossing the road near my home, and my approach frightened it. Today, I kept a watchful eye, hoping it would not attempt another crossing. I wondered how much of my garden would survive the deer and other animals living in the woods around my home.

I've been planning my garden in my mind's eye, where each flowerbed will be planted, and each row of vegetables. As I pulled up to the house, I looked into the backyard, where my vegetable garden will grow. I was taken by surprise by a bunch of daffodils right there in my own yard. These are new volunteers and are truly a gift from a loving and generous God. Thank you, Lord. Thank you again. Your mercy is never-ending.

Joyful Noises

I lift my head in words of praise
Singing songs of adulation
Grateful for my voice to raise
In fervent adoration

I care not if my voice is sweet,
I know it is to Him,
So I sing this just to please
For whom I wrote this hymn.
"All glory and praise to God!"
"Alleluia! Alleluia! Amen!"
"Hosanna!" My joyful song
Joins the everlasting hymn

Lift high, elated voices
Sing with one accord
And know that God rejoices
As you sing "Holy Lord!"

DRIVE~UP RED BEANS *and* RICE

Many of us spend a good bit of time on the go, and one answer to mealtime is to grab something at a fast-food drive-through and eat in the car. If your stomach, your conscience, or your kids are like mine, that's not your favorite option. If you distrust leaving your oven on while you're away from home, as I do, then the alternatives become even more limited. That's how I rediscovered slow cooking. Here's a favorite recipe of mine.

1	16-OZ. BAG DRIED DARK RED KIDNEY BEANS
1 LB.	LINK SAUSAGE
1	MEDIUM ONION
1	MEDIUM BELL PEPPER (OPTIONAL)
	RICE

- At night before going to bed, wash the beans, cover them, and leave them to soak in fresh water in your slow cooker. In the morning, sometime between when you jump out of bed and when you rush out the door, add some water to the beans and turn the slow cooker on low.

- You'll want to add water every few hours, so let that determine how much water you start cooking with. If you'll be home in an hour or two, then just add enough to cover the beans with about an inch or two of water on top. If you will not be home for several hours, put in considerably more water.

- Always leave at least an inch of space between the water level and the lid line of the crock to allow for expansion. The best part of cooking this way is that it pretty much takes care of itself, while you take care of the business of the day. Before the beans are done, add slices of link sausage, and make rice according to the package directions. By suppertime, or the time you get home, you should have delicious, basic red beans waiting for you.

- To spice this up a little, brown the sausage in a pan to remove some fat and add flavor. For best flavor, add Cajun seasoning and chopped onion and bell pepper. My favorite time to add these is to sauté them with the sausage and add them all together after draining.

- Mash some beans during cooking to thicken the sauce.

- Ladle the beans over the rice and serve with fresh hot garlic or French bread.

Trés Yummy, Y'all!

GOD'S BACKBEAT

"When the men were returning home after David had killed the Philistine, the women came out from all the towns of Israel to meet King Saul with singing and dancing, with joyful songs and with tambourines and lutes."

1 SAMUEL 18:6

You can find their work in most record stores, on several top-forty radio stations, and of course, in Christian book and music stores. They are the new, contemporary Christian musicians. Michael W. Smith's songs can be heard at weddings, dc Talk can be heard on local radio stations, and Stephen Curtis Chapman's music is on sale at most Wal-Mart stores, just to name a very few of these talented and faith-filled artists. Besides radio stations that specialize in Christian music, you can find them on many secular stations. Why? It's good music. There's something for almost every listening style, from light to pop to rap to rock, and even metal.

It was once believed that rock and roll was the devil's music, but contemporary Christian music has challenged and changed all that. This is rock based on the Rock of Salvation, and it appeals to people who might not otherwise hear God's message. Upbeat Christian music has been around for a while, but it seems to have gained popularity in the past few years.

Throughout the Bible, especially in Psalms, music plays an important role. We are instructed to make a "joyful noise unto the Lord." We're invited to sing and to play various instruments to praise the Lord. Music has changed quite a bit in the past two thousand years, but the Word remains constant. With the numerous references to this in the Bible, we can only gather that God is a music lover.

Once we understand that when songs are used for praise, adoration, thanksgiving, and sowing the seeds of his Word, we realize how very little rhythm has to do with it. The message is more important than the beat. Who can say exactly what music is pleasing to the Lord, and what is not? To pass judgment in his place would be, at the very least, risky and impudent. It is better to believe that God loves all music sung for his glory and honor.

An important reason to respect contemporary Christian musicians is that they are reaching a broad audience. The message is getting out there, and it's being played on popular music radio stations. Each time a song of praise is aired on one of these stations, there is a chance that seeds will be planted. If one person who hears is spared damnation because of it, then who can condemn it?

Psalm 100, among many others, instructs us to praise the Lord with joyful music. There are no restrictions mentioned about the type of music to offer to God. The psalmist David is known for his preference of percussion and stringed instruments. These in the hands of one offering praise and thanks "make a joyful noise unto the Lord."

"A Psalm of thanksgiving. Sing joyfully to the Lord, all you lands; serve the Lord with gladness; come before him with joyful song." (Psalm 100:1-2)

Although this psalmist lived many years before Christ was born, his words still ring with truth even today. Some people will always prefer traditional hymns or gospel music. If these are the songs that they choose to praise God, then they are not to be condemned, either. Each brother and sister of Christ has an equal right in him to choose what kind of music they use for praying and giving glory, thanks, and praise.

No matter what instruments are used or what the rhythm of the song, respect music with his message. It would be a mistake to judge it or the musicians as being unworthy of praising the Lord. We each serve our Lord in the way we are called, and if someone's mission has a backbeat, well, it just might reflect God's heartbeat. Only the Good Lord knows.

Bigmama's Biscuits

~ *Angie Ledbetter* ~

No matter how many times I've tried, I just can't make biscuits from scratch like those my grandmother has been making for eight decades. I know the ingredients needed and the special cooking items to use, but success eludes me.

When I first started begging Bigmama to tell me her secrets, she told me to watch her make them several times and then just try it on my own while she stood over me. She didn't use exact measurements, but she expertly added a glob of this, a glass of that, and a little blob of the other. Without fail her biscuits always rose like obedient little angels and sent the most mouth-watering aroma throughout her pink kitchen. My batch came out of the oven as hardheaded, disobedient lumps.

This experience was frustrating for a college-educated woman with decent culinary skills of her own. How could my grandmother achieve one hundred percent success and I zero? Obviously, I was in need of more training and better observation skills. Once again, I traveled miles across town to her house, determined to notice every detail of the biscuit-making process this time.

Pulling into her driveway, I am always struck by the beauty of her simple house made from specially ordered, pink-tinted Mojave bricks and the colorful array of lovingly planted spring flowers in her beds. Known for her green thumb and the ability to bring dead sticks to life, Bigmama has a mysterious way of handling plants, people, and food that few others have.

The back door is propped open, and strains of "The Old Rugged Cross" waft out with the smell of brewing chicory coffee. Bigmama is busy in her kitchen getting the cooking utensils ready. I sit at the bar attached to her work area and enjoy a cup of coffee. The coffee and chat are a mandatory ritual and remind me that time is not of the essence, and to all things there is a time. My busy working mom schedule is put aside, and we visit in the moment, not worrying about what needs to be done later. The singing of her old church hymns adds a steady rhythm to the process of gathering the items, a different approach from my harried, hurried ways.

"Now, it's important that you always have your things ready at hand," Bigmama winks at me. I'm normally scattered, dashing off to the store to purchase a bag of flour or some other staple.

"Now, you just watch me make these biscuits and you will be able to do it, too," she says, and continues humming her hymns.

I am fascinated. She prepares by heart her own grandmother's recipe, seemingly without thinking. I jokingly ask, "Bigmama, wouldn't it just be easier to get some of those canned biscuits and use them?"

I get no reply, only a small smile and a raised eyebrow as she gently sifts the flour into her favorite red biscuit bowl.

My mind wanders over the beauty of her home. It is not fancy and does not sit in a good neighborhood. It is the home my Pappy helped build in 1945. My favorite room is the back bedroom, where my sisters and I spent many childhood nights digging through her jewelry box and trying on her flowing peignoir sets as the adults visited in the parlor. The massive bed frame holds a mattress that is stuffed with cotton picked from a southern plantation more than one hundred years ago. There is no other bed like it in the world, and I am thankful that she has kept it all these years. I am proud of my grandmother for always recognizing quality, and for not discarding things just because they've gone out of vogue.

People have always felt comfortable coming to Bigmama's house, relaxing and visiting for many long hours. It is an oasis of calm from the craziness of the world.

"Are you paying attention? Are you learning anything today?" she smiles.

"Bigmama, I'm learning a whole lot today!" I tell her truthfully.

We spend the lazy afternoon going through the steps to making those one-of-a-kind Bigmama biscuits. I want to teach my own daughter and grandchildren this art of cooking, teaching, and learning that spans generations.

I will always see her hands gently and lovingly pinching the dough off just so and waiting for the beautiful rewards of the finished product. It is a privilege to help her lift the heavy iron skillet into her pink oven. Someday, I will make perfect biscuits too.

BIGMAMA'S BISCUITS

This recipe will take a few times to perfect, but don't give up. The results are worth the work.

- Use a medium or large bowl that will become your biscuit bowl forever. Sift enough Gold Medal self-rising flour to fill the bowl. The sifting must be done slowly. Singing hymns helps develop a nice rhythm. It also adds prayer to your family's food as you prepare.
- "Doodle out a 'waller hole' in the middle of your bowl." This well that you make with your fist will hold the other ingredients.
- Put one tablespoon Mazola cooking oil in the well.
- In a standard glass, mix together a half cup of buttermilk and a half cup of water. Add this to your flour well. Work the mixture gently with your fingers, pulling in as little flour as possible. Try not to handle or knead the dough very much.
- Prepare your iron skillet (required!) by pouring in a generous amount of the oil. Roll the skillet around to spread the oil evenly.
- Dust your hands lightly with flour and pinch off biscuits slowly. Place them into the skillet.
- When the skillet is full and the biscuits rest gently against one another, sprinkle on a small amount of oil to the raw biscuit tops.
- Put the skillet into a cold oven, and set temperature at 400 degrees. Be sure to put your skillet on the middle or lower rack of the oven so the biscuits will brown evenly.
- When the biscuits appear cooked, move the skillet to the top rack until the biscuits are golden brown. If your oven is true to temperature, the whole process will take about twenty-five minutes, but you will need to watch to be on the safe side.

Reflecting with the Word

My visits to Bigmama's kitchen drew me into study of the Word. You may enjoy these readings also:

SING IN PRAISE TO THE LORD:
Nehemiah 12:46

HONORING ELDERS:
1 Timothy 5:16-18

FOR EVERYTHING THERE IS AN APPOINTED TIME:
Eccl. 3:1-2

Share Your Life

Record some of your own childhood memories to pass along to your children, and be sure to capture memorable moments with photographs for the future.

Write down your special recipes, housekeeping and gardening tips, and personal graces and virtues, such as knowing how to set a table or the art of unhurried conversation and good listening.

HANDS

Her hands were wrinkled and very soft,
>From years of working chores so oft.
Hands that healed and helped all others,
Badges of a loving mother.

>From dewy youth with nails so fair,
To aged palms from giving care.
I see my own hands losing youth.
May they grow old from living truth.

(To my loving Mother.)

Forgotten Anniversaries

~ Alaine Benard ~

Snapping the stem of a brilliant magenta zinnia, I inspect it for any flaws. Satisfied with its perfection, I place it in the little basket waiting to be filled. Sitting back on my heels, I breathe in the mysterious scents of fertilizer, dewy grass, and something slightly reminiscent of sweet olive. I am at peace and content.

Moving along my planters and rows, I rip out the dandelions and other intrusive weeds. How dare they sneak in here and suck up the nutrients meant for my babies? I squish, rip, and mangle them with my trowel. "Crabgrass and nut-grass and weeds, oh, my!" replace Dorothy's "lions and tigers and bears" as the jolly tune playing in my head. Giggling at my own silliness, I continue to remove the offenders. Gerber daisies, irises, and other pretties are ready for the crystal vase inside.

As I stand and dust my knees, I hear my husband's truck come up the drive. With lunch box in hand he walks over to greet me. He kisses my forehead and we exchange minimal words about our days.

Inside, I arrange the fresh bouquet in the water-filled crystal and admire the good china and silver surrounding it. Pete fairly runs to the backyard to play with his tools and projects. I fight off the rising aggravation. How could he breeze through here and not notice all I've done today? The house is not its usual jumble of piles and half-done chores.

Checking on the pot roast and special casseroles, I review all the work I've done. It wasn't just light, necessary chores; I have really scrubbed and sweated over this house. Each and every room is immaculate.

The buzzing of one of his many saws rips across my nerves. How unfair it is that I am the one who must slave at unrewarding cleaning produced by others' careless habits! I am just the maid who has to work in fits and starts, between taxiing our child to activities, paying bills, and grocery shopping. I am The Momma: the one who is responsible for all things, the one who must be on call 24/7, the one who must deal with unpleasant teacher meetings and doctor appointments. Why is it that everything falls on my shoulders alone? I dream of being married to someone more understanding and more supportive of my needs.

Hot, steamy bubble bath waters somewhat restore my mood. Having arranged for our son to spend the night elsewhere, Pete and I will have the house to ourselves. Dressed and made-up, table ready, I call my spouse in for dinner.

He plops down at the table in his sawdust-coated, grease-stained work clothes. Through gritted teeth, I inquire, "Wouldn't you like to shower before we eat?"

I want to hurt him when he replies, "Naw, that's okay, I'm going back outside to 'fiddle when I'm finished eatin'."

Here we are, celebrating our sixteenth anniversary, I in a dress and this oaf getting dirt on Great Grandmomma's antique tablecloth. How could I have possibly married such an unaware, selfish man? I glare at him in silence. Several minutes pass before he finally asks, "What's all the fancy-schmancy stuff doing out on the table? Um. I'm starving, hope we're going to eat soon! Is that roast and gravy I smell?"

I sigh and fume throughout dinner. The lit candles and rich dessert have given him no clue. He hasn't even noticed we are without child as he digs into his second plate with gusto. I am filled with dis-gusto and boiling resentment!

After I clear away the plates, I bring out his present and card. He stares blankly and says, "Uh, what's that for?"

"It's your anniversary present," I flatly reply.

The utter look of embarrassment and humiliation on his face floods me with shame. I have put him in a terrible position.

"Oh, Honey," he says, squeezing my hand. "And you cleaned the house so pretty and the flowers and our wedding dishes," he whispers. "You did all this for our anniversary, and I forgot it-again," he says, bowing his head in misery.

My soul is overcome with love for the husband the Lord has blessed me with. I had asked for, and received, so many gifts when entering the vow of holy matrimony: a man filled with strength, skill, intelligence, honor, and deep loyalties.

I forgive him instantly. I see all these qualities mixed with sorrow shine through his hazel eyes. I reassure him of my forgiveness and turn our conversation to the time we first met. He opens up emotionally and shares memories and thoughts, better than any store-bought gift. It is hard for my groom to communicate. He is a man of few words but deep feelings, the man I wish to marry all over again.

We laugh and draw closer, complimenting, teasing, and touching each other as we do the dishes side by side. Removing the spring beauties picked earlier in the day, I remind myself to nourish my marriage with the same efforts I pour into my gardening. I will guard and celebrate the joys of our union with my wifely skills and love. The Bible truths on marriage help me put my faith into action.

"When one finds a worthy wife her value is far beyond pearls. Her husband, entrusting his heart to her, has an unfailing prize. She brings him good, and not evil, all the days of her life...She is clothed with strength and dignity, and she laughs at the days to come." Proverbs 31:10-12, 25. I want to be his prize.

I will resurrect and renew my marriage vows with the coming of each new spring. I will rise above my resentments, pride, and pettiness to see the goodness of my mate. I will honor the Sacrament of my marriage, which God has so richly blessed.

Nourishing Your Marriage

Devote thirty minutes a day to Bible readings.

The Ideal Wife:
Proverbs 31:10-31

The Way of Love:
1 Corinthians 13:1-13 & Sirach 26:1-18

Beautiful prose translated in the light of:
The Song of Songs: Solomon

God's love for his church and the sacredness and depth of married union.

Consider attending Marriage Encounter or communication seminars focusing on marital closeness.

Make "date night" an important part of your schedule.

Spend time alone treating each other to different activities.

Remember all of the reasons and qualities that originally attracted you to your spouse.

Pray together as a family and as a couple.

Champagne and Dandelion Soup

2 cups	dandelion blossoms,
	cleaned including green part (not stems)
1 egg	beaten
1 cup	milk
1 cup	flour
	Salt and pepper (to taste)
	Salad greens
	Vinaigrette dressing
1	10-ounce package frozen strawberries
	(thawed)
	or
1 1/2 cups	sliced fresh strawberries
1/2 cup	cold water
2 tbs	cold water
2 tbs	cornstarch
1 cup	low-fat sour cream
1 tsp	lemon juice
2 cups	heavy cream
3-4 tbs	fruit liqueur
	Champagne
	Whipped cream

Continues

- Place flour in shallow dish. Mix egg and milk in small bowl, add salt and pepper. Dip dandelion blossoms in egg mixture and dredge in flour. Deep fry in skillet or fryer until light brown. Drain and set aside.

- Place strawberries and half a cup of cold water mixed with cornstarch in a saucepan and bring to a boil. Simmer four minutes, and set aside to reach room temperature.

- Add sour cream, lemon juice, heavy cream, and liqueur to strawberries. Stir with a whisk, cover, and chill for two hours or more. Serve in a pretty bowl with a splash of champagne, a dollop of whipped cream, and one perfect fresh berry!

FINISHING TOUCH: Place bowl on matching china plate. Arrange salad greens and cleaned dandelion leaves around soup bowl. Drizzle with sweet vinaigrette dressing. Top salad with fried dandelions.

While preparing your special meal, contemplate the gifts of spring God sends us. Think of how you can turn your marital weeds into pleasing, sweet moments. Cultivate the intimate moments that flower from your relationship with your spouse. Tend your Holy Garden with God's love and cherish each new spring you share together.

Summer

LUKE, CHAPTER 8:15

"But the seed in the good soil, these are the ones who have heard the word in an honest and good heart, and hold it fast, and bear fruit with perseverance."

Swimsuit Season

~ *Angie Ledbetter* ~

I pulled and tugged at the shower curtain-type contraption hiding me from the world beyond. It was almost as ill-fitting on its aluminum pole as the garment in my sweating hand would soon be on my body. Too much area to cover and not enough material!

I welcomed this annual summer event as much as an unmedicated root canal. Why did I have to go swimming anyway? Who invented this stupid piece of clothing? Are these horrid mirrors in this dressing room from an old carnival? Are they making me look like a misshapen balloon when, in reality, I am just a large-boned woman? These and other questions flew through my head in rapid succession so as to put off the moment of dread-looking into the full-length mirrors surrounding me in this department store closet.

I wished again that I lived in the 1900's, when bathing attire consisted of long, striped knickers, a high-necked, long-sleeved top, heavy stockings, and ankle boots. Pulling, stretching, adjusting, rearranging, and hopelessly holding my breath did not make the lycra torture device now covering my lumpy torso look any better. Trying to think positively, I took stock of the entire picture before me in the shiny surface. No luck. The only parts of my over-exposed body that looked anywhere near decent were the portions of leg between my knees and my ankles. And they were in dire need of a shave.

Frustrated and humiliated, I hung the swimsuits back on the racks and dejectedly left the mall, fighting the temptation to pull into the nearest ice-cream parlor for a hot fudge sundae with the works. Instead, I drove to my favorite chapel to have a few moments of quiet before heading home to the family fray and the supper I had to cook.

A cool peace enveloped me as I found an empty chair. Others already there were busy with their prayers. A woman with deep circles etched beneath her eyes slept contentedly with a Bible opened on her lap. Several rows in front of me, a young student dug pen and paper from his backpack along with a small stack of inspirational reading material. Some knelt to pray the rosary, others read Scripture, and a few had their eyes closed in deep concentration on their conversations with Christ. Yes, this was a good place for me to escape the unpleasant activities of the day.

As hard as I tried, I couldn't get the experience out of my mind and pictured again and again trying on suit after suit as my disgust mounted. It was like watching a movie that was stuck in the projector, replaying a segment over and over. No style seemed made for me. I just was not a bathing suit person.

Jesus, how can you love someone who is in this shape? I have failed to take care of the temple you have given me to house my soul. I am ashamed that I am not doing a better job of keeping in shape, I prayed to my savior. Consumed by the peaceful surroundings and small sounds around me, I continued to pour out my heart to Jesus. As always when I came to this place of worship, my conversations were focused and heartfelt. No worldly distractions or interruptions followed me here except the ones in my own mind.

After sharing my thoughts and feelings for some time and concentrating on the five joyous mysteries of the rosary, I felt better. It was almost as if some relief valve had been opened and the burdens had flown. Soon, I had snuggled down in the welcoming chair and drifted off to that place that is somewhere between full sleep and wakefulness.

In my dream, I was before the Throne of God, sitting on a small footstool at his feet. He was lovingly patting my head, and the soothing touch brought instant and intense joy. It was like having days on end of gloomy rain and suddenly, the sun peeks out and the skies clear. The warmth of being surrounded by goodness and a fresh new day invades the senses.

Embarrassed, I was telling him of my failure in keeping myself in shape, and he gently asked, "Do you not know, Daughter, that I love you just as you are? Indeed, I see your interior features and they are on the whole pleasing."

Uplifted, I felt many pounds lighter. We talked on in this semi-dream state, and I saw that I did have work to do-on both body and soul-but that I was not a disgrace to the Lord. He preferred me to be healthy, yes, but that was so I could have energy to do all of the work he had planned for me, not because he considered me ugly.

I was next looking down at a small flower garden. A beautiful swallowtail butterfly with royal blue and brilliant yellow markings floated from stem to stem before lighting on a pink carnation. Beneath the umbrella of the flower's petals, a small toad sat unmoving. The fluttering of the butterfly's wings cast a moving shadow on his lumpy green and mud-colored head. I looked back and forth at the two small creatures, enjoying the scene.

A swift brown sparrow dove from some unseen tree branch toward the butterfly. In a flash, the toad leapt for cover beneath the flower's stems and was hidden and camouflaged by his coloring. The butterfly was carried off in the blink of an eye, and the frog continued on its journey.

The squeak of the heavy wooden door opening to admit someone to the chapel woke me and reminded me that I, like the toad, had better get on the road. I knelt to say prayers of thanks and to offer intentions for friends and family members in need, then I made my way to the parking lot.

A lone butterfly drifted by me toward the bank of magenta azaleas. I hoped a hungry bird would not find this lovely specimen for its supper. I was reminded that the creatures in my chapel vision had their beauty and worth, neither more so than the other. The butterfly was beautiful to behold, but the toad's strong legs and God-given hues had protected it from harm. Smiling, I drove home to prepare a meal for my waiting family.

Scripture Reference

John 2:21-

"But the temple he had spoken of was his body."

---

1 Corinthians 6:19-

"Do you not know that your body is a temple of the Holy Spirit, who is in you, whom you have received from God? You are not your own..."

Psalm 73:4-

"They have no struggles; their bodies are healthy and strong."

---

3 John 1:2-

"Dear friend, I pray that you may enjoy good health and that all may go well with you, even as your soul is getting along well."

Stewardship Tips for the Self

Stand in front of a full-length mirror if possible. Try looking at yourself with different eyes for a change. See the good things about you and play them up with make-up, accessories and/or your hairstyle. Picture yourself before our loving God, and see the goodness and beauty that he would see. Dismiss negative thoughts immediately.

Make a list of your wonderful characteristics and talents. Try to expand upon and work on these. Remember, we all look alike when we're ninety, so we might as well try to develop our inner goodness. And as Forrest Gump said, "Purty is as purty does." Developing humor and laughing more each day also helps us to shine in unexpected ways.

Improving our health, diet, and exercise routines are goals we should all strive for. Drink plenty of water, eat balanced and healthful portions and varieties, get out and move your body more often, and pray before eating. Make sure you are getting enough rest and sleep. Learning basic yoga and deep breathing exercises and listening to classical music can help soothe over-worked nerves and help prevent illness. Treat your temple as you should.

Fruity Smoothie

2 CUPS	LOW FAT OR SKIM MILK
1/2 CUP	PLAIN YOGURT
1/2 CUP	FRESH, FROZEN OR CANNED FRUIT (PEACHES AND BERRIES WORK WELL)
1	RIPE BANANA
1 TSP	HONEY

- Mix all ingredients in a blender, adding four or five ice cubes. Mix until a smooth, shake-like consistency is formed.

- Experiment with extract flavorings for different tastes. Enjoy now or freeze for later.

His Image

In His image I see beauty and worth,
Things often missed by eyes on Earth.
Straining, I spot what's hidden within.
Our Lord's view is not jaundiced by sin.

My splendor resides in a secret place,
Planted there by the Master of Grace.
In my mirror are reflections so dim,
With prayer, I see a likeness of Him.

Hot Tar in the Deep South

~ Deb Anne Flynt ~

Once you've spent quite a few years in the Deep South, you become somewhat acclimated to hot summers and mild winters. I put on my shoes, grabbed a water bottle, and headed out for my walk. If I hadn't slept late, I could have been back inside before it got hot. Now, if I was going to get a walk, I had to do it before the children came home from school with homework and before starting supper. Once the kids got off that bus, I was on mom-time only, until they were asleep. My sweet husband, knowing I was fatigued, got them off to school without waking me, but put me behind on my chores for the day. That sounds like a complaint, but it isn't. It isn't at all.

I checked my watch-12:26. This is not when I planned on walking today. I almost changed my mind and headed for the gym instead, but I wanted privacy. I had to think about something. As I started up the driveway, I set my mind to work out my problem. I had hurt a friend, and now I had to undo it. Stepping onto the road, I realized that it was hotter than I had initially thought. Small tar bubbles were tiny traps to the unsuspecting sandal wearer. I had learned this many summers ago. Once you get gooey tar on you, it's there for a while.

I remembered trying to help my son with a similar problem. He had taken a spill on his bike and landed in the road. I managed, with plenty of soap and more scrubbing, to get most of the tar transferred from his scraped leg onto a washcloth. He tossed it into the clothes hamper where it rubbed against a towel, getting a bit on it. When I washed the towels the next morning, I forgot about the tar on the washcloth. I threw it in with the rest of the load. A small amount of tar like that doesn't smell up a whole laundry room, but it does affect everything in the washing machine with it. I opened the washer and found that a few things had just a touch of tar on them, and I removed the washcloth from the load and ran it again-this time in hot water with extra detergent. I rinsed the cloth in the sink and laid it on the washer to dry, postponing my unavoidable decision to throw it away.

When I opened the washer again, the smell was more prevalent, and the tar had managed to spread. I threw away the washcloth, knowing it would only make things worse the next time I forgot what was on it and washed it with something else. It was inevitable.

I realized that I was at the halfway point on my walk, and I turned around to head back home. I thought about how that wreck and the tar had caused pain to my son, ruined a load of laundry, and cost me time and energy. "It's worse than weeds!"

I remembered then that there was something specific I had intended to think about while on this walk. I had said something to a friend that I shouldn't have. I realized that I had less than half of my walk left to think about how that might have affected her, and how I was going to make up for it. My mind kept going to the tar, though, with every little bubble I saw.

After I got home another friend called and said she had seen me walking, but I didn't even look up and wave. It was so uncharacteristic; she called to see what was wrong. "Oh, I'm sorry. No, nothing's wrong. I was just thinking, I guess." We talked briefly, since each of us had things to do before our children arrived home, but her question had touched a nerve.

I had hurt someone. No matter what I said, that hurt would still exist. Just like that bike accident would leave a scar with some unrelenting tar on my son, my words would leave a mark on my friend's heart. I could never undo that. From there, she went about her day in a less charitable mood. Everyone she might have met with her customary smile-even strangers-went without her usual cheerful greeting. I felt worse than before. If only I had been kinder, chosen my words with more care, she would not have been hurt. It wasn't a terrible thing, just something said flippantly, off the cuff, but what difference did that make to anyone?

I called and asked her if I could come over. I skipped doing the rest of the laundry and went to apologize. She was just as forgiving as I knew she would be. With that, she had thrown away the washcloth, but the residue remained. How many people did my carelessness affect?

A plaque in my grandmother's kitchen says, "Lord, let my words be tender and sweet today, for tomorrow I may have to eat them." And tar is neither sweet nor tender.

Lessons from a Long Walk

The rules are simple, but not always easy.
We know them by heart, but here's the breakdown.

1. God is God. There are no others. Father, Son, and Holy Spirit: one God.
2. Worship of anything else is unacceptable. If God is not your top priority, what is?
3. Don't call God if you don't mean it. If you say his name, be praying. If you aren't, it's a good time to start.
4. Go to church. Sundays do not belong to you, and this is the day God chose to spend with you more than any other. God owns all time, so don't say Sundays are "my time." Football is not an exception.
5. Take care of your parents and respect them. God set it up that way. He chose your parents, and he knows what he's doing.
6. Don't kill. Don't even get angry enough to think about it!
7. Have sex with only one married person-your spouse.
8. If it's not yours, don't take it. Don't take it, don't move it, and don't mess with it.
9. Don't lie. Don't gossip, don't omit facts or misrepresent them, and don't try any of the other ways that we think we get around the truth. Politics is not an exception. God is omnipotent and he is the Truth.
10. Don't wish you had what belongs to someone else. God provides you with what you need. (See numbers seven and eight above.)

If you still have questions, refer to Exodus 20:1-17, ask your minister, or pray about it.

ANOTHER GRANOLA RECIPE

2 CUPS	ROLLED OATS
2 CUPS	ROLLED WHEAT
1/4 CUP	BROWN SUGAR
2 TBS	HONEY
1/2 CUP	RAISINS
1/4 CUP	SHREDDED COCONUT
1/4 CUP	SLIVERED ALMONDS
1/4 CUP	CHOPPED PECANS
1/4 CUP	CHOPPED DATES
1/4 CUP	DRIED BERRIES (OPTIONAL)
	CINNAMON TO TASTE

- Preheat the oven to 350 degrees. Mix all the ingredients in a large bowl. Grease a large jellyroll pan or baking sheet (one with sides works best). Spread the mix in the pan and bake for ten minutes. Take it out, turn or mix it, spread it back out and bake for another five minutes, until golden brown. Let cool completely, and then place in airtight bags.

SERVING SUGGESTIONS: Pour into cereal bowls and serve with milk and honey, or eat it on the go. This makes a nice snack to take on a long walk.

Summer Learning Fun

Just because summer is a break from school, it doesn't have to be a break from learning. Your local library may provide children with a summer reading program, as mine does. The children's librarian there pointed out to me that students who read as few as five books over the summer retain most of their reading skills, as opposed to those who don't read and lose those valuable lessons learned. We both hope children will read more than that and improve their skills before returning to school in the fall. My children do read more than that, and I don't even have to make them. They love books.

They also love Vacation Bible School. They love the break from the house, that they go at night, that they make new friends, and that they learn about the Word. It seems to me that these two programs can be combined successfully. If children are going to read over the summer, what better book for them to study? Admittedly, there are no vampires or ghost dogs, but there are many fascinating stories that are appropriate for kids, and there Bibles available in more child-friendly translations for the younger readers.

THE REAL TOP TEN

I am the one True God, the Lord
Take care that you honor this.
I have given you My Word
To bow to another is remiss.

If you call Me, I will hear;
I always listen to you.
Say My name, and I draw near;
So say it with honor due.

I bid you worship on My day.
Keep it Holy and true.
Do not forget to come and pray.
I am waiting for you.

Those to whom I entrust your care
I have chosen most carefully.
I love them dearly, so do not dare
To dishonor them, or you dishonor Me.

All life is mine, for I am Life.
This you must strive to save.
I command you to respect all life,
From conception to the grave.

If by vow you take a wife,
Or if you a husband you wed,
You must keep that promise for life,
And yourself from another's bed.

I will provide for your every need,
And for everyone else's too.
This is my word, which you must heed,
Do not take what I don't give you.

I admonish you to speak the truth,
Your half-truths are only lies.
Speak honestly in old age and youth
If you will not, then silence is wise.

As you love yourself, love one another.
This I have made known to you.
If you seek to take from your brother,
Your sins, not possessions, accrue.

These are my laws, which I have given.
Honor Me, and each other cherish.
Keep my commands with your hearts, with your hands,
And seek Me, that you do not perish.

RECONCILED *by* LOVE

~ *Carol Schwartz* ~

Reconciliation means getting right with God and man in our heart, soul, and mind. Part of the process involves asking God to forgive us, confessing our wrongs to another, and asking forgiveness. In the Catholic Church we confess to a priest, in other churches people confess to one another or the minister. God looks into our hearts and sees our honest intent and desire to be forgiven. He forgives us and we become free.

Forgiving ourselves is an important part of the process. Forgetting our past hurts is the more challenging aspect of being set free. Free to enjoy, as I am this evening, the beautiful sunset with its colors of gold, red, orange, blue, and purple, surrounded by a few white clouds, amidst a baby blue sky flowing onto the colorful brown and green mountain tops.

Who could ever see such beauty and deny there is a loving and gracious God? People who have been abused, that's who. They have experienced the ugly side of life. Abuse comes in many forms, such as physical, mental, emotional, sexual, and spiritual, or as a witness to another's being abused.

There is a way out for even the most abused to find a loving God and embrace his love. The requirements are prayers for a willingness to learn and openness to change.

Change is the challenge. Because God is about love, only he makes that possible. Abuse creates distance between a person and God and between that person and others. Not having experienced love, the abused do not know there is a loving God

I was recently reminded of this when I watched the movie Angel Eyes. The gal in the movie had been witness to a family member's abuse and had become angry and resentful. Out of fear she held on to the resentment for many years, and to protect herself, she shut everyone out of her life.

The movie brought back some childhood memories that I had forgotten. My memories were of an uncle who was a drunken sot. When he drank he became abusive, especially to small and even not so small children. He abused everyone in his presence-physically, verbally, and sometimes sexually. I learned to run away and hide in the basement or outside. Sometimes I was able to take my cousin Sally with me, but not always. As a child my heart ached when I tried to fight off this huge six-foot man and couldn't save my cousins from his wrathful beatings. I suffered tremendous survival guilt for years after he killed them and then himself.

I've come to believe people are in our lives for a reason, often for a conversion or renewed connection to God through others. Sharon and I connected because of our common experiences.

My friend Sharon tells her story and how her traumatic experience left its mark on her soul. She got married to a man she loved very much, and they had two beautiful sons. Memories started resurfacing from her childhood when her husband would drink, get angry, and raise his voice. Eventually she did the only thing she'd been taught to do; she shut him out of her heart. The marriage lasted for some time after that; however, the ties were broken long before the divorce. After a number of years and numerous failed attempts to have a relationship with a man, she eventually sought counseling.

The counseling helped to some extent, but there was still something missing from her life. She had a great job and made enough money, so that was not the answer. Her sons were raised and doing well. What could possibly be missing from her life? One day at work a friend asked Sharon to go to a church concert. The friend, Cathy, was singing in the concert, and there were many other choirs. Sharon enjoyed the singing and meeting Cathy's church friends. Maybe that was it-maybe Sharon needed some friends outside of work, or maybe she needed to get back to church, or maybe both.

Sharon decided to go back to church. She tried the one closest to her house, which was the Catholic church that she and her former husband had attended. She saw some old friends and realized they were still her friends. Sharon met new friends, like myself, that welcomed her into the fold.

Over time Sharon and I became close friends. We shared many joys with laughter and sorrows with tears. I think of her often, how she overcame her fear of loving and trusting after she started going to church again. She often commented how she wished she could be more trusting of others' motives and regretted the years she had wasted in shutting out love because she couldn't trust herself to know real love.

Sharon began to see examples of God's love and blessings in her life when she finally surrendered to the idea that just possibly there is a loving God. As her friend, I learned that love is the only thing that can break down the walls of someone who is terrified to let anyone into their heart.

Love is the great reconciler of a person to God and between people. It is the only thing that opens the heart of someone whose heart is closed from abuse.

Granny

Granny was God's gift to children,
She loved Father God above,
Raised fifteen balls of energy,
Giving each her precious love.

Every time I visited Granny,
She filled me with joy and calm,
Showering love on all grandkids,
Giving us hugs all day long.

She cooked homemade soup,
Granny's chicken and dumplings style,
Like none I've ever seen,
Nor have I eaten in a while.

She answered many questions,
With loving kindness always,
Surely she was an angel,
And now rests with God all days.

In a dream some years ago,
As an angel she came to me,
On her face was a big smile,
Like when I was a child of three.

I want to be a granny like her,
To Dan, Kyle, and Tiffany Ann,
Loving these wonderful grandchildren,
Showing them God in all I can.

MOTHER'S CHICKEN and DUMPLINGS

1 1/2 CUP	SIFTED WHITE FLOUR
2 TSP	BAKING POWDER
1 TSP	SALT
3 TBS	SHORTENING
1 CUP	MILK
1	WHOLE CHICKEN
	SALT AND PEPPER TO TASTE

- Parboil chicken until the meat easily comes off the bone. Keeping the broth in the pot, discard bones and put meat back into the broth, and bring it to a boil.

- Blend dry ingredients until well mixed. Add shortening and milk and mix. Form dumplings with a spoon, and drop them into the broth, bringing it again to a boil. Do not cover. Cook about ten minutes and remove the dumplings. Thicken the chicken broth with flour and water mixture for thicker gravy, and season for your taste with salt and pepper. Place the thickened gravy and chicken into a serving dish and place the dumplings on top. Enjoy on a cool summer eve with your favorite green salad.

- If you are in a hurry, use two cups Bisquick with 2/3 cup of milk in place of the white flour, baking powder, and salt.

From Naomi Houger (her mother was my Granny)

Life's a Beach

~ Alaine Benard ~

Packing sunscreen, floats, beach towels and flip-flops, we take off for our vacation trip to the coast. It is the official beginning of summer, and screeching our feet back and forth in the sand is the joyous song we've come to hear.

The symphony of waves is the background music that lulls us into contentment. Between gathering shells and driftwood, we reapply SPF 30 sunblock to our pale skin. As we do each year, we swiftly forget about the school math and job challenges that have filled the past months. As the water rushes back into the sea, it wipes our memories clean, leaving a sea salt tingle on our emotions. The penetrating warmth of the white sun bakes us fresh and clean-invigorated.

Buckets in hand, our little family trots off down the shoreline to capture sand dollars. Dodging the jellyfish left high and dry by the tide, our son speculates why God made such a terrible creature. Not too far into the ensuing discussion of good versus bad, we encounter a group of wild drunks. Vulgar, cursing, half-dressed partiers taunt and heckle us as we try our best to ignore them.

Out of earshot, I struggle to pick up the thread of the "lesson" we had started. Mind back on the group behind us, our son melds the two offensive categories into one; "Hmmm, those people back there are just like the jellyfish, hunh, Mom?"

"How so, son?" I ask, intrigued. "Well, jellyfish are nasty and so are people when they act like that. Jesus must be awfully ashamed of what they're doing," he answered quietly as he looked back over his pink shoulder.

My super-intelligent husband reels off a list of positive benefits gained from the jellyfish; how they help the chain of ecology continue, and so on. Other than boosting hotel business and alcohol sales, we couldn't think of any constructive benefits derived from the group of people we had observed. That evening, we prayed for their safety and for their souls to reawaken in the light of God's love by following the commandments. Pulling the cool sheet over our sleepy, freckled-faced boy, his last words were to remind us to 'hate the sin but love the sinner.' Kissing his forehead, we agreed wholeheartedly.

Unlike the stinging sea critters, we humans do have a choice as to what type of life we will lead. We can use our free will to be either jellyfish or sand dollars on God's earthly beaches. Each and every minute we opt to commit sin or to do what is pleasing to the Lord. Free will is the power to make a choice between two opposites.

Studying the Parables shows me just how striking the contrast is. Jesus gave us the example of the weeds among the wheat; "The kingdom of heaven may be likened to a man who sowed good seed in his field. While everyone was asleep his enemy came and sowed weeds all through the wheat, and then went off. When the crop grew and bore fruit, the weeds appeared as well." When questioned by the slaves, Jesus replied, "No, if you pull up the weeds you might uproot the wheat along with them. Let them grow together until harvest; then at harvest time I will say to the harvesters, 'First collect the weeds and tie them in bundles for burning; but gather the wheat into my barn.'"

So, the angelic "harvesters" will be the ones in charge of separating the bad from the good, under God's direction. We must not make judgments, as God will do that according to his justice. The "wheat" is expected to be patient and share thoughts on repentance and living according to God's word while cohabitating with the "weeds." We should strive to bear good fruit and not think of others as excluded from the Heavenly Kingdom.

What a joy walking upon the sands of life is when we keep things in proper perspective! Avoid the jellyfish stings and concentrate on the beauty of giving and receiving the sand dollars God provides. His mercy and forgiveness are the ever-continuing and comforting wave-hymns that fill our spirit with sweet sound.

Sand Sculptures

For each day of your trip, try a different theme. Some suggestions worth creating are: the Crucifix, the Holy Spirit Dove, and other religious symbols. Ask each person participating to make a sand sculpture representing his or her favorite parable subject. Try your hand at designing your most beloved spiritually inspiring subject in nature.

Sun and Sand Inspirations

Shell collecting is especially good if a storm interrupts your activities. Read about the sand dollar, and when the weather clears, start gathering. The best time to comb the beaches is when the tide recedes. After a heavy storm, many different shells are dredged up by the increased wave action.

Legend of the Sand Dollar

The Sand Dollar's legend
That I would like to tell
Is of the life of Jesus
Found in this lovely shell.

If you examine closely
Four nail holes will appear
And next to them a fifth one
Made by a Roman's spear.

Behold the Easter Lily
Its center is the star
That shone above our Saviour
For the travelers from afar.

The Christmas Poinsettia
Etched on the other side
Reminds us of his birthday,
Our happy Christmastide.

Now break the center open
And here you will release
Five white doves awaiting
To spread good will and peace.

This simple little token
Of faith and purity
Becomes a living symbol
Of Christ's love for you and me.

Reading and Sharing

Footprints in the Sand,
Daily Meditations for Women/Men Who Do Too Much

The Life of St. Bernard
(Being non-judgmental and loving all you meet)

Matthew 13, 24-15
(Parables)

The New St. Joseph Baltimore Catechism
(Our free will)

BEACH SALAD

3 CUPS	FRESH SPINACH
1	BANANA, PEELED AND SLICED
1/2 CUP	RASPBERRIES
	or
1	ORANGE, PEELED AND SLICED
1/2 CUP	SLICED RADISHES
1/2 CUP	SLIVERED CARROTS
1/4 LB.	BARBECUED OR SMOKED DELI CHICKEN, SLICED
1 TBS	GRATED PARMESAN CHEESE (OPTIONAL)
1/4 CUP	LIGHT ITALIAN SALAD DRESSING
2 TBS	CHOPPED RED ONION

- Arrange spinach on two salad plates. Arrange banana, berries or orange slices, radishes, carrots, and chicken over spinach. Sprinkle parmesan cheese over each serving, if desired. Stir together salad dressing and onion in small bowl or cup. Serve over salads.

From the Dole Recipe Collection

Time to Slow Down!

~ Deb Anne Flynt ~

Part 1: Dealing with Everyday Stress

Yesterday, I was joining a virtual town that a hometown friend of mine wanted to take me to through my computer. I was told I'd need a nickname for it. I've had plenty of those, but some I'd prefer not to be called. I looked at hers, which was an expression of her motherhood. I jokingly asked if I should call myself something similarly mom-ish, and wondered if "stressed_mess" would be available. I never tried it.

I felt guilty for that, because my children are real life miracles, and they are a blessing. I love them, but they do stress me out-especially the oh-so-teenage boy. No matter how wonderful children are-and mine are-they are a source of stress. They are not the only source of stress in my life by far, but they contribute generously. I have learned, especially in the past year, that this is not necessarily a bad thing, that stress can be good for me. A few years ago, I would have had my husband commit me to a psychiatric hospital just for thinking that. A few years ago, I had no clue as to how clueless I was.

In college, I wrote some papers on "The Physical and Psychological Aspects of Stress." I was an expert, I thought, on how to deal with everyday stress. I knew how to prevent and overcome headaches, backaches, stiff muscles, neck cramps, and several other symptoms. I offered exercises, stretches, diets, relaxation and breathing techniques, and advice on how and when to sleep. There was no tension that could not be relieved by taking advantage of my marvelous expertise.

A few years later, I got married. It didn't take long to discard the papers I had previously held in such high regard, and the delusion of wisdom with them. Then I had kids. That's when I learned the meaning of the word "stress." I spent my son's terrible two's with my shoulders against my ears. I couldn't get my neck muscles to unlock.

It took a while, but I found what was for me a surefire cure. I returned to creative writing, and I came back to the church. I returned to God and made friends with similar interests, including my friend mentioned earlier. I found myself in a good place with great company.

My relationships have deepened to a point that I am now nearly comfortable. Well, it's a point where my goals are always just barely within my reach, so I keep stretching-mentally, emotionally, spiritually, and even physically. There is now satisfaction, where before I would have found disappointment, and I would have been terribly stressed out about failing to meet every goal.

After all the years I spent convinced I was fine, and that I always would be with all the knowledge I had attained, I finally realized that the most important thing I had to learn was how little I knew. Once I got that, I began learning again-in earnest. I began to look at things differently, to set higher standards, and to expect more from myself.

I suppose the irony of all this is that I couldn't gain wisdom until I recognized my ignorance. I couldn't rekindle my spiritual life until I noticed that the embers were cooling. It's a lesson that would be easier to take earlier in life, with the humility of a child, but in his infinite wisdom, God makes us work for this knowledge.

PART 2: SEEKING TIME

Many people have never sat in a porch swing in the late afternoon with a sweating glass of tea in their hands, slippered or bare feet dragging along the worn wooden porch boards. Everybody's in a big rush, and we let the simple pleasures go when other things crowd our time.

I used to love to sit on the porch swing, my feet making that old familiar fft fft fft on the floor as they skidded the edge of each weatherworn board. Droplets would spill from a cold glass of tea or lemonade onto my shorts-clad legs, sending shivers up my spine and often waking me from a reverie.

I had a favorite stump that I sat on while I daydreamed for hours. I spent much time with God there, and I could hear and see him all around me. And there was a spot on the bank of a pond where I could sit all day just thinking. It didn't matter about what, or how important or frivolous.

What happened? Days are short now! They seemed to have more hours before. I have more to fit into the few hours I have left of these days, but the more timesaving conveniences I acquire, the less time I have. Is this someone's cruel idea of a joke?

Where is all that time that I'm saving? Where is it stored? It seems like it would be there at the end of the day, but I'm just as hurried then. What's the point of saving time if you can't have the time you saved?

With all this fancy stuff, my saved time ought to be a nice chunk by now. If it's sitting in a time bank somewhere collecting interest, I'd like to make a withdrawal so I can spend an extra weekend with my kids this month.

Who owns time? I hear people talk about "my time" and "your time" and "company time." I've heard the phrase, "making time," a few times, and I want that recipe! I'm always trying to find time to do things, and I can't even find my car keys sometimes.

My theory about time is it's all God's. There's no such thing as "my time" or "your time" or anybody else's time. Now, if I'm right, and it is all his time, then what are we supposed to be doing with it?

If you don't know the answer to that one, then take the time to figure it out. The way I see it, we're all living on borrowed time, so we may as well slow down and make the most of it, which for me means spending more time with God.

Part 3: Too Busy for God?

Mary and Joseph were obedient to the law of Moses and had completed their days of purification, according to the law. When this was done, they took Jesus to the temple in Jerusalem. The law stated that since he was the firstborn son, he must be consecrated to the Lord, and an offering be made of "a pair of turtledoves or two young pigeons." In the temple they found Simeon, who was a devout man. The Holy Spirit had revealed to him that he would not die until he had seen the Messiah. When he saw Jesus, "he took him into his arms and blessed God, saying: 'Now, Master, you may let your servant go in peace, according to your word, for my eyes have seen your salvation, which you prepared in the sight of all the peoples, a light for revelation to the Gentiles, and glory for your people Israel.'" (Luke 2:28-32)

Simeon had opened his heart to the Lord, and he was a great prophet. He wasn't too busy or in the middle of a phone call when Jesus was brought in. He didn't have them make an appointment and come back later. He was totally devoted to the Lord and to the Lord's work.

In my life, I find that I am frequently too busy for one thing or another. I have a family to tend to, a house to clean, and places to go. In my rush-rush life, I sometimes forget to walk to the woods or be alone with God. I go to church, but I usually leave as soon as it's over. I feel like I need more hours in the day, but would that help? If I had more time, would I spend it in prayer, meditation, adoration, and service, or would I fill it up with more housework, kids' activities, and rushing here and there? I would like to think that I would spend more time talking with my family, in communion with the Lord, and doing his work. The truth is, I don't know what I would do.

I know some people who also have only twenty-four hours in their days who work eight- to ten-hour jobs, spend much time in community service and stewardship, cook, clean, spend time with their families, exercise, spend time in meditation or in adoration, and still spend hours in prayer. I am not one of those people. They get more done every day than I do in a week, and yet they are not as rushed as I am. Oh, and they sleep, too. One even takes naps! They have mastered something that I still struggle with but am working to overcome. I want to take control of my life, make my own choices, do what I think is right. They are not in control of their lives, and yet their lives are far better controlled than mine! How? They have surrendered it to God. He is in control of their lives.

Okay, so maybe I am a control freak. I've been called that. My goal is to turn every day over to God. Put him in the driver's seat and see where he takes me. When I do accomplish this, my days are fuller, I get more done, but I'm not as busy. He usually takes me on the scenic route, too. Now if I can only remember to do it every day-before mid-afternoon.

When I was a child, I would daydream for hours on end. I would love to have that back. Right now, though, I just don't have time. What I do have time for is to turn the rest of this day over to God. Maybe then I'll have time to daydream. ❦

Bible Verses for Dealing with Stress:

Psalms 118:24-

"Today is the day the Lord hath made; let us rejoice and be glad in it."

Philippians 4:13-

"I can do everything through Christ who strengthens me."

Proverbs 3:5-6-

"Trust in the Lord with all your heart, and lean not unto your own understanding. In all your ways, acknowledge Him, and He will direct your path."

Philippians 4:6-

"Do not worry about anything; instead PRAY ABOUT EVERYTHING."

Psalm 4:1-

"Answer me when I call to you, O my righteous God. Give me relief from my distress; be merciful to me and hear my prayer."

Psalm 94:19 -

"When anxiety was great within me,
Your consolation brought joy to my soul."

Part of the Burden

Have you ever noticed that the same group of people does most of the work in a church? It may not be true of all churches, but it's probably true of enough of them for the point to be worth making. There are many things that must be done, but only a few that do them. You know who they are, if your church is like this. You may be one of them. If you aren't, though, ask yourself why not. Are you embarrassed? Are you unconcerned because someone else always does it? Are you afraid that they have a secret club that you won't be welcomed into? Maybe it's too far to drive more than once a week. Or are you just too busy?

It's time to question your reasons for not helping. Picture yourself explaining it to Jesus. Could you justify your reasons to him? If you have a real reason for not being able to shoulder part of the burden, he knows, but if you think your reasons would sound lame to the King of Kings, then maybe it's time to get busy.

Cloves for Busy~Day Stress Relief:

Buy cloves from a health food store, since they are generally more potent than those found in a grocery store.

Clove tea is a stress buster. Put one teaspoon of clove buds in a cup of filtered or distilled water. Simmer for ten minutes and promptly strain. Put the cloves in the refrigerator-you can use them again. Sip slowly as you listen to some soothing music, burn a calming floral scented candle, and allow yourself to relax.

Clove baths can overcome insomnia. In a large pot (non-aluminum) combine three quarts of water with four tablespoons of cloves-use buds or powder. Simmer this for twenty to thirty minutes and strain. Pour the clove water into your hot bath, and relax. Sip your tea while you soak for no more than twenty minutes. (Soaking longer may result in oversleeping, so don't overdo it.) It's normal to feel a slight numbing and warming all over your body. This tells you that the cloves are working. Climb out, dry off, stay warm, and crawl into bed. Sweet dreams.

The Stars *that* Came Through My Room

As I lay there in the strange world
between consciousness and sleep,
I began having the most unusual dream,
Thousands of stars moved across my ceiling,
Filled my room with a luminous stream.

I asked them what they were there for;
Why they had visited me,
They answered in a gentle voice,
That they were all prayers for me.

And then the stars began slowing,
Though streamers now followed them through,
The ones with the tails not as bright as
Their cousins had been, but they were blue.

These stars I asked very gently,
Their hearts all seemed to be broken.
"We are the prayers that you offered to say,
But never by you were spoken."

I thought of all the times I started,
All the prayers I'd started to say,
When I would fall asleep too soon,
Or something got in the way.

Of all the people I'd prayed for,
And all the times I'd prayed,
I found it hard to believe that
This many had gotten away.

Right then I prayed for all of them,
And again I'll pray for them still,
I don't know the names of most of them,
But in my heart, I know God will.

The names of the nameless, God knows,
It doesn't matter if I do,
And whenever I offer a prayer,
I pray for the nameless stars, too.

I pray for the weak and the lost,
Because sometimes no one else does,
And I pray for the lonely and friendless,
That they, too, feel the warmth of God's love.

I pray for the helpless and hopeless,
I know that God knows who they are,
And I pray for the many unprayed for,
For everyone else's star.

Perfecting Job

~ Angie Ledbetter ~

"Shall we indeed accept good from God and not accept adversity?"

Job 2:10

In reading about the long-suffering Job, I laughed when I thought about my daily dreaded chores-job-having the same spelling. A free flow of thoughts made me sit down with pen and paper to make a list of the similarities between poor, faithful Job and my own version of a job.

Job (the man):

He was an upstanding person and top-notch Christian, fearing God in all he did. He was a faithful father of many children for whom he prayed daily and an owner of huge herds of livestock and servants. Job walked with God. With that many kids and responsibilities, I know he had his hands full, but still he persevered and lived a life of example in his humility and trust in the Lord.

Satan, being the deceiver and troublemaker that he is, tells the Lord that Job is only righteous because he has been blessed in every way and never tested through hardship. When God's hand is withdrawn from Job, plagues and natural disasters take some of his children and possessions, yet he does not curse the Lord. Satan is allowed to attack Job's flesh and puts him through unimaginable pain and suffering. Living through a crucifixion of sorts, Job remains steadfast. In a way, Job's trials are a foreshadowing of what will happen to Jesus at his crucifixion. He, too, wondered if he'd been abandoned in his hour of need.

Even as his friends and family turn against him in his afflictions, Job does not listen to their bad advice and discouragement, but clings to his hope in the Lord. After years of suffering and just barely alive, Job is rewarded by God for his faithfulness. His earlier riches, health, and offspring are multiplied until the end of his life at age 140.

Job (my daily work and chores):

Many days I tend to see my own career and roles as heavy burdens. Small children often wreak havoc on my sanity and peacefulness. The activities my family partakes in sometimes strain my van's mileage and the allotted 24-hour daily time frame. I catch myself whining impatiently at the scheduling duties I have for a family of five. I grouse at waiting in a carpool line in the heat of southern summers, or the minor pain of sitting on scorching metal bleachers at another of my son's baseball games. Anger often overtakes me when my husband and I are not communicating well, and I feel that the brunt of family and kiddy responsibilities are piling up on my shoulders.

When friends or relatives fail to act as I think they should, I sometimes get weepy. Why can't everyone just see what needs to be done and jump in to help out fairly? Why are my own children intent on rollerblading over my last nerve? Why do they seem to be allergic to one another and love to squabble and tattle so often? These and many other pity-drenched questions jangle my mind often as I struggle to keep our family life in balance. Trying to maintain our home as an oasis safe from the invasion of a crumbling moral society outside our doors adds to the burden.

Then there is my so-called profession. My work/job life is also a mishmash of competing interests. On any given day of the week, I am called by pager to run to a job for a furniture company in between cleaning houses. I complain about having to be a maid for others, but in truth, it is an excellent way to earn money and still have time at home for my family, or to be available for school volunteer projects. I have trouble remembering the advantages when my lower back is screaming from mopping, vacuuming, sweeping, or cleaning potties and tubs. I've also been tempted to listen to others who think that housecleaning is a demeaning profession of no glory or worth, until I realize that these same people devalue the choice of being a stay-at-home parent.

If I chose to view my jobs-at home or in the world-through a negative lens, I could have one heck of a pity party! But, if I see the many blessings that come from my jobs, I surely have a wealth of reasons to rejoice. After my babies were old enough to go to school, I prayed hard and long for God to send me the perfect job. I asked that it not be back in the legal profession or secretarial, as those were hard, long days that would require before, after, and holiday childcare.

My top priority was to be the one who raised my kids. I then asked God to find me work that would allow time for lots of ministry work and school volunteering. To further load my request, I also prayed for a job that would allow me time to pursue my passion-inspirational writing. The Bible tells us to be specific in our prayers, and so I was.

Thinking this was an impossible to-do list for the Father, I prayed in faith anyway, thanking him in advance for that perfect job to come. The job came to me with lightening speed, but not in the form I'd expected. Sometimes our dreams and the life we envision for ourselves is not what God has planned for us at all. I'd been daydreaming of finding some cushy job that would allow me to leisurely sit at my computer all day and never require me to leave home. But my "perfect job" was a combo plate of three separate jobs. Together, these jobs filled my prayer to a tee.

I have time for my family, my stewardship activities, the children's goings-on, school helping, and even writing. I'd suffered through a bad time (albeit not nearly as severe as biblical Job) and was fruitfully rewarded for my faith in God's power to arrange my life perfectly. My prayers on the job situation also taught me to pray with open-mindedness so that I do not miss future opportunities and blessings. Praying and then accepting God's answer instead of my own preconceived outcome has helped me see his hand at work rather than my own.

The naysayers and scoffers at my in-home and work-world jobs can snicker all they want to. I am happy, fulfilled, and thankful to have my hard work. I am cut out for it and empowered by God's strength to accomplish it. I've been blessed with housecleaning clients who understand my need for rescheduling and/or the interruptions of my plans when "Mom Responsibilities" call my name. On the days when I am at maximum stress level, I just take a few seconds to remember the life and times of Mr. Job, and all things fall into perspective. Counting my blessings never fails to help.

Faith in Action

There is someone in your life who is unable, due to physical restrictions or time constraints, to clean their home or apartment. Think of new mothers, friends having surgery, a family member too bogged down in work to do a deep cleaning, a super-volunteer person who gives most of their free time to others, an elderly or shut-in person, or someone who is hard to buy a "normal" gift for. Get a few friends together and plan a surprise cleaning for him/her.

You will only need two hours and simple supplies, but your gift will be so appreciated. The time goes quickly as you work together as a team. Another friend can be enlisted to take the clean house recipient off to a movie or out to eat while the cleaning team goes into action.

Recipe for a Basic Cleaning Kit

- Sturdy plastic-handled bucket
- 10 good cleaning rags (old T-shirts make excellent dust rags and used towels cut into squares are great all-purpose cleaning cloths)
- Large bottle of window cleaner (plus a refill bottle)
- Furniture polish spray
- Multi-purpose cleaning spray (409, Clorox Clean-up, Simple Green)
- Can of Barkeepers Friend, Comet, or Ajax
- Crest O Mint, Mr. Clean, or Pine Sol liquid

Ode to the Bucket

I drag my bucket to and fro,
Praying simple prayers I go.
The kitchen will be sparkly clean,
Elbow grease of Cleaning Queen.

I think of Martha, Job, and self
As I mop and dust the shelves.
Lord, lend me strength to do my chores
As I praise You and adore.

This work of mine is Your fine gift.
Many thanks to You I lift.
My heart's desire You have covered.
My bucket surely runneth over.

THE DARK MAN

~ *Alaine Benard* ~

The Dark Man came to her aid right after her seventh birthday. Running down the hall, she had fallen across the floor furnace grate. Her Buster Brown sandals somehow caught the metal and had thrown her down. Alone and not knowing what to do, the hurt child curled into a ball and wept while her body went into shock.

Her next thought was surprise at being lifted by a man with coffee-colored skin. She remembers hearing the whir of the ceiling fan and the way her thin blonde hair flew across her face and blocked her vision. The smell of some unnamed oil filled her nose as she become aware that her shredded knee was numb. Happiness flooded her little soul at the disappearance of the burning pain. So grateful was she that she didn't realize she was standing on the grass in front of her beloved grandfather, Pappy. Squatting down, he was applying ointment and unrolling gauze.

Pappy rode her on his piggyback, through the Louisiana breezes and cricket chirps. Off to the Pac-a-Sac they went to get a treat. In the excitement and relief at the trauma's passing, she forgot about the Dark Man. She smelled a coconutty smell all the way to the store.

The Dark Man made his mysterious appearance off and on throughout her youth. The gawky girl could put no face to her black knight, but she knew he would find her each time she encountered a crisis. At twelve, not paying attention, she'd walked into the path of an oncoming car. Standing frozen like a deer trapped in the headlights, she'd waited for the impact. A blur of sound and time, she came back to herself on the opposite side of the street. As her heart beat furiously, she looked everywhere for her secret friend. She'd run circles around each azalea bush in search. Where could he have gone? She whispered thank-yous into the dusk and prayed that he'd heard. The incident faded as her best friend pulled her away to their clubhouse.

College days came and brought with them temptations of all sorts-many in which the woman indulged. Whenever terror entered her life, usually brought on by those very same temptations, her protector was there reaching out. Flashes of his smooth white palms, so in contrast with his beadle nut skin, danced across her mind.

At the age of independence, his presence wore on her nerves. Why on earth would she need the likes of this shadow man? He skulked around, spied on her, and often irritated her with his over-protectiveness. She no longer wanted a mentor, a knight. She wanted life without interference from him, or anyone else for that matter.

For the next several years, the Dark Man vanished. The only times he came to her were in brief dream-snatches. She would wake with misty remnant knowledge of her head resting upon his shoulder soaking up the comfort of him.

She'd be drying her hair, daydreaming, or zooming around town in her old Volkswagen Bug when she'd catch his unique aroma. "Sandalwood Oil" is what she had named it in her head. Upon "feeling him" she would concentrate with all her might and try to bring him to her. Other than the rare dream snippet, he never fully materialized.

Marriage and maturity took the place of a freewheeling lifestyle, and she soon forgot about him altogether. She had a husband and her own household and career to manage; she needed nothing else.

Or so she thought.

The Dark Man found his childhood charge when she returned to the church of her youth. On Christmas Eve of her thirtieth year, he brought the woman a gift sent straight from God. He delivered the message that his friend, the infertile woman, would bear a son in nine months.

She thanked him profusely through tears and hugs. He promised to be with her through the upcoming difficult labor and delivery. Twenty-six hours of natural childbirth brought forth the couple's perfect baby boy. Stressed and exhausted, she drifted off holding him to her breast, but not before she felt the Dark Man kiss both her and the newborn's brows.

Through the remainder of her years, she never again hid from the Dark Man. For she now knew with certainty that he had never left her. They formed a partnership and accomplished many works together. The middle-aged woman came to understand that her son had not been the first miraculous gift sent from heaven. The Dark Man had been with her since birth. Through the entirety of her life, he had guided, protected, and prayed for her.

The Dark Man is her personal guardian angel-the epitome of faithfulness and perseverance. He walks beside me daily.

St. Gertrude's Guardian Angel Prayer

O most holy angel of God,
appointed by God to be my guardian,
I give you thanks for all the benefits,
which you have ever bestowed on me in body and in soul.
I praise and glorify you that you condescended to assist me
with such patient fidelity,
and to defend me against all the assaults of my enemies.
Blessed be the hour in which you were assigned me
for my guardian, my defender and my patron.
In acknowledgement and return for all your loving ministries to me,
I offer you the infinitely precious and noble heart of Jesus,
and firmly purpose to obey you henceforward,
and most faithfully to serve my God.

Amen.

Guardian Angel Studies

Psalm 103:20-

"Bless the LORD, you His angels, mighty in strength, who perform His word, obeying the voice of His word!"

Psalm 91:11-

"For He will give His angels charge concerning you, to guard you in all your ways."

Exodus 32:34-

"The Lord answered, 'Him only who has sinned against me will I strike out of my book. Now, go and lead the people whither I have told you. My angel will go before you.'"

Genesis 24: 6-8-

"The Lord, the God of heaven, who took me from my father's house and the land of my birth, and who spoke to me and who swore to me, saying, 'To your descendants I will give this land,' He will send His angel before you, and you will take a wife for my son from there.'"

Exodus 23:19-21-

"Behold, I am going to send an angel before you to guard you along the way and to bring you into the place which I have prepared."

Continues

Judges 13:6-

"Then the woman came and told her husband, saying, 'A man of God came to me and his appearance was like the appearance of the angel of God, very awesome. And I did not ask him where he came from, nor did he tell me his name.'"

Psalm 34:7-

"The angel of the Lord encamps around those who fear Him, and rescues them."

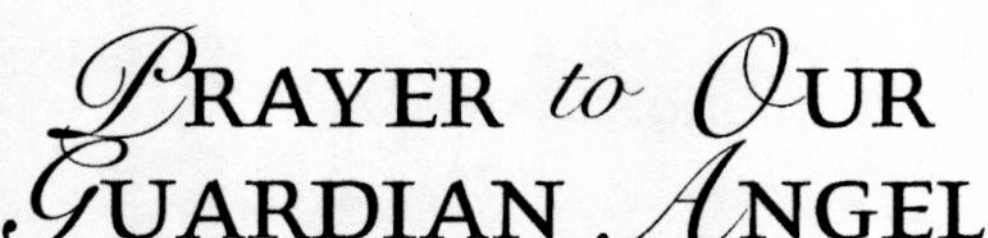

Angel of God,
My guardian dear,
To whom his love commits me here;
Ever this day be at my side,
To light and guard,
To rule and guide.

Amen.

Angel Salad

1	6-OZ. PACKET LIME FLAVORED GELATIN MIX
2 CUPS	HOT WATER
2	3-OZ. PACKAGES CREAM CHEESE, SOFTENED
1	8-OZ. CAN CRUSHED PINEAPPLE
20 OZ.	DICED, DRAINED PIMENTO
1 CUP EA.	DICED CELERY, PECANS
1 CUP	HEAVY WHIPPING CREAM

- In a small bowl, dissolve the lime gelatin in hot water. Allow it to cool for ten minutes. Mix together the cream cheese, pineapple, pimentos, celery, and pecans. Fold in the gelatin. Chill for one hour, or until thickened but not firm. Whip the heavy cream in a small bowl until thickened. Fold into the gelatin mixture. Refrigerate three hours, or until firmly set. Serves twelve.

Angels in Our Lives

~ *Carol Schwartz* ~

Have you ever dreamed about the person you would like to become? Possibly you would be something like an angel, a spiritual creature of the greatest perfection.

In my imagination I would be like my favorite Bible story character, Ruth. I imagine her to be a slim figure of five feet, seven inches with soft, olive skin, flowing dark brown hair, and piercing brown eyes. An image of my own mother, Naomi Ruth Houger, at age seventeen comes to mind. These two Ruths share similar characteristics: a soft and gentle nature, strength and sturdiness, devotion to others, hard work, and faithfulness to family, friends, and God.

The Bible story of Ruth is a charming love story. After Ruth's husband died and left her childless, she became devoted to her mother-in-law, Naomi. She attempted to live a normal life, although she had experienced the painful loss of her husband. Because she believed in God, she became determined to make the best of her life.

She'd moved from her own country to the strange land of Bethlehem. Ruth's choice to stay in this foreign land forced her to establish a new life. She went to work in the fields picking up grain after the sowers had taken all they wanted. It was a hard way to live, and she chose it because she was totally dedicated to Naomi. Naomi had lost her own husband and both her sons, and Ruth could not bear to leave her dear mother-in-law to suffer alone. Ruth was a kind, caring, trusting, giving, and peace-filled person. Everyone in the village noticed how well she took care of Naomi.

One of Naomi's wealthy relatives, named Boaz, noticed this as well. Ruth went into his field's daily and labored from sunrise until dark. He watched how she toiled all day long, never complaining of the back-breaking work. Boaz was kind to her and supported others' acceptance of her. He became interested in her. Eventually they married and had a son, providing Naomi with a grandson to care for. They had a good life, centered on God.

Ruth's spirit of self-sacrifice and high moral integrity pleased God. This angelic lady had earned her place in life and was given God's blessing to the end. Her story indicates that surely she was like an angel, like so many others to be found in the Bible.

If we examine the Bible, we find several places where God indicated that prayerful asking brought his angels to the aid of his servants. Several examples of God's messengers can be found in Exodus, Acts, and Luke. God sent an angel to guard Moses while he guided his people to the Promised Land, as related in Exodus 23:20. An angel opened the prison doors and guided the apostle Peter to freedom as found in Acts 5:18-20 and 12:5-10. Also, according to Acts 10:1-8, there was an army officer, Cornelius, a God-loving man, who was visited in a vision by an angel telling him to seek and find a man called Simon Peter.

In the first chapter of Luke, the angel Gabriel appeared to an elderly Jewish priest, Zacharias. The angel told him that God had heard his prayer and that his wife, Elizabeth, would bear him a son called John in her old age. An angel appeared to the Virgin Mary and informed her that she would give birth to a son named Jesus, that Jesus would become very great and be called the Son of God, and the world would be forever changed.

Just as God sent his angels to help those of long ago, he will send his guardian angels to help each of us. Our guardian angels come through the power of daily prayer and meditation. They are God's heavenly spirits whose job it is to help guide and guard us. Guardian angels have been known to lift spirits during life's tragedies, maintain daily closeness during times of unknowns and change, and to perform extraordinary events beyond human powers.

With our guardian angels by our side we are attracted to the good. They provide strength and encouragement and help us live with love and trust. Most of all, our guardian angels provide our souls with serenity here on earth.

Summer Angel Food Cake

- Buy an angel food cake at your local grocery store. Cut pieces into pie-shaped wedges and place on pretty serving dishes.

- Wash ripe, fresh, seasonal berries and trim if necessary. If not quite sweet enough, add a dash of sugar and let the berries sit in a bowl and soak up the sweetness for an hour or so.

- Place a healthy helping of berries on each cake slice. Top with light whipped cream. Garnish and serve.

My Guardian Angel

With words of wisdom from on high,
My guardian angel came to me.
She said, "Now Carol, pay attention,
For this you must do to become free."

Each day follow this path,
You will have something to do.
You will not be lonely or lost,
God's grace will carry you through.

Ask Him in your morning prayers,
As the day gets under way,
What you can do for others,
The lists include give and pray.

Ask Him for knowledge of His will,
So you can fulfill His plan.
He will shine blessings upon you,
With His loving, mighty hand.

And when you go too fast,
He will work to slow you down,
By whatever means He chooses,
God's lessons will abound.

CONTINUES

As your angel shall be here,
To guard you against the storm,
To inform you of God's will,
Giving you strength to perform.

Thank God for what He provides,
At the end of each lovely day,
Be grateful for what you have,
You are the Potter's perfect clay.

~ Carol Schwartz

Mom's Heavenly Dessert

As one of fifteen children, my mom, Naomi Houger, has become the celebrity cookie and dessert maker for our large family reunions, because she makes such scrumptious treats of all types. This is her recipe and one of my favorites (they are all favorites when she's cooking, whatever she's cooking or baking!)

1 cup	flour
2 tbs	sugar
1 cup	chopped walnuts
1/4 tsp	vanilla
1 tbs	butter
1 cup	powdered sugar
1	8-oz. package cream cheese
1 cup	Cool Whip
1 pkg.	chocolate instant pudding
1 pkg.	vanilla instant pudding
3 cups	milk

- Mix first four ingredients and cut in butter. Spread in 9x13 cake pan and bake at 325 degrees for 20 minutes. Let cool completely. Cream together powdered sugar, cream cheese, and one cup Cool Whip. Spread over first layer. Combine pudding and milk and spread over second layer. Top with Cool Whip and garnish with chopped walnuts and grated milk chocolate. Refrigerate two hours before serving.

Swattin' Skeeters

~ *Alaine Benard* ~

"After all, it is those who have a deep and real inner life who are best able to deal with the irritating details of outer life."

- EVELYN UNDERHILL

Judging by the quote, Ms. Underhill must be personally acquainted with my parents, Carroll and Peggy DiBenedetto.

My earliest childhood memory is of the six of us sitting down to dinner. Baby brother Buck and sister Dee (one in the highchair, one perched atop a stockpot), twin and I sitting side by side, and our parents holding down the end seats. With clean faces, slicked-back hair and growling bellies, we waited with arms folded on top of the boomerang-patterned Formica tabletop. When the Melmack bowls of macaroni and cheese (with hotdogs sliced into it), string beans, and applesauce were set down we all joined hands. Grace followed, and even the babies added their made up prayer-words to the blessing. We listened closely for our favorite rendition; "Bwess us, Oh Lord and Dee's hour grits..." Smothering our giggles and kicking each other's scrawny legs, we twins got a stern look.

"Swatting mosquitoes..." Daddy said in his deep bass voice.

We knew that we were treading the thin line between acceptable and unacceptable behavior. Or, at least this is how we interpreted our parental catchall phrase, associating "swatting" with the action our sassy little behinds were facing.

Before eating, the Bible was opened and Daddy read a passage. The enjoyable descriptions of foreign lands and holy servants, added to the smell of our feast, made us squirm. The simple fare was often subsidized by government cheese and peanut butter. The neighborhood kids all begged to be invited to eat at our house because they had yucky food. Having eaten at their houses, I certainly agreed. Pot roasts, peas with little onions, pineapple rings sprinkled with grated cheese, and rolls replaced the gummy, yummy, white bread and goodies we got.

Each Sunday, dressed in our best clothes and shoes, we'd take the ever-changing vehicle to church. We'd whine about the "itchiness" of our skirts and the way the heater blew from the Rambler station wagon's vents. Before too many complaints were voiced we would hear, "Swat those mosquitoes!" from one of our parents.

Once inside the doors of the church, I would watch Daddy scan the crowd. Crossing our fingers and locking our elbows together, twin and I would pray silently that he would find what he was searching for; an Asian, Hispanic, or African American family. If we were lucky enough to have a minority visitor share our pew, we were allowed certain latitude regarding our behavior. We got away with whispering, playing with little treasures from our vinyl purses and even an occasional game of tic-tac-toe could be played with the tiny pew pencils without fear of Mother's pointed nails twisting our soft skin. This was a much more favorable choice than the alternative, which was sitting in the very first pew in the church-an unbearably embarrassing fate.

Around the time we inherited our seventh or eighth hand-me-down car, I came to realize certain truths, the main one being that we were different from the typical, early 1960's, Baton Rouge, Louisiana family. Mother gave up her own dreams to stay home and support Daddy's college career. To supplement the income, she took in typing jobs and part-time work she could do at home. She raised four children virtually single-handedly while Daddy worked night jobs and paper or milk routes while earning his masters' degree. Feminism was just beginning to present itself to the world. I'm sure Mother faced humiliating torments for opting to stay barefoot and pregnant.

Our family's practice of "colorblindness" was about as accepted as my parents' choice of supporting each other and putting family first. At the time, we kids were oblivious to the nasty looks and comments heaped upon our parents for teaching us to accept all whom we met as equals. Differentiating between skin color was not tolerated. We grew up knowing prejudice was not a quality to admire. Never a night went by that we did not kneel and include the end of racism in our prayers.

Peggy and Carroll live the simple rules they taught us. Give thanks for all things. Love the simple things in life. Keep the Sabbath. Remember to do good works and love all mankind.

Their deep faith in God and in each other turned every action into a blessing: simple meals, inexpensive clothes, trials, and graceful sacrifices. Complaints, challenges, and un-Christian attitudes are the pesky insects we shoo away from our enjoyable barbecues of life.

Sundays, when my son plays "rock, paper, scissors" with Jermelle in the front pew at church, I pretend I don't see them. After all, he does come from a long line of "skeeter swatters."

Natural Mosquito and Bug Repellent

For the environmentally conscious who want a safer alternative to some OTC bug repellents, try Basic-H, from Shaklee. It may be safely applied full-strength to the skin. For outdoor area use, try mixing Basic-H in a spray bottle after diluting with tap water in a one-to-one solution. This is valuable information to keep in mind as the West Nile virus continues to spread.

Ordering and further information can be found at:
https://www.shaklee.net/specneeds/member

EnvironSense at:
http://es.epa.gov/new/contacts/newsltrs/shopping.html

NURTURING MATRIMONY and FAMILY

In order to provide our families with strong role models, we must make sure our marriages are built on solid foundations. Christ instituted the sacrament of matrimony when he attended the wedding feast of Cana. Through his preaching he taught that the union of a man and woman in marriage should be permanent until death.

Matthew 19:4-6 reads, "Have you not read that from the beginning the Creator 'made them male and female' and said, 'For this reason a man shall leave his father and mother and be joined to his wife, and the two shall become one flesh'? So they are no longer two, but one flesh. Therefore, what God has joined together, no human being must separate."

This passage teaches us that we are to help and serve each other by forming marital partnerships. In the intimate sacrament of marriage, the mutual giving of each spouse and the good of their children demand total fidelity from each.

In our own time, in a world often alien and even hostile to faith, believing families are of primary importance as centers of living, radiant faith. The Second Vatican Council calls the family the "domestic church." It is in the bosom of the family that parents are "by word and example...the first heralds of faith with regard to their children. They should encourage them in the vocation, which is proper to each child, fostering with special care any religious vocation."

It is here that the father, the mother, children, and all members of the family exercise the priesthood of the baptized in a privileged way "by the reception of the sacraments, prayer and thanksgiving, the witness of a holy life, and self-denial and active charity." Thus the home is the first school of Christian life and a school for human enrichment. Here is where one learns endurance and the joy of work, fraternal love, generous-even repeated-forgiveness, and above all the divine worship in prayer and the offering of one's life. (Catechism of the Catholic Church, 1656-1657)

By nurturing your marriage, you will build stronger foundations for your entire family and community by your example.

Noah's Obedience: a Childlike Faith

~ Deb Anne Flynt ~

"As long as the earth endures,
seedtime and harvest, cold and heat, summer and winter,
day and night will never cease."

Genesis 8:22

This is what the Lord promised Noah, who survived the Great Flood with his wife and his sons and their wives. They were the eight survivors of mankind.

Think about all that Noah must have endured in his six hundredth year when the Lord spoke to him and told him to build the ark. In reading the dimensions of the boat-a massive ship in Noah's time-I am amazed that he was able to build it.

"So make yourself an ark of cypress wood; make rooms in it and coat it with pitch inside and out. This is how you are to build it: The ark is to be four hundred fifty feet long, seventy-five feet wide and forty-five feet high. Make a roof for it and finish the ark to within eighteen inches of the top. Put a door in the side of the ark and make lower, middle and upper decks." (Genesis 6:14-16)

To build a vessel that size, he must have hired workers to help. He would soon have no need for the money he would have to pay them. His faith would sustain him while they laughed about him behind his back, thinking they were taking advantage of his eccentricity. He probably felt pity for them.

As difficult as pitch is to remove, several workers must have drowned still wearing it. Without God's protection, it did them no good. Although it made the ark watertight, it only burned their skin and itched-for a while.

How did he manage all the animals? He must have had a hard time with the animals of prey. The storage of food certainly would have posed problems. He had to have so many different types of holding pens and cages. Was keeping the animals out of the humans' food supply laborious? Surely some of the animals escaped from their areas and caused trouble.

These and many, many more questions flood my mind when I put myself in Noah's position. And as usual, I'm thinking too much. Noah didn't question the Lord on details. He simply obeyed. What faith he had! This is my goal, too. I seek to do the Lord's will, and I wonder if I'm failing. I seek details and ask too many questions. While I'm trying to make sure that I do everything just right for him, God is waiting patiently for me to simply obey. My Father in heaven asks the same thing of me as I do of my children.

"And he said: 'I tell you the truth, unless you change and become like little children, you will never enter the kingdom of heaven.'" (Matthew 18:3)

We must strive to be more like children every day, and simply obey. I remember looking into my parents' faces and seeing perfect love. Of course, only God offers perfect love, but that's what I thought I saw when I looked at them with my heart full of love for them. They'd give me the simplest tasks and praise me for helping them. I must confess that as a parent I gave my toddlers such chores, too. I'd ask them for something that was easily within my reach, and then pretend they had been such a great help for bringing it to me. The look on their faces was my reward.

I think when Noah first saw the olive branch, he must have felt very much the same as a small child rewarded for a good deed-consumed with gratitude and delighted at being allowed to serve.

God doesn't really require our help. He who can do all things doesn't need assistance. However, when he calls me to do his work, I can think of his glorious, sacred face, and there I see perfect love-or as close as I can imagine-and I want to do his will. Sometimes I still ask too many questions, thinking I have to plan everything to do it well. I'm learning to trust him, though, and it gets easier each time. He will not fail me. He never has and never will. "For the Lord is good; His mercy is everlasting, and His truth endures to all generations." (Psalm 100:5)

Growing in the Lord requires us to become more child-like. Trusting in God is the first step on a journey that will last the rest of our lives here on earth. Each day, seek to see the world as a child does, with innocence. And when our Father asks us to do something, just obey.

Victims Need a Flood of Support

We all know how devastating floods can be, but hopefully not from firsthand experience. Just watching the news gives us a clear enough picture of what the victims must be going through. Help is usually on the scene quickly, but more support is needed most of the time. In the case of serious flooding, in which people are left homeless, much more is needed than a safe place to sleep.

If you are in a position to volunteer, one of the best things you can do is to load up old blankets, toys, children's books, food, clean water, a can opener, and some bibles, and head for the nearest shelter. When people are at such a low point, offering the hope that comes from God can change their whole perspective. Read to the children, hold hands with the elderly, and be a compassionate ear to all. Food, shelter, and clean blankets are not enough to heal the spirit. Be a light in their darkness, and bring the message of hope to those who feel hopeless.

GOING DOWN *with* *the* ROWBOAT

~ Deb Anne Flynt ~

Some of my greatest memories were made at a small cabin that my parents rented for several years, in a rural area of our home county. We spent weekends and most of our summers there. Many warm nights were spent dancing with my sisters to our favorite vinyl records and playing games in that big front yard. I remember the first time I heard a whippoorwill, the smell of the woods after a rain, and the beauty of the stars unencumbered by city lights. It was situated deep in a beautifully wooded area, with a small pond about a quarter of a mile behind it. Naturally, we spent many hours in and around that pond, especially since that rustic house had no air conditioning, and was not wired for it. >From the source stream to the dam on the other end, the pond was about three hundred yards, but it was only about a hundred yards across at the widest point.

One day my dad and his youngest brother found a small wooden boat sunk several feet from the bank. They struggled to get it out of the muck in which it was embedded and finally pulled it ashore. It was only about four feet long and about two and a half feet across, if it was that big. It wasn't much to look at, plain wood painted black. After it dried out for a while, though, it proved to be more seaworthy than it looked-it floated. My cousins, my sisters, and I each made several trips across the pond in that boat.

During one stay at the cabin, one of my aunts wanted her sons for something, and I set off across the pond to get them. Since the boat would only carry one person at a time, I made them walk around the pond, and I rowed the boat back-well, about halfway back. That's when it started taking on water, and not just a tiny little bit seeping in, either! I decided that it might be a good idea to paddle faster, and I did-for a while. Of course, I wasn't making much progress because the water coming in created too much drag. It wasn't very long before I realized that at the rate at which it was sinking, I'd better start bailing instead of rowing. It seemed like a simple and obvious solution, except that the only bailing equipment we had on board was a small tuna salad bowl that was in there for small jobs, and this job was growing by the second!

I bailed as fast as I could for about a minute and a half before I knew that I was sunk. I couldn't make it back by rowing, and bailing wasn't getting me any closer to the bank. Somehow, the scene of me frantically bailing and hopelessly rowing had managed to draw a small crowd. My whole family, including aunts, uncles, the cousins who had beaten me back across (and evidently gone to gather spectators), my parents, and my sisters were all standing, leaning on trees, or sitting on the ground, helplessly laughing at me.

When I saw them, which was shortly after I had realized the hopelessness of my situation, I knew there was only one thing left for me to do, besides swim. Fortunately, the boat was sinking straight down and keeping steady, although continually getting lower in the water. Before I started swimming, I turned to the bank and all my relatives, brought my hand solemnly up, and absolutely straight-faced, stood saluting from the boat until it was completely submerged and sank out from under my feet. They lost any self-control that they had left. My cousins were practically howling with laughter! As soon as my feet were clear, I swam to the shore and joined them in what was, and probably still is, the best laugh we have ever had together.

BASIC PIZZA for EIGHT

CRUST:

4 CUPS	UNBLEACHED FLOUR, DIVIDED
1 1/2 CUPS	WARM WATER
1 TBS	REGULAR ACTIVE DRY YEAST
1 TSP	HONEY
1/2 TSP	SALT

- In a large glass mixing bowl, combine one and one-half tablespoons flour with yeast and honey. Mix gently while adding the water. Cover with a clean damp dishtowel and leave for thirty minutes in a warm place. Keep your towel clean.

- The mixture should now be foamy. Mix in the remaining flour and the salt. Knead gently but firmly for ten minutes, adding small amounts of flour if dough is sticky.

- Transfer the dough ball into a lightly-oiled large glass bowl. Cover with the damp towel and leave in a warm place to rise for about forty-five minutes or until doubled in size.

- Preheat the oven to 450 degrees. Punch down the dough and pull and press it into two sixteen-inch disks. Do not use a rolling pin.

- Carefully place the dough into pizza pans, top with marinara or pizza sauce (see below), olives or your favorite toppings, mozzarella or goat cheese, and bake at 450 degrees for fifteen to twenty minutes on the center rack. More toppings require more cooking time. Meat toppings should be pre-cooked or cut in small pieces or very thin slices.

Quick and Easy Pizza Sauce:

1	16-ounce can tomato sauce
1/2 tsp	oregano
1 tsp	basil leaves
1 tbs	garlic powder, or one clove, chopped
	Salt and pepper to taste

- Mix all ingredients and spread lightly to moderately on pizza dough, then add toppings and bake.

The Prodigal Son Comes Home

~ Carol Schwartz ~

I once knew a young man, Chris, with whom any lady would be proud to be. He was a fine Christian, went to mass daily, prayed, and was what every Christian gal would want to have in a husband. He stood tall, had a confident walk, and looked great in his Sunday suit. He had an outgoing personality and his friendliness made him well-liked.

Chris had a lot of energy and was always extremely active. He was the type of person who would stop and help a stranger fix a flat tire, loan money to a friend, or walk an elderly lady safely across a busy street.

As a young lad growing up in the city he picked up some not so nice things from his companions. He learned to cuss, steal, and be mean to other kids smaller than he was. His home life was sometimes chaotic when his father would come home from work drunk and yell at the family. He tried his best to shut it out and not listen to the arguments. He sometimes stayed away from home.

In high school Chris started drinking, and it often got him into trouble. One day he and his friends stole his father's car without asking or letting anyone know they were taking it. The joyride ended at the police station after the car was reported stolen. Things in Chris's life continued to get worse.

He was drinking more and not showing up for work, so he was fired from his part-time job. His friends started using drugs and introduced Chris to them by offering him some free stuff. Then he was hooked. Because he had lost his job he couldn't afford to pay for the drugs, so he started stealing from his parents and their friends to pay for his daily marijuana.

His mother noticed things were missing, especially money from her purse. His father thought that was nonsense until he realized some of his things were also missing. Chris's father threatened to call the police on Chris, but he never carried through with the threats because he often came home so drunk that he couldn't find the front door.

Then one day everything changed! His mother announced that she had had enough of the chaotic and Godless living and was leaving them to fend for themselves. She packed her suitcases, walked out the door, and never looked back. Chris grew worse and got into weekly scrapes with the local police. Chris's forty-year-old father was losing the battle of convincing Chris to grow up when he couldn't grow up himself. There was a warrant out for Chris's arrest, so he decided it was high time to skip the state and move to where his mother was now located.

Chris called his mother in California and asked for a one-way airplane ticket to Los Angeles. Within one week he was on his way. His mother told him he would have to get a job or go to the local community college. She bought him a car so he could look for a job. Chris enrolled in the college and almost flunked out. However, he did meet a couple of nice young men who liked to have a beer now and then but weren't party animals like he was. For some reason they liked Chris, so they all hung out together while studying.

Chris went back to drinking lots, although he gave up the drugs. These new friends of his told him the drunken behavior was going too far and that he would have to stop drinking around them or they wouldn't be his friends anymore. A few nights later, they confronted Chris about his obnoxious behavior. When Chris got drunk, he became a different person-one no one wanted to be around.

His mother was also growing tired of the late-night arrivals and being told Chris was flunking out of community college. She discussed his behavior and asked him to leave if it was going to continue.

Even Chris was beginning to see that maybe his drinking was messing up his life and his relationships with other people. He was put on academic probation and only returned to full student status after proving he had changed and agreeing to take two life skills classes.

His mother had a friend whose daughter was in Alcoholics Anonymous (AA) and Narcotics Anonymous (NA). He looked up the friend, Sara, and asked her how she had been able to give up the wild party life.

The next night Sara took Chris to an NA meeting. He found friends there like himself.

Chris has been clean and sober now for fourteen years. He did graduate with an associate's degree from the community college and continued on to get his doctorate.

What happened over the past fourteen years to change Chris's life?

Chris found acceptance and love in NA, which convinced him that he was a lovable person. His relationship with his mother changed a lot, as did all his other relationships. Chris's mother and father helped him through college. Not only did they provide monetary support, but they also gave him tons of emotional, mental, and spiritual support.

Chris's parents were proud of their son and loved him very much. His mother cried all the way through his graduation ceremony when he received his doctorate; at one time she had been sure she would lose him to a drug overdose, a terrible drunken car accident, or death at the hands of some dealer like so many of his old friends.

Chris had been on a one-way path to self-destruction, very similar to that of the prodigal son in the Bible, Luke 15:11-32. The rancher in Jesus' story had two sons. The oldest son worked hard helping his father. The youngest son was adventurous and enjoyed partying with his friends. The father loved both sons very much. When the younger son asked his father for his portion of the inheritance so he could travel and see the world, the father agreed and gave him what he would inherent. The young man went off to play, squandering his money on friends who also loved to party. When the money was gone, so were the friends. The young man dejectedly staggered back home to his father, willing to be a servant in the fields just to have a place to sleep and enough food to eat.

The father welcomed the prodigal son with open arms. The son who was lost and believed dead was now safe at home. The father had a party for him and all their family and friends welcomed him home. Just as God loves us and totally forgives what we do, so we should love him and our children.

Chris, the prodigal son, came home! God had become a big part of Chris's new life. God had given him a whole different perspective, as the responsible loving parent to his ten-year-old son and in holding down a good job. His devotion to living a better way of life included helping those less fortunate than himself. It has led him to help other parents and grandparents of troubled youth, trying to convince them to encourage their children to attend AA or NA or at least practice the principles of tough love.

A big crowd of Chris's new friends and his family gathered for his graduation, and everyone celebrated the new life.

Dedication

This story is dedicated to my brother and sister-in-law, Del and Jo Ann, with lots of love and prayers at the loss of their only son, Andrew Houger, who died at a young age this past year when he was hit and killed by a drunken driver.

We pray that if you have a son or daughter who's acting out in the world of alcohol or drugs that you will seek help in Al Anon, attend your favorite church, and find a loving God to help you through these times. God is the answer and has all the answers, even when we do not understand.

Help References:

Alcoholics Anonymous

Grand Central Station
P.O. Box 459
New York, New York 10163
Local phone book under Alcoholics Anonymous
http://www.alcoholics-anonymous.org/

Narcotics Anonymous

World Service Office in Los Angeles
PO Box 9999
Van Nuys, California 91409
Telephone (818) 773-9999
http://www.narcoticsanonymous.org/

Al-Anon Families Group

Al-Anon Family Group Headquarters, Inc.
1600 Corporate Landing Parkway
Virginia Beach, VA 23454-5617
888-4AL-ANON
http://www.al-anon.org/

Red Carpet Fruit Salad

2 cups	cold cooked rice
2 cups	miniature marshmallows
1 cup	drained pineapple tidbits or
1 cup	fresh pineapple cut into small pieces
2 cups	drained fruit cocktail
1/2 cup	red maraschino cherries
1 cup	heavy cream, whipped, *or*
1 cup	Dream Whip

- Combine rice, marshmallows, pineapple, fruit cocktail, and cherries. Fold whipped cream into rice-fruit mixture and refrigerate for one hour before serving. Makes eight to ten servings.

- For variety add one can drained mandarin oranges, 1/2 cup chopped walnuts, or 1/2 cup chopped pecans.

I have served this on many occasions, and it has always been a great hit at women's luncheons. It goes well with your favorite green salad and fresh rolls and butter.

~ *Carol Schwartz* ~

Daddy's Teachings: A Father's Day Tribute

~ Angie Ledbetter ~

"A wise son heeds his father's instruction..."

Proverbs 13:1

Many people in many ways have blessed me throughout my life, but none compare to having been reared by the best of parents. My dad has always been there for his children, friends, coworkers, and anyone in need of his talents, but that is not what makes him unique. What lifts him above the crowd of other good people is his humility and ability to jump into a situation and do what needs to be done at any given moment without being asked. It's an automatic reaction on his part-like breathing to the rest of us. And my simple words of platitude will always be insufficient in describing and thanking him.

Daddy made sure we had all of the things we needed, not necessarily the things we wanted. This helped assure that we didn't become spoiled adults. He taught us to be self-reliant members in good standing within our church and community. He taught us fairness by handing down punishment and praise in equal measure as merited. He taught us love and selflessness through many acts of personal sacrifice, by spending time with us, and by never failing to show that he was proud of us. Daddy taught us strength by being strong.

We knew we could count on him at all times. Dad is a sturdy, indestructible oak. He showed us consistency by never swaying under any type of influence or pressure from what he knew to be good and right. "If you don't stand for something, you'll fall for anything," is a motto that encapsulates his beliefs.

Our Father taught us faith by living the Gospel. He educated us in the art of forgiveness by forgiving us daily and by never holding a grudge against anyone. We learned honor by witnessing his honorable behavior, and character by the same method. He also taught us patriotism and the definition of "gumption" by being a loyal citizen of this country, and by showing a strong worth ethic. Living examples of these wonderful virtues and the Golden Rule taught us-not lecturing or pop-psych experimentation.

Outside the home, Daddy made sure we were involved in good, clean, healthy activities, many of which he volunteered for or participated in himself. Scouting, sports, religious education, and several ministries still enjoy his membership. He is a leader of men. He is firm, but fair. He does whatever it takes to get the job done. If that means getting up at 3:00 a.m. to deliver milk so that he could attend college during the day and work other odd jobs to support a wife and four children, so be it.

Before I make him sound like a drill sergeant, I'll add that Daddy also has his softer side, too, which shows itself at unexpected moments. How many dads would get down on the floor and play jacks with their kids? Not many. All of these things, and more, he still is to his four children, eleven grandchildren, and many "surrogates."

I can only hope to infuse my own children with some of these characteristics. Daddy's shoes are some big ones to fill. Those shoes are also one-size-fits-all, because he'd never expect to be anyone's role model or believe that he was better in any way. And Daddy's shoes of choice are soft, well-worn moccasins-so symbolic of his quiet walk down the good path that comes so comfortably and naturally to him.

This Father's Day, I will take a few minutes to write down my thoughts about the precious gifts he's shared with me. Hopefully, he'll realize how much he means to me.

I will also get him a brand new set of jacks.

Father's Day Stewardship Tips

Recall those men who have shaped your life in some positive way and remember them this Father's Day. Coaches, teachers, stepfathers, uncles, older brothers, mentors, and pastors are some you may consider. You do not have to buy them a costly gift, but give them the benefit of your time and talent. Being a good shepherd of your resources is one way to bless others.

Think how special the loving men in your life will feel when they are remembered for a small kindness or help they provided at one time. A nice letter, a shared cup of coffee, a video or tape recorded message, or an unexpected phone call are simple gifts from the heart that help make others feel loved, needed, and appreciated. Could you take someone for a trip down memory lane to enjoy the reliving of good times on a balmy summer's evening?

Make time in your hectic schedule to let all of the men who've cared for and about you know that they've meant something. As simple as this activity is, surprisingly, not many take the time to do it! Set a trend. Rekindle the gentle art of kindness "just because." I'm sure the recipient will be much more impressed with your thoughtfulness than with another ugly tie.

SCRIPTURAL REFERENCE for ACTS of BROTHERHOOD:

Romans 12:10-

"Be devoted to one another in brotherly love.
Honor one another above yourselves."

---

1 Thessalonians 4:9-

"Now about brotherly love.
Honor one another above yourselves."

---

2 Peter 1:7-

"and to godliness, brotherly kindness;
and to brotherly kindness, love."

My Father's Image

A son to make a father proud
Never one to boast aloud
Serene
Steady
Strong
Ready
A son to fill a mother's heart
Or to pierce as he departs
Willing
Resigned
Blessed
Benign
A son who molded children well
Even as they often fell
Humble
Pious
Giving
Righteous
A son whom no one will forget
A man who remembers no debt
Eternal
Forgiving
Sacrificial
Living

DADDY DAY PROJECTS

Gather old and new photos and mementos from past vacations and events. Arrange and glue them onto a sturdy backing (check craft stores for materials). Have your collage matted and framed for a one-of-a-kind gift.

Another lovely gift idea is to have your dad's family and friends fill out questionnaires about your dad and send them back to you to bind into a unique book. Sample questions:

Let your imagination loose. This special project is an excellent way to honor a man in your life. You can make it simple (photocopied questionnaires, three-hole punched and tied with ribbon) or elaborate and elegant (professionally bound or placed in plastic sleeves in a fancy decorated binder). Check your options at local printing shops.

Heart Healthy Pizza

1	16-oz. can tomatoes
	(or use summer ripe), finely diced
2 tbs	tomato paste
1 tsp	minced garlic
1 loaf	French bread (sugar-free types
	are now readily available)
1 tbs	high quality olive oil
3/4 lb.	low-fat mozzarella
	(or cheddar cheese, finely grated)

- Drain the tomatoes, reserving half a cup of juice. Mix juice with tomatoes, garlic, tomato paste, and olive oil. Slice the bread in half lengthwise. Spread loaf halves with the sauce. Sprinkle with cheese. Bake at 400 degrees for about fifteen minutes or until all of the cheese has melted well.

- Slice and serve hot. Note: pizza may be cut into small slices to serve as an appetizer.

Autumn

2 Corinthians, Chapter 9:10

"Now He who supplies seed to the sower and bread for food will supply and multiply your seed for sowing and increase the harvest of your righteousness."

Big Yellow Aspirin: Relief from Summer Kids

~ Deb Anne Flynt ~

Okay, I admit it. I was counting down the days. What can I say? It was a long summer, and many times it was too hot for the kids to go out and play here in Mississippi. I love my children, I really do, but I was so glad to hear that school bus run on the first morning of school! I kissed my little ones, hugged and blessed them, sent them to the big yellow aspirin, and yelled from the front stoop how much I loved them as I flashed the ASL sign for "I love you."

They reciprocated-thumbs, index fingers, and pinkies extended. Then I watched the bus pull away, and I went back to bed. Now you may think I'm a terrible mom and you might wonder how I could sleep at a time like that. Well, I'll let you in on a little secret: my kids have great guardian angels, and I have faith in God, so why worry? Sure I'm concerned, but not worried. I also have faith in my children-which isn't easy, but is fairly well-deserved. I know my children will do the right thing most of the time, unless I'm present for them to rebel against.

That, and I was tired. Like I said, it had been a long summer. The previous school year, I had asked my youngest if she had been remembering to pray before her meals at school. She said she had. I asked her if anyone had said anything to her; she said no. Had anyone said anything about it? Had they been giving her looks? "I really don't know. I wasn't looking at them. I was praying!" Okay, I got a "duh" look, but I didn't care to fuss at her about it just then. I was too busy thinking, that's my girl.

My children go to a public school. They don't say a blessing in class as a group before going to lunch anymore, they no longer have a morning prayer and devotional, and the Lord's Prayer has ceased to be broadcast to every student over the P.A. system. Now my children usually have to do this alone. One year, my daughter was saying the blessing before eating, and the boy across from her asked, "Are you some kind of Christian or something?"

She finished what she was saying, crossed herself, and said "Yyyes!" while giving him a defiant look that dared him to say or do anything about it. She was quite small for her age, but he backed down. Now they're starting school again. They have new classmates, new challenges, and new teachers. I pray for them to have the courage to stand up for what they believe in. I pray for them to be strong in their faith. I pray for their safety and peace of mind, too.

I'm proud of my children and what they do as Christians. As a mom, I hope my children never suffer persecution for their beliefs-but I know I don't really mean it, not entirely.

My daughter's small example of faith may one day have a profound effect on someone's life-maybe even on that of the boy who taunted her. I'm glad they have the chance to meet new people and make new friends. The class camaraderie that they develop in school now may lead to some real, lasting friendships. They have new opportunities to help others.

My son told me he hasn't found his new best friend yet. "That's okay," I told him. "You may not have one this year, or it may be a while before you find someone that you want for a very best friend." I wonder about his choices. What is he looking for in a best friend? Please just don't let it have anything to do with cartoon characters or trading cards! What are his goals this year? And why doesn't he go through that "girls are yucky" stage?

I asked him if he too had been praying at school, and he said yes, and that several of his classmates now joined him as he blessed each meal before eating. His eyes brightened as he told me this, and the light of the Spirit radiated from him. His courage to persevere in this when he was initially scorned has helped many hearts make those first steps toward a faith-filled life.

My dear son is the kid on the playground who takes up for the smaller ones. He's bigger than most of the kids, not only because he's older, (he has "teaching difficulties"), but because he comes from "big people," meaning the shortest man on either side is "only six feet even."

It pleases me to know that he has taken this semi-heroic role for himself, although I dread the day the principal calls and says, "we have to talk," while I wonder if he's been suspended. He was sent home before for "fighting" while defending a child who was waiting with him for the buses to come to take them home. I had to come pick him up, and he was allowed to return to school the following day. I got the idea that they didn't really want to punish him. I didn't either-not for that.

I like the schools here on the whole, and I believe in public school education. My children have learned to respect diversity. They choose friends according to who they are, not what they wear, what their fathers drive, skin color, or denomination. That makes me proud. Now if I can just remember to do that all the time, too.

I have to admit it, but I don't really want to: now that the summer is over and the kids are finally out of the house and out from under my feet, I miss them. I wait for the sound of the bus to bring them home, just as anxiously as I wait for it to take them to school.

Now there's only one thing left for me to do after I wake up from a little nap-plan next summer's vacation! Panama City, Memphis, or Santa Fe? Just somewhere at least a hundred miles from here!

Maybe I'll just take a bubble bath instead-and then a nap. ❦

A Mother's Haste

"I'll be there in a minute! Let me finish washing these dishes."
"But, Mom, it'll be over by then!"
I wished for a genie to come and grant me all my wishes,
And a small voice behind me said "Amen. "

I cringed and grabbed a towel as I turned and
dropped to my knee,
And that dear, sweet child did the same.
"I'm glad that we're going to pray together, Mommy.
Let's start with Jesus' name."

I carefully, watching him, made the sign of the cross,
And my darling baby mimicked me.
I tried to speak a prayer, but I was at a loss,
And fresh tears were soon blinding me.

What I had begun, with exasperated haste,
Trying to get on with my too busy life,
Now made me realize what a terrible waste
Was my hurry, anxiety, and strife.

Oh how could a child, so inexperienced, so young
Have taught me so valuable a lesson?
When for so many years, to my wisdom, I've clung,
And not realized how much did lessen.

CONTINUES

I wiped a tear from my eye with the back of my hand,
The same one I'd used shortly before
On him in discipline of that corporal brand,
The mark on his thigh he still bore.

Dear sweet child of my heart, gentle, pure, and kind,
Forgive me for not knowing more.
But as the sun rises tomorrow, just you and I
Will sit and watch at the patio door.

On a wall in her kitchen,

my wise grandmother has a trivet that states,

"The Hurrieder I go,

the Behinder I get!"

Parents would do well to remember this as we

busily hustle through the lives of our children

instead of spending time with them

while they quickly grow up and out of our lives.

Thanks for the reminder, Nana.

EASY PULL ~ APART (MONKEY) BREAD

2 CANS	REFRIGERATED BISCUIT DOUGH
1/4 CUP	BUTTER OR MARGARINE, MELTED
1/4 CUP	SUGAR
1 TBS	CINNAMON
	CHOPPED WALNUTS OR PECANS (OPTIONAL)

- Preheat oven according to biscuit directions. Mix cinnamon and sugar in a shallow bowl. Coat the bottom of a round cake pan with butter. Sprinkle with a little of the cinnamon sugar, and nuts, if desired.

- Cut each biscuit into quarters. (It's quicker to cut a few at a time.) Dip biscuit quarters into melted butter and drag through cinnamon mixture. Place them in the cake pan in a single layer. Squeeze them together if necessary. Sprinkle more of the cinnamon sugar on top and drizzle with melted butter.

- Bake according to biscuit directions. Cool for a minute, then invert pan onto a plate. Serve warm.

Making it through the Summer with Kids

When I get mad at my children over simple things like slamming a door-a personal pet peeve, perhaps inherited-I have to remind myself to keep things in perspective. I should be grateful that they are safe at home, angry with me, instead of sneaking around doing whatever it is I told them they couldn't do that made them mad enough at me to slam a door. And I am grateful.

Proverbs 22:6 tells us to "Train a boy in the way he should go; even when he is old he will not swerve from it," and verse fifteen says, "Folly is close to the heart of a child, but the rod of discipline will drive it far from him."

There is no excuse for child abuse, but these verses do mean that we should instill self-discipline in our progeny. Key words to remember in this endeavor are love, understanding, humor, firmness, constancy, concern, and gratitude. At no point should anger, fear, rigidity, indecision, indifference, or obstinacy replace them. Being consistent doesn't mean you can't have some flexibility within a range.

Loving a child doesn't mean giving him everything he asks for, or even most of it. If children associate material possession with love, how will they learn to love God, who provides for their needs but not every little want? Love your children with your time, your patience, your understanding, and your discipline-not just with your paycheck.

Discipline is a two-part effort. It is positive and negative. We quell the negative behavior and instill values, while we support and encourage positive behavior, which also supports those same values and more. Corinthians 13:13 says "faith, hope, and love remain, and the greatest of these is love." Toys, games, bicycles, and cars are not love. They can't replace faith, and the only hope they offer is for more toys, games, and cars.

*F*LY *with the* *E*AGLES

~ Carol Schwartz ~

"Do you not know or have you not heard? The Lord is the eternal God, creator of the ends of the earth. He does not faint nor grow weary, and His knowledge is beyond scrutiny. He gives strength to the fainting; for the weak he makes vigor abound. Though young men faint and grow weary, and youths stagger and fall, they that hope in the Lord will renew their strength, they will soar as with eagles' wings; they will run and not grow weary, walk and not grow faint."

Isaiah 40:28-31

I have always been in awe of our national symbol, the bald eagle, for its strength, courage, beauty, and ability to soar high on the slightest of winds. They appear so serene and peaceful just floating in the air.

Remember when our elders used to say to us, "Birds of a feather flock together, so be careful of the company you keep." Let us take a look at the lives of eagles and see what we can learn. They build lasting relationships, have great vision, continuously renew themselves, and face storms without fear.

What do these four characteristics symbolize for those wanting to live peace-filled lives?

In its primary relationship an eagle has security by building one nest and living there for life. 2 Corinthians 6:14-16 is indicative of what our relationship is to become. "Do not be yoked with those who are different, with unbelievers. For what partnership do righteousness and lawlessness have? Or what fellowship does light have with darkness?...Or what has a believer in common with an unbeliever?" Oh, the glory to connect spiritually with another person. A loving God allows that to happen when we place him first in all of our affairs, including values, beliefs, and actions.

An eagle has great vision, and if we know God, we will seek out his vision for our lives in ways such as praying daily, sharing with a dear friend, attending our favorite place of worship, or taking a walk alone to be in quiet meditation with God.

Eagles constantly clean themselves by pulling out damaged feathers. In Psalms 103:5 we are told to fill our "days with good things; your youth is renewed like the eagle's."

Eagles are strong, courageous, and fearless. Recently, after having completed two major cross-country moves with tight finances, I equated flying with the eagles to being monetarily rich. I met someone whose life appeared to be full of joy, happiness, security, and peace, partly because he was wealthy. As time went on, a closer look revealed something very different.

What does it take to live in the world of today's average millionaire? Do their resources bring them peace? From what I observed, it is not the kind I want-"the peace of God that surpasses all understanding" as God promises in Philippians 4:7. Peace and joy of this type cannot be given by the world.

The rich may say they are happy and joyous. What I actually witnessed was people being pleased and jolly as long as things were going their way. As long as everyone and everything was within their power to control, they were content and cheerful.

I am not a millionaire, although I've often wished I could be. What I've seen has changed my mind. Oh yes, most of us would like more money than we normally earn, but the price is too high.

Jesus Christ, the wisest among men, said to his disciples, "It will be hard for one who is rich to enter the kingdom of heaven. Again I say to you, it is easier for a camel to pass through the eye of a needle than for one who is rich to enter the kingdom of God." (Matthew 19:23-24)

Why is that true? Jesus answered in Matthew 6:24, "No one can serve two masters. He will either hate one and love the other, or be devoted to one and despise the other. You cannot serve God and mammon." Some affluent people act as if they are God, and for others, riches become their god. What matters to them is whether they win or lose in investment deals. The almighty greenback and getting more of it takes priority.

They worship, but they worship possessions. God taught us to observe a day of rest and worship him. Jesus clarified when he said, "Your heavenly Father knows that you need them all. But seek first the kingdom of God and his righteousness, and all these things will be given you besides. Do not worry about tomorrow; tomorrow will take care of itself." (Matthew 6: 32-34)

Peace is the quality that characterizes all who have received a new life from God and continue daily to live in that relationship with him. It is the condition of the heart, mind, and soul that leads to everlasting calm and soaring with the eagles to heights unknown. This interior peace creates external peace within families, communities, societies, and the world.

Fly High with God

Ever since I was a little girl,
Wanted to pilot an airplane,
One day in the Mojave Desert,
Got in a Cessna and did train.

Oh it was such a beautiful day,
Away into the blue sky,
Over the Sierra Nevada Mountains,
Snow covered peaks we did fly.

Down into the valleys we went.
Even the one called Death Valley,
Flew out of Reno one time,
Where pilots gather for a rally.

Touch and go's we did a lot,
Practiced so I could solo soon,
It was at the Inyokern Airport one day,
In the desert almost went one noon.

I was a student pilot for quite a while,
It was wonderful to live my dreams,
Thanks to a patient instructor,
Who saved us from a spiral it seems.

Continues

If you have ever taken four G's,
Your heart is in your throat,
And your stomach better be empty,
Or 'twill be nothing to gloat.

Flew many hours over the desert,
Watched the golden sun rise and set,
What a glorious place earth is,
Especially from a pilot's jet.

Whatever your dreams as a child,
Hopefully some have come true,
If not, what are you waiting for,
Fly high with God, make things new.

Close your eyes and wander,
Let your dream come into mind,
Let go and head forth to fly,
Trust God, to yourself be kind.

Tuna Delight

1 CAN	TUNA, PACKED IN WATER
1 TBS	SALAD DRESSING
2 TBS	PICKLE RELISH
1/4 CUP	CHOPPED CELERY
8	TOMATO SLICES
4 CUPS	LETTUCE, TORN INTO BITE-SIZED PIECES

- Put tuna into a bowl and add salad dressing, pickle relish, and celery. Mix well. Put salad lettuce in the bottom of two salad bowls and add four tomato slices to each. Put a big spoonful of tuna mixture on salad.

- Invite a friend to lunch and serve Tuna Delight, Tasty Bars, and Soothing Herb Tea.

Children love to make this because it's easy. It encourages them to help and then to eat healthy food.

TASTY BARS

1 CUP	BUTTER
2 TSP	BAKING POWDER
1/2 CUP	DARK MOLASSES
1/2 TSP	SALT
1/2 CUP	BROWN SUGAR
1 CUP	ROLLED OATS
4	EGGS
1 CUP	RAISINS
2 CUPS	FLOUR
1 CUP	NUTS
1 CUP	WHEAT GERM

- Beat butter with a mixer until fluffy. Beat in molasses and sugar. Stir in eggs and remaining ingredients.
- Spread in 13 x 9-inch pan. Bake for thirty minutes at 350 degrees.

This recipe was a favorite snack on Scout camp-outs.

Soothing Herb Tea

- Place tea leaves or tea bag in a preheated pot. Use one teaspoon tea leaves per six ounces of water.

- Allow the leaves to steep for three to five minutes. Serve tea while it is hot.

A favorite in the evening as you are relaxing and reading before calling it a night is a cup of chamomile tea sweetened with one-half teaspoon of honey.

A fine afternoon tea is chai green tea with lemon, adding cream or half and half. This rich taste will bring enjoyment to your taste buds as if they were experiencing a delicate dessert.

FABRICS of a LIFETIME

~ *Alaine Benard* ~

My long-awaited, prayed-for child finally arrived, shortly after I turned thirty. The first hint of fall in the air showed itself through my hospital window, and I watched the leaves begin their trip from branch tips to ground.

Angels to my aching arms delivered my infertility-denying baby. As he lay naked upon my chest, I wept at his perfection. Initial kisses, caresses, and counting done, I wrapped his tiny body in the softest blue receiving blanket. I remember the exact feel of his warm, content body through the downy cover-how the smooth edges felt under my fingers as I wrapped him up like the tiny gift he was. I'd have no wrinkles or unsightly folds mar the sight. Had I ever breathed in and exhaled so contentedly before that gesture? No. This was the moment for which I had been born, my destiny. I had accomplished the job of producing a healthy baby boy. I was completely satisfied with the realization that I was a mother.

As the years unfolded, I kept fabric mementos from each milestone he passed. Every autumn I pull out the trunk and fondle those items so reverently. I begin with his beige linen christening outfit, lifting it to my face. The light of heaven shines through the fine eyelet, bringing tears to my eyes. I recall the friends and family who gathered under our magnolia tree to celebrate. A low-looping branch hung down perfectly to support the swing he so loved to ride in. We took turns pushing him back and forth through the gentle smells of hickory leaves burning down the street.

The navy and white conductor's overalls, complete with hat, comes out next. I rub the embroidered bib between my thumb and fingers. The rough feel of the cotton ticking brings a smile as I recall that this was the little outfit he wore for his nine-month picture. How exuberant he was taking first steps toward the wooden train, turning at the precise moment for the photographer to catch his glee!

Sipping on orange pekoe tea, I reluctantly move on to the next item. The "terrible two's" are represented by a hooded, purple and green jogging suit. How many, many miles did we go with him in the fleecy suit? Kicking leaves and feeding the ducks on windy November days, I recall rodeos and petting zoos as I pull the drawstring into even-sized ties. The brightest memory is of my little man deciding he was going to ride the circus elephant. No size or age restriction was going to stop him! Marching across the straw-covered floor, he confronted the trainer and demanded a turn. The lead rider, he was, with five terrified school-aged children behind him. I followed his progress around the ring, my eyes trained on his pointy little hood.

Cub Scout uniform, heavy white tae kwon do ghee, nylon slick, raggedy football jersey with the number thirty-seven on the back, and silk first communion tie all wait their turn for my attention. I return to my trunk with a second cup of tea. I want the fabric memories to last all day. This is my private autumn party and time is of no consequence today.

Some of the cloth sends me back in time. With my son's team jersey, I smell the sweat of victory, hotdogs, and pungent grass in the fibers. I remember the shock of seeing him squash an opponent during a grueling defensive play. When did my baby learn to play like this? Where did he get the knowledge and techniques of the game? Why is he hobbling to the sidelines in pain? I remember standing and heading down the bleachers as he signaled he was okay. Who is the pretty classmate applying ice and bandages to his knee? Oh, when did he turn into a young man and leave boyhood behind?

I fold the collage of fabrics and return them to the cedar trunk. Not ready for my mother's celebration to end, I carry the box outside to the porch sofa. Pulling my cardigan tighter, the precious memory of the night before floods me. On the antique loveseat, my son and I had spent a most tender moment. He came to join me, wrapped in his favorite old patchwork quilt, with handpicked cotton tufts peeping out of seams. Laying his head in my lap, he wanted to snuggle and watch the stars. I smoothed back his hair as he quietly pointed out the Little Dipper. I'll never forget the way the moonlight pushed through the wicker X's to tattoo his awestruck face. What a miracle fabric that will always be-a swatch I'd give anything to hold.

The late afternoon shower begins to patter in the rock garden. Fall weather provides rain almost daily to us southerners. I let my mind drift away as I watch the American flag dance from its position, hanging off the eave. The chilly air turns frigid and I clutch the trunk to my chest. The flag brings visions of impending violence and war. I catch myself in the grip of fear as the wooden edges dig into my breastbone.

A horrid scene on an imaginary bolt of material has unrolled itself inside my head. I cringe away from the thought of my baby, my son, wearing camouflaged military attire. The whipping of the red, white, and blue nylon sends terror through my heart. Knees drawn under chin, I huddle upon my treasure box and weep for what the future may hold.

I actually hear his deep, mature voice cry out, "Mom, I love you!" as he lies in a puddle of muddy, bloody grime. Smoke and haze fill the missile-filled air as he lies fighting for breath and comfort. He's so all alone! My baby, my world, is ending. I want to hold him and make him well and whole. The grief and pain are too much to bear. Subconsciously I rock myself, back and forth, holding my trunk of scraps. It has become my replacement infant in the black, lifeless world.

A mother's worst nightmare has become a possibility for us all. September 11, 2001, made us face the knowledge that our children may be called to war. Our sons may never wear caps and gowns, tuxedos, and work suits, now. Our pachyderm riders now mount tanks, black hawks, and stealth bombers.

But isn't this what our children have been raised for? My most stringent lessons were about duty, responsibility, and generosity. Did I not teach my son the very skills needed to fulfill his obligation to God and country? I did.

I promised the Lord on the day of my son's birth that he would understand the values of morality, justice, honor, and overcoming adversity. It is my turn to send him to God's path, God's plan, God's will. How must Jesus' mother, Mary, have suffered, knowing the fate of her son? Yet she willingly sacrificed all to do what was necessary. We must pray for her consolation. We must pray for St. Michael to defend us in all of our battles-even those in which we fight our selves. Parents must pray unceasingly to have the grace to move forward into any future with strength and trust in God's promise. We can do nothing less than put our sacrifices aside and release our children back into the arms of the angels who brought them to the earth from the Lord.

We must rest in the assurance that our children are known and named by God before their birth. Tears will turn to joy on the day we are reunited with our precious sons and daughters. The days of strife and sadness will be replaced with the glorious sight of our "babies" standing at heaven's gate to greet us. They will have on the finest raiment, robes of golden threads, as they reach for our hands and welcome us home. We must, with thanks, allow angels to carry back to God's aching arms what he lent to us for a season.

War Within

Month one flashes from minute, day
Righteous, rubbled debts yet unpaid

Left hand waves Old Glory, right holds cross
Missiles launch, governmental coins toss

Drop donated contribution;
Seeking justice, retribution

Political bands mete out the urge
Heavy feet dance patriotic dirge

As each one sings Jihad songs
Assuring rights, repairing wrongs

End time's apocalypse spreading fear
Don His breastplate, faithful visions clear

As Jesus hangs from our cross haired sites
Living proof of sacrificial fights

Honor overtakes Calvary's hill
The march of Love to do His Will

Cadence set by hearts' own content
The sum of beating prayer intent

PRAYER *and* CONCLUDING MEDITATION

Today, I will reflect on that on which I have declared war. I will seek to discern which of my personal Jihads are worthy and which are dishonorable. Who do I battle-and for what purpose?

Would our Father approve, or would he advise me to break down my war camps? What weapons and graces have I been given to use? Am I making the most of them by growing healthy, more faithful, and more admirable in my actions? Am I leading others into dark, dead-end caves, or am I a guide toward lightness and God's word? Lord, give us graces to overcome our useless wars and senseless fears. Send us gifts of the Holy Spirit so that we may battle for your goals and not our own.

Show us how to march the path of your will, especially when it concerns our children. Send us strength, abundant faith, love, and protection. Multiply our faith. We ask this through our Lord Jesus Christ, amen.

Take time for quiet reflection; perhaps after browsing through your loved ones' pictures or other special keepsakes, do an honest appraisal of your heart. What are the areas that cause you fear? What are your God-centered strengths? Are you capable of totally entrusting your spouse, children, family, security, and needs to God's will? How can you win the war against doubt and lukewarm faith?

Berry Good Muffins

1 cup	flour
1 cup	oatmeal
3 tbs	sugar
1/2 tsp	salt
3-4 tsp	baking powder
1 cup	blueberries, washed
1 cup	whole milk
1/4 cup	vegetable oil
	Cooking spray

- Preheat oven to 400 degrees. Mix together in a large bowl flour, oatmeal, sugar, salt, and baking powder. Add the berries and mix well.
- In a separate bowl, mix egg, milk, and oil. Add to flour mixture and mix for about two minutes with a large spoon. Don't worry about the lumps.
- Line mini muffin tins with paper cups or spray lightly with cooking spray. Fill each tin about two-thirds full with muffin mix.
- Bake for about twenty minutes, or until just brown.

Enjoy while warm with your favorite tea.

Hope in a Crisis: a Little Peace on Earth

~ Carol Schwartz ~

If you doubt God, ask him to prove that he is. Take a stroll by the ocean or a river, take a long walk in the city park or the mountains, or go sit under a large southern oak tree; you will see the splendor he created.

I recently spent a couple of days with a friend and colleague doing just that, taking a walk in the wilds on a warm fall day. From Galena Overlook we viewed it all, Idaho's Sawtooth Mountains rising majestically to nearly 11,000 feet above sea level. It was like viewing a little piece of heaven here on earth. Its beauty was strikingly peaceful.

The autumn colors gloriously shone forth with different shades of gold, yellow, orange, rust, red, and green. The various colored Quaking Aspen trees, glowing through the everlasting greens of the fir and the pine, made it the perfect picture that only a loving God could have created. I took pictures of it, and even though they are beautiful, they do not do justice to God's handiwork.

I was experiencing this overwhelming, awesome love of God in the high country, viewing the deep valleys with clear blue waters below, and reveling in the slight fall breeze. For what seemed like a fleeting moment, it created love, peace, and a hope within that will endure anytime my mind wanders back to that little piece of heaven here on earth.

Standing there reminded me of the story I'd recently been reading about St. Francis of Assisi. What can we learn from his life that relates to life today?

St. Francis is famous worldwide for having written the "Instruments of Peace" in the thirteenth century. It is a favorite prayer as quoted:

LORD, MAKE US INSTRUMENTS OF YOUR PEACE.
Where there is hatred, let us sow love;
Where there is injury, pardon;

Where there is discord, union;
Where there is doubt, faith;
Where there is despair, hope;
Where there is darkness, light;
Where there is sadness, joy.

O Divine Master, grant that we may
not seek so much
to be consoled as to console;
to be understood as to understand;
to be loved as to love.

For it is in giving that we receive;
it is in pardoning that we are pardoned;
and it is in dying that we are born to eternal life.

Amen

It has been this writer's joyful opportunity and a true challenge to capture the essence of St. Francis of Assisi. This most humble man devoted twenty-five years to following the guidance of a loving God. His religious lifestyle would probably not attract the majority of today's Christians.

St. Francis of Assisi was born as John Bernardon in 1182 at Assisi in Umbria, Italy and died there on October 4, 1226. He grew up in the family of a wealthy silk merchant. His Italian mother named him Giovanni after John the Baptist. His father, Peter, was infatuated with France, so he renamed his son Francesco. As a young boy he was nicknamed "Francis" and sometimes called "Frenchy" because he liked to play a French instrument similar to the guitar.

Everyone loved Francis with his consistently cheerful attitude. From his younger days until his death he was charming, witty, and joyful. Later in life, peace, truth, and love were added to his watchwords.

Francis was a leader, and during his wild youth, he was quoted as having "lived in sin." He wanted to be a noble knight and had that chance during a war between Perugia and Assisi. His glory was short-lived when he was captured and spent one year in a dark, dreary dungeon until ransomed.

Francis' next war experience changed his life forever. He had the finest horse that money could buy, was decorated with gold armor, and wore a magnificent cloak. One day's ride out of Assisi he had a dream. God spoke to him about this wrongdoing and told him to return home. This vision was so intense that Francis obeyed.

Francis began to earnestly pray and ask God what he wanted him to do with his life. He went off to a cave and wept for his regretful behavior, but soon God's grace overwhelmed him with joy.

Francis loved beauty and detested deformity. One day while riding through the countryside, he came face to face with a leper. The gross appearance and stench of this decayed body was almost more than he could bear. However, he quickly said a short prayer and dismounted his horse. God gave him strength beyond his own to kiss the leper's hand.

Later in life he would learn to eat supper from the same platter as the lepers, although some had body parts destroyed by the disease. God had given Francis the special gift of seeing beauty in all living things.

Francis felt connected to all living things. He is known for his love of animals, especially birds. It is said that a flock of them listened intently to one of his sermons and waited until he had completed speaking before they all flew away. Once in a small village, a wild wolf was killing domestic animals and attacking citizens. Francis was said to have preached to it, and thereafter the creature retreated back to the wilderness.

Francis received another message from God, to repair his church, so the obedient servant took that literally and began to rebuild damaged places of worship. He even confiscated fine silk from his father's shop and sold it for money to use on the restoration of these ancient ruins. His father discovered it missing, considered it theft, and was furious enough to have him arrested. Francis returned all the money and disowned his father's greedy ways.

Francis begged for stones and rebuilt many of these old churches with his own hands, not realizing quite yet that God's intention was for him to reform the Church from the inside. God wanted Francis to preach the gospel, talk with the people about changing their lives, and lead them to reconcile with him.

Francis came to believe in true equality and showered every person with honor, respect, and love whether a barefoot beggar or the Pope. His companions came from every walk of life-field hands, town politicians, nobility and common people, university professors, merchants, and members of the Church.

He was a saint different from all the others. First, he was never ordained as a priest and yet he preached. Second, in a pilgrimage to Rome, wearing his usual beggar clothes, he eventually received blessings from the Pope as a brother. Further, he founded the Franciscan orders for both men and women and became the patron saint of ecologists and merchants.

Francis was born to wealth, chose to give it up, and devoted his life to living in poverty to care for the sick and the poor, which made him an unusual individual. All accounts of St. Francis indicate he never lost his joyful attitude toward life, whether in prison or in very ill health at the end of his short forty-five years.

Francis enjoyed an impoverished lifestyle and tried to make it holy by taking the vows of simplicity, humility, obedience, poverty, and chastity. Francis' final years were filled with more supernatural events accompanying his suffering. It is reported that he received the stigmata in a vision while praying to share in Christ's passion. Visible wounds similar to those of Christ appeared on his body. His eyes began failing him, and it was in response to blindness and final suffering that Francis wrote the glorious Canticle of the Sun.

Canticle of the Sun

Most high, all-powerful, all good, Lord!
All praise is yours, all glory, all honor
And all blessing.
To you alone, Most High, do they belong.
No mortal lips are worthy
To pronounce your name.
All praise be yours, my Lord, through all that you have made,
And first my lord Brother Sun,
Who brings the day; and light you give to us through him.
How beautiful is he, how radiant in all his splendor!
Of you, Most High, he bears the likeness.
All praise be yours, my Lord, through Sister Moon and Stars;
In the heavens you have made them, bright
And precious and fair.
All praise be yours, My Lord, through Brothers Wind and Air,
And fair and stormy, all the weather's moods,
By which you cherish all that you have made.
All praise be yours, my Lord, through Sister Water,
So useful, lowly, precious and pure.
All praise be yours, my Lord, through Brother Fire,
Through whom you brighten up the night.
How beautiful is he, how gay! Full of power and strength.
All praise be yours, my Lord, through Sister Earth, our mother,
Who feeds us in her sovereignty and produces
Various fruits with colored flowers and herbs.
All praise be yours, my Lord, through those who grant pardon
For love of you; through those who endure
Sickness and trial.

Happy those who endure in peace,
By you, Most High, they will be crowned.
All praise be yours, my Lord, through Sister Death,
From whose embrace no mortal can escape.
Woe to those who die in mortal sin!
Happy those She finds doing your will!
The second death can do no harm to them.
Praise and bless my Lord, and give him thanks,
And serve him with great humility.

French Vegetable Soup

4	small carrots
1	large onion
2	medium tomatoes
7	small potatoes
	Salt to taste

- Cover carrots, onion, and tomatoes with water in large kettle. Boil until carrots are almost soft; add potatoes. Boil until potatoes are soft. Add salt.

Serve hot.

Serves six.

Crop Gathering

~ *Angie Ledbetter* ~

A rare, cool crispness has entered the air, right along with the beginning of a new school year. Watching the big, yellow school bus pull away from our house brings mixed emotions for me-a sigh of relief after a long, hot summer, worries about the new teachers and classmates my children will encounter today, and my own goals for a more productive and peaceful period as our fall routine is established. This morning will be a time spent in reflection and putting things in order.

I seek out my favorite church chapel and enjoy the feeling of my senses being bathed in peace and quiet-two things that are not abundant in my life during the summer months. It has been a season of many activities and a lot of hard work for me. I begin a silent conversation with Jesus as I lower to my knees. "Lord, I pray that you renew my body, mind, and spirit so that I can accomplish all things you put before me to the best of my abilities, and for the benefit of the most people. Please guide me and give me direction. I thank you for all of my many blessings. Amen." There are very few people in church this morning, and the line to the confessional moved quickly.

Sitting back upon the worn pew in this calming oasis, I want to evaluate the last several months and my actions/reactions to those summer events. Taking a small tablet from my purse, I see where I've written a quote on the top binding. I don't recall when I had written it, or the circumstances that prompted me to record it, but this morning it is a lovely thing to read and ponder.

"Sorrow looks back,
Worry looks around,
And faith looks up!"
- AUTHOR UNKNOWN

I want to look back, not to dwell on the negatives or to mourn for the passings, but so that I can learn from events and to try to avoid repeating mistakes. I will look ahead in bright optimism and faith, but without foolish expectations. I will continue to look up, for I know all riches and bounty come to me from God's generous and loving hand. My hope is there in this life and the next. I am in the right frame of mind after prayer and this small, inspiring quote, so I draw small apple baskets on the tablet. I smile at the crude attempt, as I have no artistic ability. Even so, the containers will serve their purpose. In fact, the baskets are like me-not very appealing to look at, but functional and open to whatever bounty may fill them.

One basket I label "Pray for!" and list a crop of the names I've held up in prayer recently: my grandmother, who has been having hellacious medical problems, a friend who is very ill, another friend who is having a dogged time with a job search, and family members with various personal struggles. I write the names so they appear to be going into the container and put a small cross on the basket's front. I ask the Lord to fulfill their prayer needs according to his will and ask that any small sacrifices I can make for their intentions be applied to my prayers for them.

Next, I write "Give to God" around the rim of another apple basket. Streaming into it are such things as "financial worries," "sale of house," "using my talents well," "direction with ministry projects," and "physical, mental, and emotional strength." The gatherings I've put into this container are things that I spend too much time worrying over. By placing them in God's basket, I intend to stop giving time to them and let God handle the outcomes of these concerns. I draw a round lid (without a handle) on top of the basket so that I'll be reminded to quit peeking in and checking on the progress of the items.

Another basket reads "Disappointments" and requires more thought and prayer. Several events during the summer had unsettled me. They were things I could continue to work on and attempt to make better over time, such as establishing more and regular family time, reading more Scripture, getting to church more than once a week, sleeping more at night, getting more exercise, having a better diet, helping bring about more peace in the home and in relationships. I made notes beneath the basket about specific things that were in my control with each unsatisfactory item listed. For good measure, I drew in a small paring knife and a long ribbon of apple peel beside that basket. I would work steadily and with patience until these goals were achieved.

I left for home feeling centered and hopeful. Stopping to get a few items from the grocery store, for some reason I was drawn to a display of ruby red apples and picked out a gleaming specimen. At the checkout register there was a small display of magnets. Smiling, I plucked off one of a stylized apple that read, "An apple a day..." and put it with my purchases. I'd have a visual daily reminder of the baskets I'd drawn in church. Some of my crop still needed work from me, others would be left alone for the Master to tend to, and there were still good seeds left to be planted at some future date.

Prayer and Goal Building Activity

At the end of a particularly trying time or hard season, make your own list of worries, prayers, goals, and ideals to put into drawn baskets. This exercise will help you bring your thoughts and visualizations into more concrete terms for action. You may even consider buying a few small baskets that are available for less than one dollar each. Write your concerns on paper and cut them into strips. Distribute to appropriate category baskets and look at the contents periodically to see how you are doing.

Did you take some of your projects or troubles back from the Lord's basket? Do you need to add a few more prayer intentions? Is your goal bucket empty or too full? This could also be a good project for children who need help getting organized with school work, or who want to have prayer baskets of their own. Display your efforts in a prominent place so that you will be easily reminded of them.

Parable *of the* Rich Fool

Luke 12:16-21

And He told them a parable, saying, "The land of a rich man was very productive. And he began reasoning to himself, saying, 'What shall I do, since I have no place to store my crops?' Then he said, 'This is what I will do: I will tear down my barns and build larger ones, and there I will store all my grain and my goods. And I will say to my soul, Soul, you have many goods laid up for many years to come; take your ease, eat, drink and be merry.' But God said to him, 'You fool! This very night your soul is required of you; and now who will own what you have prepared?' So is the man who stores up treasure for himself, and is not rich toward God. And He said to His disciples, 'For this reason I say to you, do not worry about your life, as to what you will eat; nor for your body, as to what you will put on.'"

Think *on* This:

"It is the height of absurdity to sow little but weeds in the first half of one's lifetime and expect to harvest a valuable crop in the second half."

~ *Percy Johnston*

HARVEST

Harvest me Lord from Your majestic fields.
Gather me in, and take what I yield.
Pluck from my bounty the weeds and the chaff.
Bundle me tight and bind my two halves.

Harvest me Lord as this season does fall.
Share Your fruits through me with those who call.
My roots grow deeply in Your verdant earth.
Let them remain 'til Fall yields my worth.

Harvest me Lord before winter sets in.
Shield me from the dark storms of my sins.
Rain down Your spirit of love on my soul.
Send the Son's rays, my stalk to unfold.

Harvest me Lord at the end of my days.
After the seasons have had their way.
Leave fertile seeds of me buried in loam.
Shoots left behind when I am called Home.

Autumn Bounty Pie

Filling:

4 cups	rhubarb or apple, sliced
1/2 cup	sugar
1 tbs	all-purpose flour
1/4 cup	Grand Marnier
2 tbs	orange marmalade
2 1/2 cups	strawberries, sliced

Crumbly Topping:

1/3 cup	unsalted butter
1/3 cup	packed light brown sugar
1/2 cup	all-purpose flour
1 tsp	cinnamon
1/2 cup	shredded coconut
1/3 cup	pecans

- Preheat oven to 350 degrees. Using your favorite pie crust recipe or refrigerated pie crust, line a lightly oiled nine-inch pie dish with the dough, crimping the edges, then pierce the bottom with a fork. Weigh down with foil and dried beans and bake for twenty minutes.

Continues

- For the filling, place the rhubarb or apples in a baking dish, sprinkle with sugar, and bake at 350 degrees for thirty minutes or until tender. In a saucepan, mix flour, Grand Marnier, and orange marmalade into a paste. Drain the liquid from the baked rhubarb/apple into a saucepan, add flour mixture, and stir over low heat until the mixture thickens. Remove from heat and combine with the rhubarb/apple. Set aside to cool slightly.

- For the topping, cut the butter with the brown sugar. Process with the remaining ingredients until crumbly. Place the baked pie shell on a cookie sheet. Fold the berries with the rhubarb or apple, then pour into the crust. Smother with topping and bake for thirty minutes or until the top is browned and juices are bubbling.

FROM CARYL WESTWOOD'S
Angels in My Kitchen: Divine Dessert Recipes, Celestial Arts Publishing

Epeche, the Unchosen

~ Deb Anne Flynt ~

Epeche watched as her brothers and sisters were plucked from the limbs of her mother as soon as they reached their prime. She envied them that they would be enjoyed by the family who lived in the little farmhouse nearby, and joyously awaited her turn.

But Epeche was too high in the branches for the children, so they never reached for her when they picked a ripe fruit to eat in the shade of Tree Mother's arms. The plump farm wife was not even as tall as the oldest boy, so she never chose Epeche for cobblers, pies, or preserves. The old farmer who loved pickled peaches would choose carefully the exact ones he wanted, but never Epeche. Autumn trickled by one day at a time while she hoped and waited.

She thought of summer, and one of her favorite memories played itself over in her troubled mind. Tree Mother recounted the tale of her children's births. She told them how they all began life as lovely little flowers. The honeybees and butterflies flew all around her and danced in and out of the sunshine among her branches. Sometimes they would come from another peach tree that lived right down the road, then visit her blossoms.

"My pretty little blooms would be washed away by spring rain or borne off on a gust of wind. This didn't bother me at all, because I knew what it meant," she'd tell them. "Once the flowers fell off, I could see tiny fruitlings. Do you know what those were?"

All the young peaches on the tree would say "Us! Those were US!"

"That's right my sweet ones." A bird landed on her twig and brought Epeche out of her reverie. She listened as the bird chirped and sang. Some of the birds would leave when the days grew cooler, but Epeche somehow knew this red one would stay. She hoped he would come visit her again. He flew away as suddenly as he had arrived.

Epeche knew her time was short, because she could feel the sap slowing. Nearly all her brothers and sisters were gone. She had been a late bloom, one of the last. She knew this because there were many peachlets on the tree when her flower fell. She was ripe nearly to burst, but still she was not chosen.

"I am no longer a child," she told Tree Mother. "I will fall off and rot on the ground. I have served no purpose. Even the birds did not choose me. I have failed you, Tree Mother. Please forgive me."

"My dear Epeche, you are younger than you know. You are but a fruit now. You have failed no one. Your presence is a delight to me every day. I love you, child. Believe what I say. When you were all still but flowers, I kept count of every blossom, and which ones were visited by the bees and butterflies. I kept count of every one that was visited after my Tree Cousin. I put on my best blooms. This is how I invite the winged ones. This part is most important, my darling Epeche. You are special. You were one of my most beautiful blooms. You were visited many times. The little bees would fly all through my branches visiting my children, but many came back to you-perhaps because you are so high in my branches."

"Tree Mother, I still don't see how I can bring you any joy now!"

"Listen to me and hear this now. You ARE special. All that live will die, but not all that die will live. Tomorrow I will tell you more, but it is nearing dark and I must rest."

Epeche knew tomorrow she might fall, but she would wait and trust Tree Mother. The air turned cool, as it did every evening lately. She would be heavier with dew, but she would try to hang on and wait. A soft thud below indicated that another of her siblings had fallen to the ground beneath her mother's branches.

The next morning, the farm wife came and gathered the ones that had fallen during the night. She took a long look up into the tree. "Only a few good ones left. I guess you're the last ones, then," she said to the peaches in the basket. Tree Mother knew that she would not be back tomorrow, and Epeche sensed her thoughts.

"Oh, Tree Mother! How can you be so happy? Now I will never be chosen! I can't even hope to be picked up now!"

"Because now you can die, my dear one, so that you might live!"

"I don't understand."

"Today, you will fall. I can no loner hold you. Try to hang on until the children go in tonight. You may not understand why, but believe what I tell you and do as I say."

"I will do my best, because I love you and I trust in you," Epeche said, heartbroken that her mother did not understand her strong desire to be chosen.

Tree Mother knew her child's thoughts as she always did, because they were connected in so many ways. "Have you already forgotten what I taught you yesterday?" She knew she had not, but that she didn't understand it. "You sorrow because you will not be chosen, but I have told you that you already were chosen."

"How can that be, since I am still here?"

"You were chosen by the butterflies and the bees. This is far more important than being chosen by people! Do not be so proud, daughter. You have been blessed to be among the last. Now you must stop worrying and focus your energies on hanging on until nightfall."

"But," Epeche began, but stopped and did as her mother instructed. She might not understand, but she knew Tree Mother's love and had faith in her. She stopped thinking and worked on hanging on, though she knew it was her last chance.

Evening came and the dinner bell called the children inside. The farm wife had not come out that afternoon to gather the fallen fruit. Tree Mother shook softly. "Epeche, it's time."

"Yes, somehow I know this. Will it hurt?" she asked.

"It may, but only for a short time. Do not forget what I have taught you. After you fall, we will not be able to hear each other as plainly anymore. You are not alone, though. I am here and I will watch over you. I love you always. Good-bye, daughter and friend."

"Good-bye, Tree Mother. You have been my delight all my life. I love you," she paused, "and I trust in you." With that, Epeche released herself from her mother's limbs and fell. She bounced off a few branches, and it did hurt, but not for long.

She landed in the first fallen leaves, and that didn't hurt so badly. During the night, a small animal came and nibbled at her. Another one picked her up and carried her off a little way before taking a few bites.

She was no longer beneath Tree Mother's branches, but a breeze came up and she heard the familiar voice. "It's nearly time, dear one, for you to sleep. You can no longer live unless you die." The voice trailed away as the wind shifted. Epeche still did not understand, but she trusted.

That night, the breeze turned into a strong wind, a hard rain began falling, and it turned colder than Epeche ever remembered! Soon, she was spattered with mud and covered with leaves. "I will die now," she said to herself. "I will become part of the earth." Her last thoughts were of Tree Mother as she allowed sleep to overtake her.

She slept the rest of autumn and all through the winter as rain, leaves, dirt, and even snow covered her, and as insects and worms feasted on what was left of her once beautiful fruit, yet only part of her became part of the earth.

It seemed to Epeche to be only a short time before she awoke, but when she did, she understood all that Tree Mother had told her. Somehow she knew much more than this, too. She stretched upward and downward with all her might. "Ah, that's it!" she thought as her first rootlet popped out of her pit and dug into the soft earth. Always, she pushed her root deeper into the ground and reached up. She knew it was what she had to do, and it felt wonderful!

One spring day a short time afterward, the sun shone warm on the blossoms of a peach tree on a small farm. Honeybees flew from blossom to blossom and Tree Mother counted each one. From the other side of the yard, another, much younger tree watched.

Super Easy Peachy Cobbler

7-8	RIPE PEACHES (TO BE SURE YOU HAVE PLENTY LEFT AFTER THE KIDS GET A FEW)
2 CANS	REFRIGERATED BISCUIT DOUGH
1/3 CUP	SUGAR PLUS THREE TABLESPOONS
	CINNAMON TO TASTE
	BUTTER OR MARGARINE
1/4-1/3 CUP	WATER

- Scrub and stem peaches. Have the children wash them again. Peel what's left of the peaches. Cut them, and remove the pits. Give pits to the children and tell them to make up a story about a peach. Cut the peaches into about one-inch cubes.

- Grease or spray a 9x13-inch cake pan or casserole. Stretch out the biscuit dough to cover the bottom of the pan, or let the children do it and then patch the holes. Place the peach cubes on the bottom crust. Send the kids outside to plant the pits.

- Cut up about one tablespoon butter and scatter over peaches. Stir one-third cup sugar into the water and pour over peaches. Cut remaining biscuits into quarters and stretch them out on top. It's okay if they don't cover the top. Brush with melted butter. Sprinkle with sugar and cinnamon.

- Bake at 400 degrees until bubbly and golden brown-about fifteen minutes. Go outside and repair your flower garden, removing the peach pits. Cool slightly before serving with ice cream.

CONNECTING *with* KIDS

I love reading to children. When mine were younger, I would go and read to their classes in school. The teacher welcomed the break and the children welcomed the change. I usually carried several books from my own children's library in case the teacher hadn't chosen something ahead of time.

With familiar books, I could use different character voices or even act out some parts. These little tricks never failed to delight them. In teaching children to enjoy stories, they are more anxious to learn to read. Reading to children encourages children to read.

Read for a class of five- to seven-year-olds sometime. Do it once and you'll be glad you did. Do it twice and you'll be hooked. Do it weekly, and you'll be someone's hero.

Listening Eyes

How I love their little faces
Excitement dances in their eyes.
Each story that I read to them,
I try to bring alive.

I start with one I know quite well
An elephant on a nest
Bird's lines I read in whining tones.
The children like that best.

Elephant sounds so dignified,
His plight becomes so clear
As I read the familiar book
These children hold so dear.

They laugh at all my antics
They're quiet when things look bleak.
And at the end, quite backwards,
They yell, "An elephant with a beak!"

Inspired by Dr. Seuss's Horton Hatches the Egg

Working the Arbor

~ *Angie Ledbetter* ~

Have you ever gotten one of those brilliant ideas and acted on it immediately, later regretting the rash spur-of-the-moment decision? I get a lot of those, and am trying to temper those spontaneous "Hey, so-and-so would be great to do. I'm gonna go for it!" thoughts by at least considering the ramifications and possible consequences of leaping before looking. I don't want to completely squelch that side of my personality, because it adds such fun to life and racks up funny stories I'll be able to recall in my golden years. Realistically, though, a little moderation and thoughtfulness go a long way in helping me avoid disasters.

About ten years ago, I got the harebrained inspiration to try a project that could be done at home with my then one-, two-, and three-year-olds. It would be cheap, creative, and wonderful domestic fun. In hindsight, I should have realized that I was stretching the bounds of possibilities, but with baby-engineered sleep deprivation, I only saw the positives of my scheme.

One morning when it was autumn in the south, but you really can't feel it much yet, I loaded up the kids and drove to my parents' house. Getting Mom to watch the babies, I went out into the backyard to begin my adventure. Behind the massive fig tree was a small grape arbor Daddy had built from wood and chicken wire. The sturdy vines grew thick on and over the arched structure, and clusters of greenish-purple fruit hung their dewy heads proudly.

A cooling breeze rustled the crispy leaves around in the yard and made mini leaf tornadoes against the worn backyard fence. I enjoyed the feeling of freedom, as the opportunity to be kidless didn't come along often. It was a strange feeling, being alone, and I kept wondering what I was forgetting. Moms of small children often say the same thing. Not having those little arms and legs constantly entwined around you, after having been there for so long, kind of makes you feel floaty and free but also like something is missing. I wondered if the grapevine would feel the same after I plucked the fruit from her limbs.

I carefully gathered what I considered to be the choicest grapes in my bucket, realizing that my country gal experiences were limited. I prayed that I was picking the right ones, and remember thinking, Even if I'm picking unripe grapes, it's still nice to be out here alone and free to do something that does not directly relate to taking care of one of the kids!

Back home an hour or so later, I set out all the items I'd need to make my first delicious batch of grape jelly. If my project worked out well, I'd have something inexpensive to make and give to loved ones on my Christmas list! Paraffin wax to seal the sterile jars, cheesecloth to strain the cooked-down grapes from their hard seeds, a huge vat, sugar, and other things soon filled my limited countertop space.

I began the jelly making process with a smile on my face and a happy tune on my lips. Four hours, two bottles, three diapers, baby meals, a potty-training attempt, and several tugging-over-a-toy-refereeing sessions later, the purple goop in the big pot did not look at all appetizing. In fact, it had a fermented, sour smell that matched its oozy appearance. I sat on the sticky kitchen floor and cried tired tears into my stained apron. All that time, effort, money, and hope looked like it was literally going to go down the drain.

In my disappointment, I moaned about the fact that my husband, father of the three angels now howling with me on the floor, was thousands of miles away in Nova Scotia. Sometimes I hated Dennis's career. It took him away from us for months on end as he traveled about to work on electricity-producing turbines across the United States. On days like those, the only comfort I had was praying my mantra-the Serenity Prayer.

Leaving the kitchen mess until after the kiddies would be tucked into their bed and cribs, I boarded the circular treadmill that took me around the house on a rapid succession of pit stops-the trash cans full of dirty diapers, the kitchen sink, the washroom overflowing with clothes to be done, the bathroom with the leaking commode, and various spots where toys sat like waiting traps for my feet. I finally disembarked the chore train at about 12:30 a.m. and sat in my favorite chair with a cup of hot, soothing tea.

Looking down at my forgotten apron with all its evidence of menial duties and failed culinary attempts with the jelly-making, I tugged it off and threw it in the nearby trash can. Grabbing my black Bible for comfort, I put my slippered feet up on the baby's carseat on the floor. The quiet was a blessing after the disastrous day. I leaned my head back and deeply inhaled the peace. The only sounds I could hear at that moment were the low hum of the dishwasher and the leaves stirred by strong breezes underneath the dry azalea bushes outside the house. Praying for inspiration, I opened the Good Book and my eyes fell on Exodus 23:16: "Also you shall observe the Feast of the Harvest of the first fruits of your labors from what you sow in the field; also the Feast of the Ingathering at the end of the year when you gather in the fruit of your labors from the field."

What did that mean? My grape harvesting was certainly nothing to celebrate and my labors had all been in vain! I wasn't even doing a good job keeping up with the daily laboring of motherhood and housewife. Many times, I just saw my days stretching out in front of me like an endless field in constant need of tending. My efforts seemed to make no impact. I was not a very good farmer and I balked at the yoke many a day.

In prayer, it came to me that I was looking at the wrong harvest. The physical work and even the wonderful grape jelly-making adventure were not my only crops. My most important work was being done in my children. Yes, they were the "first fruits of my labors." The field God had helped me plant and given me charge over would need many seasons of work and toiling before I'd see the yield, but what a unique and special harvest it would one day be!

I would rejoice for the small "Ingatherings" I'd have between now and our children's adulthoods. I'd also make it a point to always consult my Farmer's Almanac (the Bible) when I had questions, doubts, or needed directions.

Closing my Bible and draining my cup, I was struck by the thought that I was blessed to come from such a long line of harvesters. The grape arbor Daddy had lovingly and carefully planted was in the tradition of his Sicilian forefathers. Their hard work had produced generations of harvesters. And I was going to be one of them! In the meantime, grape jelly is cheap, and the wine-colored stains of imperfection are easily washed from my apron with the help of a most merciful and loving heavenly Father. I dug my old apron from the trash and tossed it into the washer as I made my last rounds to softly kiss my babies goodnight. ❦

Faith in Action Tip

Could God be trying to show us things and teach us lessons through our mistakes? I learned powerful ones during the jelly-making. Try to see where he could be leading you when things fail to go as planned, instead of just wallowing in disappointment and self-ridicule. Sometimes, what we learn through our errors is much more important that the project we had originally planned. Remember, the Lord turns all bad into good!

Vineyard Scriptures

Genesis 40:9-

"So the chief cupbearer told his dream to Joseph, and said to him, 'In my dream, behold, there was a vine in front of me.'"

Leviticus 26:5-

"Indeed, your threshing will last for you until grape gathering, and grape gathering will last until sowing time. You will thus eat your food to the full and live securely in your land."

Deuteronomy 24:21-

"When you gather the grapes of your vineyard, you shall not go over it again; it shall be for the alien, for the orphan, and for the widow."

---

1 Samuel 8:15-

"He will take a tenth of your seed and of your vineyards and give to his officers and to his servants."

Psalm 107:37-

"And sow fields and plant vineyards, And gather a fruitful harvest."

Isaiah 5:4-

"What more was there to do for my vineyard that I have not done in it? Why, when I expected it to produce good grapes did it produce worthless ones?"

Jeremiah 2:21-

"Yet I planted you a choice vine, A completely faithful seed. How then have you turned yourself before Me into the degenerate shoots of a foreign vine?"

Matthew 9:37-

"Then He said to His disciples, 'The harvest is plentiful, but the workers are few.'"

Luke 6:44-

"For each tree is known by its own fruit. For men do not gather figs from thorns, nor do they pick grapes from a briar bush."

John 15:5-

"I am the vine, you are the branches; he who abides in Me and I in him, he bears much fruit, for apart from Me, you can do nothing."

Concord (Conquered?) Grape Jelly

5	POUNDS GRAPES
4 1/2 CUP	SUGAR
1 BOX	FRUIT PECTIN CRYSTALS

- Remove stems and wash grapes. Crush well and add two cups of water. Cover pot and let simmer for about fifteen minutes. Pour off the juice and reserve it (it will make about seven cups of juice).

- Mix fruit pectin crystals with 1/4 cup of sugar. Slowly add this mixture to the fruit or juice in your pot, and put on high heat until it comes to a full boil. Boil for one minute, stirring constantly.

- Immediately pour jelly into sterilized jars. Add lids quickly and screw tight.

Recipe makes about eight cups of jelly.

If all else fails, go to nearest grocery store and purchase Bama grape jelly!

Queen of Quotes Finds the Truth

~ Alaine Benard ~

"Personal freedom, love, happiness and experimentation are the only four ingredients in the recipe of truth. Truth feels good."

- Z. Murray

Quotes, such as this one, are my number one weapon. I stockpile them in my arsenal of self-deceptions. I cannot simply make a life choice and live it. I must have logical reasons, backed by written material, before proceeding. The written word rings the bell of intellectualism! With a life as important as mine, I deserve all the bells and whistles I find. For whatever purpose I am searching, I can pull an appropriate author, book, or expert's advice out of my hat.

Who wants to be looked upon as a wing nut? Not I! I back myself up with proper quotes. Others will be convinced by my righteous ramblings of academia. When I choose my paths, I want those surrounding me to approve of my choices. Yes, I want cheerleaders, or at the very least, respectful admiration from the sidelines. (I have provided legitimate quotations for my decisions, so, therefore, I am not to be doubted-certainly not to be questioned.)

Alcohol, loose morals, and a steady diet of caffeine and nicotine; not a thing wrong with that! "If it feels good, do it!" Yep, all of it felt good, so I did it. While I was out kickin' butt in the bars, I would rise the next afternoon and read all manner of self-help rationalizations. From Sartre to daily horoscopes, I located all the justifications my rebellions required. That and a pot of coffee helped settle the queasy roll of my guts.

Moving the empty beer cans off the coffee table, some overnighter's copy of Life hit me in the bleary eye. Through the red haze I read the fact that "God was Dead." Hmmmmmm, well, I had to go back to bed and give serious consideration to that one.

After some heavy contemplation (while getting ready to go out again), I resolved to find God's replacement. As it was Thursday night, and thirty-six more hours of partying were ahead of me, I'd start looking on Monday. Yeah, "Monday is the first day of the rest of your life." Cool. I'd find him on Monday-late Monday.

With a short search, I soon found the perfect new god. She was loving, all-powerful, all knowing, and omnipotent! The new age Unitarian church made the introductions. After months of studying philosophies of N.A.U.G.H.T. at the New Age Unitarian god's Happy Thoughts Church on the corner, I knew I'd found nirvana. That wonderful new god was...Me! Ahhhhhhh! How right was that?

I was my own Dali Lama Ding-Dong! It was just what I had suspected all along. There was no mean old Daddy-Man sitting up on a throne judging me with stern eyes. No way. I was a good princess-goddess/god who knew all the answers, complete with quotes.

Along with my innovative religion came a new diet plan. After all, "You are what you eat!" Swinging crystals and chanting mantras, I was enlightened to the fact that animal products weren't good choices. Eating them meant we were eating our brother cows and sister chickens. Books like, Healthy Food for Your Chakras had all the answers. The diet would decrease the negativity surrounding my aura. Oh, my. I could dig that! (Long-neck Lites and Virginia Slims weren't mentioned, so again, I had literature to back up my dietary choices, lifestyle, and spirituality.)

"Your Body, Your Choice!" emerged shortly after Roe vs. Wade. Although the slogan became the war cry to propagate abortion, it came in handy when I succumbed to the call of the tattooist's needles. "My body, my art!" became my personal twist to the saying.

I do dearly love them quotes! Such handy, dandy bullets to shoot down arguments against the recipe I used to cook up a pot of "truth."

Time has marched on. Marriage, childbirth, and middle age have not changed my love of written word and quotes. Re-examining Z. Murray's example, with the experience of motherhood and forty-one years, I notice a word I had previously left out. "Feels." Hmmm, I hadn't read that closely. What the heck does feel good have to do with what's right?

Truth is simple, all right. Truth is intelligence for sure. Truth IS the Bible-simple, clean, and right. I had just chosen to dismiss it, for it did not offer me any affirmations regarding my feel-good rebellious life.

Just as my parents' belt swung down to spank my sassy behind, the truth isn't always nice and pleasant. It means consequences for our actions, both the good and the bad. The real ingredients are: truth is hard and solid and offers unconditional love.

For those ready to accept the responsibility to grow up and really live, the Bible has all the truth we need. (Great quotes, too.) Its pages give examples, reasons, lessons, commandments, and the promise of our Father's love. Very simple, indeed. The Book of Life has nada to do with what feels good. Living the Word is hard work-admitting guilt, striving to do our best, no matter what our old rebellious minds would rather us do! "Where's the Beef?" It's in the Book! We also get the best author and the number one seller of all times. All the answers and justifications we need are within those pages.

"Oh what tangled webs we weave, when first we practice to deceive!" Yes sir, I can quote with the best of 'em. "And you will know the truth, and the truth will make you free." (John 8:32)

N.A.M. INFORMATION (NEW AGE MOVEMENT)

Red flags for NAM involvement include interests in the following: witchcraft, Satanism, or cult activities. The individual may show a fascination with or actually attempt suicide. Other influences to watch out for are Jungianism, I Ching, astrology, occult books, musical group influences, channeling (people "speaking" for deceased spirits), meditating, crystals, reincarnation, horoscopes, palmistry, fortune-telling, zodiac, Ouija boards, UFOs, numerology, Wicca, and enneagram diagrams.

Arm yourself with the best knowledge there is. Father Mitch Pacwa, S.J. is the four-star general in the battle against NAM.

Arm yourself with his book, *Catholics and the New Age* (Servant Publications, Ann Arbor, Michigan). The back of the book lists recommended and non-recommended sources for further reading.

Father Pacwa's "weapons" against NAM are outlined and include having hope and trusting that the Church, with the help of the Holy Spirit, will prevail against all. "Our growth in Christ requires an active sacramental life and a daily prayer life to nourish our relationships with God," he says. Frequent reflection on biblical morality is strongly encouraged. We can refer others to read the biblical passage to you rather than quote it or read it to him/her. Use the rosary and devotion to Our Lady to keep you firmly rooted in scripture. Her intercession and motherly care is a tremendous grace for ourselves, as well as those to whom we witness. Reading good, Catholic theology and apologetics will help in refuting NAM arguments. Always pray for protection when reading/listening to NAM material in your research.

Helpful Cult and N.A.M. Resources:

American Family Foundation:
(617) 893-0930

Catholic Answers:
(619) 541-1131

Center Research Institute:
(714) 855-9926

Prayer to St. Michael

St. Michael the Archangel, defend us in battle. Be our protection against the wickedness and snares of the devil. May God rebuke him, we humbly pray, and do thou, O Prince of the Heavenly Host, by the power of God, cast into Hell Satan and all the evil spirits, who prowl about the world seeking the ruin of souls.

Amen.

This is a powerful prayer to offer for those involved in NAM, as well as any other type of spiritual attack you may encounter.

AUNT ALFIE DIBENEDETTO'S BEAN PATTIES

3 CANS	GREEN BEANS (ANY KIND)
1	ONION, MINCED
1	CLOVE GARLIC, MINCED
3/4 CUP	ITALIAN BREADCRUMBS
1/2 CUP	PARMESAN CHEESE
10	EGGS
	SALT AND PEPPER TO TASTE

- Wash and boil three cans of green beans (any type) for about ten minutes with minced onion, garlic, salt, and pepper. Drain well and put into large bowl. Add bread crumbs, cup cheese, and eggs.

- Stir to mix well. Shape mixture into small patties and drop by the tablespoon-full into hot oil. Mash like a pancake with spatula. Brown well on both sides and drain well on paper towel. Makes a big platter full!

Mercy Me! The Lightning Struck the Tree

~ Deb Anne Flynt ~

"...Holy God, Holy Mighty One, Holy Immortal One, have mercy on us and on the whole world. In the name of the Father, and of the Son, and of the Holy Spirit. Amen."

BOOM-CRACK!

A flash of bright red-orange light flashed through the doorway of my bedroom where my children and I still sat on my bed, having just finished our daily three o'clock Divine Mercy Chaplet. It caught our attention, to say the very least. Six bare feet simultaneously hit the ground as we flew off of the bed, thumping across the floor almost as fast as our hearts were pounding in our chests.

We rushed to the doorway and all managed to crowd through at once-bending a law of physics as we did. My son ran off to unplug everything as quickly as he could, but I had to hurdle my daughter, who, for some unforeseen reason had abruptly stopped halfway to the door. Using more agility than I thought I ever had, I finally made it across the room to the back door and looked out.

Gray-black clouds stampeded across the sky, pushed by stronger winds than the ones that were beating the branches of the trees and bushes in the backyard against each other. I scanned for damage, seeking out the most obvious targets.

A tall oak grew draped over the roof, its roots practically part of the house's foundation. It shuddered in the wind and rapid-fired acorns down onto the tin in short bursts, but it was undamaged. The skeleton of another tree stood practically motionless against the wind. With no leaves and only a few stumps of branches left, it offered little resistance. It too was unharmed. The huge pine, which had survived the crash of a larger, ancient pine that had been removed because it was a lightning hazard, also seemed unscathed-besides the old scars. The aged sweet gum and the younger oak appeared okay, too.

I scanned back over them again, suspecting that I wouldn't find anything because it must have been farther away than I could see from inside the house. There was a small mark on the pine, just a faint line, but nothing on anything else. I moved to my left. Clear of the privet that had blocked my view, I saw it. The small mark was the inside of the tree, not just some thin stream of sap. It extended upward into the branches, and down into the underbrush. The entire tree was split open, tip to toes!

I looked away to call the children when suddenly a second bolt struck, filling the room with blue-white light and instantaneous thunder! I didn't see where it hit and never found evidence of other damage. It might have struck the same tree again.

Poof! Both kids appeared at the door beside me.

"Children, look at this!" I pointed out the mark and they followed the line all the way up and down.

"Mom, is that the tree's insides?" my young one asked, full of concern. I nodded, but explained that trees aren't made like animals.

"Is it gonna make it?" asked my practical one, but his eyes revealed sadness.

"That's up to God." I let that soak in, then added, "It's a strong tree, and it's survived hardships before. Remember how that gigantic pine stripped half the branches off that side when it fell on it? It kept growing."

"Yes ma'am, but..." The question faded away.

"Yeah, lightning is different, isn't it? I really don't know what will happen to it. Like I said, it's a strong tree, but a lightning strike is a pretty traumatic event. We'll have to wait and see."

I stood there thinking of the time I'd spent under that tree. There had been a bit of it, and when the time came, we had even chosen its shade for a nice place to bury the dear animal friends we lost.

It's been a nearly a year since the Mercy Tree was struck and I first wrote this. During the winter, the temperature dropped below freezing a few times, and it snowed more than once. I guess it was more that a South Mississippi tree could handle with that kind of injury. We checked on it often as it slowly changed to never-green and its needles fell, and then limbs.

The stump will be used for sitting and thinking or praying, and it will have a rosary design carved into the top before it is treated and sealed. For now it still stands as a reminder of the pets who passed away, of the day it was struck, and especially as a reminder to pray daily for mercy!

To Pray the Divine Mercy Chaplet, Using a Regular Five~Decade Rosary:

Say the Lord's Prayer ("Our Father..."), a Hail Mary, and the Apostles' Creed ("I Believe in God...").

On the large beads, pray, "Eternal Father, we offer You the Body and Blood, Soul and Divinity of Your dearly beloved Son, our Lord Jesus Christ, in atonement for our sins and those of the whole world."

On the small beads: "For the sake of His sorrowful Passion have mercy on us and on the whole world."

Conclude by saying three times, "Holy God, Holy Mighty One, Holy Immortal One, have mercy on us and on the whole world. Amen."

"Jesus, I trust in you!"

If you don't have a rosary:

Some of my friends who don't own a rosary or have one with them use their fingers to count the prayers. After the opening prayers, pray one large bead prayer ("Eternal Father...") then say ten small bead prayers ("For the sake of His sorrowful passion..."). Repeat the large bead prayer, followed by ten small bead prayers. There are five large beads and five decades (sets of ten) of small beads. The large beads come before the decades.

Although the rosary is still usually considered a Catholic tool, many non-Catholics are learning the joy of using it for various prayers, including the Divine Mercy Chaplet. More and more people are coming to appreciate it for what it is-a means of praying available to everyone-no matter your brand of faith.

LIGHTNING FAST DIVINITY

2 1/4 CUP	SUGAR
1/2 CUP	LIGHT CORN SYRUP
1/2 CUP	WATER
1/4 TSP	SALT
2	EGG WHITES
1 1/2 TSP	VANILLA EXTRACT
1/2 CUP	CHOPPED PECANS

- Combine sugar, corn syrup, water, and salt in a microwaveable bowl. Cover and cook on high in microwave for five to six minutes, until boiling. Uncover and cook an additional eight to ten minutes, until a small amount dropped in cold water forms a hard ball.

- Beat egg whites with a mixer until stiff. Pour hot mixture over egg whites while beating on high. Add vanilla and beat for four or five minutes until candy holds shape. Fold in pecans and drop by spoonfuls onto waxed paper.

Awe at God's Light Show

Lightning is beautiful, but it's dangerous. It kills at least three hundred people in the U.S. every year, but most people who are struck survive. Around the world it strikes about one hundred times per second. It can precede or follow a storm for several minutes, and it can strike before you ever see it or hear the first thunder.

When a storm approaches, turn off electronic equipment. Even a surge protector doesn't stand a chance against a direct hit. Lightning can follow water and electrical lines into your home, so stay out of water and off the phone. A cordless is safe, but fairly useless if the power goes out, and you can get a loud pop if a line takes a hit. If you're outside, stay away from trees and water and avoid open spaces. And yes, lightning can strike the same place twice-and sometimes it does. This myth can be dangerous.

The wonder and beauty of lightning remind us of God's presence, even if we are afraid. His majesty is displayed in the intensity and splendor of it. It is amazing to watch! Gary and I love sitting at the back door just admiring a magnificent storm. I feel safe there, but I also sometimes fear the fierceness of it. When storms feel threatening, I have a powerful prayer that was sent to me by a friend.

THE PRAYER or BLESSING AGAINST STORMS

Jesus Christ a King of Glory has come in Peace.†
God became man,†
and the Word was made flesh.†
Christ was born of a Virgin.†
Christ suffered,†
Christ was crucified.†
Christ died.†
Christ rose from the dead.†
Christ ascended into Heaven.†
Christ conquers.†
Christ reigns.†
Christ orders.†
May Christ protect us from all storms and lightning.†
Christ went through their midst in Peace,†
and the word was made flesh.†
Christ is with us with Mary.†
Flee you enemy spirits
because the Lion of the generation of Judah,
the Root of David, has won.†
Holy God!†
Holy Powerful God!†
Holy Immortal God!†
Have mercy on us.

Amen!

Grace Amazing

~ Carol Schwartz ~

"Amazing Grace! How Sweet the sound,
That saved a wretch like me!
I once was lost, but now am found,
Was blind, but now I see!
'Twas grace that taught my heart to fear,
And grace my fears relieved.
How precious did that grace appear,
The hour I first believed!
The Lord has promised good to me,
His word my hope secures.
He will my shield and portion be
As long as life endures.
Through many dangers, toils, and snares,
I have already come.
His grace has brought me safe thus far,
And grace will lead me home."
When we've been there ten thousand years,
Bright shining as the sun,
We've no less days to sing God's praise
Than when we'd first begun."

- JOHN NEWTON, 1725-1807

"Amazing Grace" is my favorite hymn to sing with a group of friends. A favorite Amazing Grace memory is of a women's retreat I made in Redlands, California.

We were told on Saturday morning that we would have a special treat that evening before Father Bill shared his twelve-step talk. I had no idea what kind of surprise was in store for us.

They wheeled Jean in and turned on the tape player to accompany her. Out of her mouth came the most melodious voice I have ever heard as she sang a beautiful rendition of Amazing Grace. There wasn't a dry eye in the place after she made the words come alive. I felt like I had visited heaven listening to her, and that particular retreat weekend was a very peaceful time.

Later on I learned that it had been Jean's first appearance since a near fatal car accident. She had been engaged to be married, and after the car accident she turned away from everyone, including her fiancé. She ended up in the wheelchair and couldn't exercise, so she had gained a lot of weight and was very unhappy with herself. At one time she had been an opera star.

Jean said she had been suffering from not knowing how to adjust or cope with her new life. Friends had introduced her to a small church that supported twelve-step recovery programs, and that's how she wound up at our retreat singing and crying her heart out.

She eventually returned to a singing career. It was not the opera world she had known before, but one of teaching young girls how to sing. The last I heard she was enjoying her new life, giving God and her new friends praise and thanks for saving her.

Jean gave us all hope that day that it is possible to recover from even the worst of tragedies if we seek and believe in God's amazing grace.

Sisters' Soda Bread

The Sisters at Redland's Franciscan Retreat House made mouth-watering soda bread and served it to us on spiritual retreats. Many of us put in a request to buy loaves to take home to our families and treat them to this special. Their recipe was quite similar to the recipe below.

3 CUPS	SIFTED FLOUR
1/4 TSP	CREAM OF TARTAR
3/4 TSP	SALT
1/3 CUP	BUTTER
1/4 CUP	SUGAR
1 CUP	BUTTERMILK
1 TSP	BAKING SODA
1/3 CUP	SODA WATER
1/2 TSP	BAKING POWDER
1/3 CUP	RAISINS, OPTIONAL

- Sift together the first six ingredients. Cut in the butter. Add buttermilk and soda water. Stir until moistened. Add raisins if desired. Shape into a ball and knead about fifteen minutes. Place on lightly greased cookie sheet.

- With palm of your hand flatten dough into a circle about seven inches in diameter and one and a half inches thick. With a sharp knife, cut a cross on top, about one-quarter inch deep and five inches long, to prevent cracking during baking.

- Bake at 350 degrees for forty-five to fifty minutes. Cool on wire rack. Makes one round loaf (about twenty slices).

GOD'S BLESSINGS

He provides for the sparrows,
Surely He will provide for you,
Ask Him for what is in your heart,
He has the power to make dreams come true.

He is the glorious Gift giver,
Blessed gifts from above,
To one and all of His children,
With unconditional forgiving love.

He promises us peace within,
Whenever we choose to obey,
The laws He's laid before our hearts,
With grace each and every day.

We can have all our freedoms,
So gracious and kindly given,
Reaping His grace always,
Since He walks among the living.

We learn to give love to others,
Through our actions and attitudes,
We know the cost could be great,
To reap all of God's Beatitudes.

Partakers of divine nature,
We walk each God-given day,
Through life divinely inspired,
Choosing good and loving His way.

Our morals and standards are high,
Because we choose to live in His graces,
Blessed above all else with joy,
We see His love in our sister's faces.

He asks that we give our all,
And become fishers of men,
With lots of gratitude,
We say thank-you God, and Amen.

Cowgirl's Sparrow

~ *Anonymous* ~

Resting her head on the faucet, her tears joined the scalding water falling into the tub. Although the hot knob was the only one turned, she did not notice the skin-burning temperature. Cowgirl had never been so cold in her entire life. She sat with arms wrapped around her body, rocking and shivering in a hunched-up little ball, trying to disappear down the drain. "Oh, God. Oh, God," she repeated, unable to stop herself.

The sparrow-spirit launched into furious flight. The poor little creature was trapped inside the fortress of her skull. Out, Out! Which way to go? No direction, no opening found, causing it to continue careening into its prison walls.

Cowgirl felt the tiny wings, claws, and beak thrashing in the dark. Her pity for the terrified bird unleashed a fresh set of tears from her swollen eyes. "God! Oh, God, how do I set it free? It's dying! Help me, help me, pleeeeeease," she wept. Whatever answer came was not heard, the commotion and drama of the bird within her blocked out all sound. Rocking, rocking with the rush of the water eventually put Cowgirl and the sparrow into a calmed state. Wings cease to beat as an undetermined amount of time passed by.

The woman who slept in the cooling water thought herself to be a good person. She had always tried to be generous, loving, and kind when dealing with others. She was tall, lithe, and had a long mane of auburn hair. Talented beyond her share, she could draw, paint, create poetry, dance, and make every person laugh and feel important. Cowgirl was a sassy, self-assured natural-born leader who attracted friends at every turn. She considered herself to be in possession of "okay" looks, but those who knew her labeled her uniquely beautiful. Her mirror never reflected back what others saw. She was humble yet proud; her personality and dreams were magical.

Why, then, was Cowgirl lying in chilly tub water with a blackened eye, a split lip, and fractured ribs? What had she done to deserve such brutal treatment?

"Oh God, Oh God..." the mantra returned with her awakening. Her violent shaking spooked the bird into desperate twirls. Cowgirl shook and helplessly watched the tiny sparrow exhaust all energy and in shock, lay down to die. Covering her battered, swelling face, the girl went into deep inconsolable mourning. Her spirit-sparrow, with her the twenty-one years since her birth, was gone.

Cowgirl crept to her twin bed and pulled the quilts tightly around her. Someone (herself, probably) had opened the tiny bedroom window. October blew its wet breath into her room. Alone, so singularly alone, the woman wanted comfort. She wanted understanding. She wanted him. The admission made her run to the toilet and empty the bile from her stomach.

For three days she refused to rise from her quilted nest. Door locked, she would speak to no one. Roommates worried and tried to coax her from the bed, but self-hatred and depression kept her there. She also had to invent an explanation; the condition of her face would demand it.

Between sleep and in dreams, Cowgirl would replay the events prior to the beating. She remembered the thrill of wearing "his" jacket to ward off the evening chill. For weeks they had looked forward to the Sugar Cane Fall Festival. It was the town of Plaquemine's one claim to fame. Farmers, Dow plant workers, and families anticipated the annual celebration. Buses from neighboring Baton Rouge and Lafayette delivered the hordes to the gates.

A twenty-acre field with converted warehouses, stages, and rides spread throughout the area. Bright pumpkins and crawfish-shaped lanterns brought charm to the site. A different aroma was found every couple of steps: roasting peanuts, spiked café au lait, and damp hay mingled with spicy gumbo smells. Cajuns, Choctaws, city dwellers, and country folk kicked up their heels to the sizzling Zydeco bands. All came to "pass a good time, cher!" as the local saying goes.

Under a perfect harvest moon, their date began perfectly. Helping Cowgirl from the truck, he warned her to watch the mud. She took her black felt cowboy hat off to peck him on the cheek. (He hated for her to wear it, because it emphasized the difference in their height.) No matter how many times she told him it didn't bother her, he was never convinced. She never stopped to consider that his shortness was a sore point to his pride. At five feet, ten inches, she had gotten past the teasing and tall jokes. She quite enjoyed the altitude ribbings and took them in jest, as they were meant to be. He, however, could not accept his height being shorter than hers.

Ferris wheel rides and romantic touches warmed Cowgirl's heart. She was so deeply in love, her first love, that she overlooked his troubling temper and lack of self-esteem. She'd convinced herself that her devotion would change his mistrust, once he was sure of her commitment. It thrilled her that he could be jealous; it made her feel so special, and oh so pretty. He could make her feel like an undeserved prize. He evoked such tender feelings from the redhead's heart that she would give anything to dispel his insecurities.

He left Cowgirl smiling, rearranging her turquoise feathered hatband, to get her a café and himself a draft beer. She took in the sights and tapped her boot to a Merle Haggard oldie. Huge hands surprised her as they covered up her eyes from behind. "Guess who, stranger?" didn't give her a clue. Twirling around, she squealed as her old friend lifted her in the air and swung her around. Catching up on the news, Cowgirl and the LSU football player enjoyed their chance meeting. They laughed and remembered the chemistry class in which they had met and nearly failed the previous semester.

Out of the corner of her eye, she saw her beloved standing about ten yards away. As she smiled and signaled for him to come to her, she wondered why he was standing so statue-like. Her eyes widened and her smile froze as she watched him fling the drinks to the ground. Shock kept her from moving. Her mind registered her friend's voice, but not the words. Cowgirl was watching him picking up speed and fury as he closed the ground between them. She reached her hand out to hold his massive bicep with the intention of introducing him to her college friend. To explain it all.

He pulled her hand behind her back and crushed it with all his strength. She struggled to get loose but was caught in a vice that was now dragging her in the direction of the parking lot. Cowgirl's friend sensed something was wrong and trotted after them. He grabbed her free hand and asked if everything was all right. With lightning speed, and before she could make a sound, he jerked her other hand away from the man's polite hold and proceeded to squeeze it just as hard as the first one. She was in such pain her mind would not work to tell her how to react. "Yeah, you. Every ting is juss fine, juss fine and ain't none of you damned bidness," his menacing Cajun voice hissed out.

The whole scene happened in less than one minute. The next thing Cowgirl was aware of was being shoved roughly into the truck, where she confronted him and demanded an explanation. She wasn't afraid, she was angry!

She never got the answers to her questions. He began to scream at her as he pushed the gas pedal to the floor. The Chevy pickup swerved in and out of the highway traffic, causing a car to run into a ditch to avoid being rear-ended. Fishtailing onto a country road, they careened into the night as he cussed and slammed his fist into the seat, occasionally hitting her thigh. Each time Cowgirl scooted toward the door, he would yank her back to his side, causing the truck to swerve more.

Finally, she sat stone still and refused to speak or look at him, thinking this would calm him and keep them from crashing to their death into the cane fields that were racing by on both sides. This only infuriated him. She knew he was not sane as his screaming voice fogged up the windows. Without thinking, she opened the truck door and tried to roll out, somehow realizing that she would survive the rough fall but might not live through the conclusion of the drama they were flying toward.

Before she got all the way out, he jerked her back by her long hair and slammed on the breaks, skidding them into the high stalks. They traveled forty yards or so before coming to a stop. She was still ricocheting from dashboard to seat when he brutally attacked her.

Boot heels, closed fists, head-butts, and slapping palms all blended together in the assault. She could do nothing to defend herself but try to keep her head and face covered as best she could.

His fury spent, he began to weep as he saw his destruction. Semiconscious now, Cowgirl became a stone as he begged and apologized. She heard some of the words as if she were in a long tunnel. Time passed and he drove the truck back toward town. At the first stoplight, she heard the engine of another vehicle next to them. She simply opened the door and walked away. With witnesses, he could do nothing but circle around her and yell for her to get back into the truck. "I just want to talk to you," he kept repeating. She neither looked at him, nor spoke to him, but continued walking down Highway 1. Whenever she sensed him closing in, she walked directly into the line of oncoming traffic. He cursed, begged, blew the horn, and pounded the window glass out as Cowgirl continued making miles.

She walked six miles and on across the Mississippi River Bridge. When she stepped onto the bridge, she knew she was free. He could not circle or stop in the lanes. She never looked back.

Twenty years passed before I saw Cowgirl again. Though her auburn hair was shorter and colored to cover the gray, her smile was the same. She had changed; she was older, solemn, but I still recognized my old friend. I told her I often wondered about where she was and what her life was like after she'd left him. She reassured me that her life was now full of blessings and good times. She had married a loving, honorable man and they had a tall, handsome son. Her husband had not, nor ever would, touch her violently, she assured me. She was content and fulfilled. She never spent a moment of her day thinking of the abuse she'd gone through, or the abuser. I told her how much I admired her for the lack of bitterness in her heart.

"Oh, I was bitter, angry, and self-destructive for a few years after the fair," she said, only able to refer to the beating as simply, "the fair." Many things had changed inside. It was only after she returned to her religion that her heart began to grow. She was now harvesting God's tender mercies through her life works and her family. His grace had healed her angers and her fears. They had been mercifully erased.

Watching her healthy child and respectful husband work together to build a Plinko board for the school fair brought her full circle. The pride and pleasure she experienced at the sight, made her send up prayers of thankfulness. The prayers included the Lord's Prayer, said for "him."

When Cowgirl silently spoke the words, "forgive us our trespasses as we forgive those who trespass against us..." something happened inside her mind. The long-dead sparrow that was her spirit was released and replaced by a strong, wise eagle. Inside the nest of her heart and soul it roosted for the years she had left on earth. The insightful eagle guided her through sureness and grace to times filled with love, faith, and hope. Cowgirl's spirit bird would always lead her to the abundant blessings of the Lord, sent through the Holy Spirit. She was strong. And she was sure.

Forgiveness Scripture:

Matthew 6:14-16-

"For if you forgive others for their transgressions, your heavenly Father will also forgive you. But if you do not forgive others, then your Father will not forgive your transgressions."

Psalm 31:243-

"Be strong and let your heart take courage, all you who hope in the LORD. Blessedness of Forgiveness and of Trust in God."

Kings 8:30-

"Listen to the supplication of Your servant and of Your people Israel, when they pray toward this place; hear in heaven Your dwelling place; hear and forgive."

Betty Bosarge's Texas Two~Step Chicken

1 1/2 cup	Picante sauce, preferably medium (can use hot or mild)
2 tbs	Packed light brown sugar
1 tbs	Dijon-style mustard
4-8	Boneless, skinless chicken breasts or thighs
1	Small can sliced black olives

- Place chicken in large baking dish sprayed with non-stick cooking spray. Mix first three ingredients and pour over chicken to cover completely. Dot chicken with black olive slices.

- Preheat oven to 400 degrees. Bake chicken uncovered thirty to forty minutes, depending on your oven. Serve with Spanish rice, refried beans or corn, and a salad and warm tortillas. Serves six or more, depending on appetites.

Leftover chicken cut into bite-size pieces can be used for filling burritos, or stuff tortillas and pour remaining sauce over the top to make enchiladas.

Crunchin' Acorns!

~ Angie Ledbetter ~

I love the way my feet crunch the acorns scattered about on my morning walks. They carpet the ground in brittle lumps, and smashing them is therapy akin to the popular bubble wrap popping pastime. Hearing the small, brown nuts pop and crackle as their orange guts squish out onto the pavement is almost as satisfying as eating an entire bag of greasy potato chips.

My mind always associates the season of autumn with acorn smashing and the annoyance of huge hickory nuts falling from colorful branches far above my house and noisily plinking down the roof. Both types of nuts are aggravations. The hickory nut banging disturbs my infrequent naps as they ricochet off the bedroom A/C window unit. The littering of acorns ruins the serenity of my solitary prayer walks. My aggravation at these nuts is also more deeply rooted. These same pods feed the enemy-squirrels, deer, wild boar, and all those other critters that make up the sought-after game of Louisiana's main season-hunting season.

I used to have a ratty camouflage t-shirt that said, "We Temporarily Interrupt this Marriage to Bring You Hunting Season!" That slogan pretty much stated how I felt about the sport. For many of the men I know, hunting is more than a mere sport or hobby; it is a way of life. The be-all of existence. The raison d'être. A birthright. A pursuit much like seeking the holy grail. The event around which all other events rotate.

More than a few men folk choose their jobs and also fix their work schedules around the time frames of hunting season, often "dragging up" from their jobs when that golden opening day of the hunt rolls around. Normal, rational, productive men seem to lose all perspective each year, and it's not uncommon to hear of marriages breaking up because husbands have chosen the thrill of the woods over the comforts of home and hearth.

A popular joke reads like a classified ad: "Single man seeks wife who cooks, loves dogs, has hunting lease and bass boat. Send photo of lease and boat." An often-seen door sign and bumper sticker says, "A bad day in the woods is better than a good day at home!" The abundance of these jokes speaks to the common problems that this "sport" often breeds.

I'm sure that these nuts (acorn and hickory, not hunters), innocent pods of God's bounty, get unfair associations from me because they happen to feed the sportsman's game. But when I add up the hours, days, weekends, and holidays that the hunting seasons they represent take from my family life, I can't help but be a bit provoked. Believe me, valiant attempts to impart guilt on the head of the hunter will not deter him from his wooded sanctuary. Lord knows I've tried for years!

It's not the premise of the activity to which I object. My husband and relatives are excellent gamesmen and women. They obey the laws and rules, take care with safety responsibilities, and make sure all the hunters-to-be (young sons and daughters) get proper training and safety courses through the Wildlife and Fisheries agency. They do not hunt for sport alone. They clean and butcher what they kill, proudly filling freezers with their booty.

I'm not jealous of the male bonding for days on end, or annoyed that Thanksgiving and holiday meals are interrupted or have to be served cold or piecemeal. The part I find hard to justify is all the time I spend alone with the kids while Dad is at the hunting camp, especially considering that he's away often for work.

It took years of behavior modification training and prayer power to squelch the urge to scream like a banshee whenever I heard the first rumblings of hunters gearing up for their seasonal hiatus. The three-wheelers, four-wheelers, target practice, banging and sawing on hunting stands and blinds, and other assaults on the ear were all just gigantic acorns under my skin!

Before I make myself sound terribly uncharitable, let me explain that hunting season does not just cover a few random weekends each fall. There are the preseason mandatory work weekends during which the hunters must get the camp and deer stands ready, the meetings pertaining to rules and membership, and the occasional gatherings that really have no purpose other than talking about the coming excitements. One year I put red X's on the calendar for nights spent at the deer camp or on a hunting trip of any kind, and there were 56 in one "season." No, I don't begrudge the extensive time my husband spends in the wooded wonderland. I'm just envious and in need of a little respite and R&R time myself. I also am saddened to be without him when the kids and I attend church alone.

There are some things that help me make it through nut-stomping season without going off my nut altogether. Daily prayer helps tremendously. Reception of the holy sacraments gives me strength and grace. Trying to understand that my mate needs time away from a stressful job also gets me through about the first three weekends fairly intact. Distracting myself with activities with our kids or doing fulfilling ministry work also eases the stress of being a "hunting widow."

I also remind myself that like all seasons, this one too will eventually end at some point and life will return to a somewhat more normal pattern. I know, too, that as the kids get older, they will soon be accompanying Dad on these forays. It helps to see the bigger picture if you can dislodge yourself from in-the-moment hissy fit tendencies. I know that's easier said than done, but it is possible with a lot of practice.

One of my favorite remedies for the symptoms of H.S.O.D. (Hunting Season OverDose) is to plan and execute quarterly getaways, retreats, a few days at a nearby B&B's where I've become friends with the owners, or spiritual retreats. Hanging on to my humor is also helpful.

In fact, giving myself one of those try-to-see-the-bright-side-and-at-least-he's-not-out-in-the-bars-carousing pep talks, I relax the hold on my clenched jaws long enough to make a profound discovery. An epiphany, if you will, ushered in on the wings of humor and grace.

How many people know that the venison obtained during a single deer hunting season ends up costing only $978.50 per pound? Add in license fees, equipment, food, club dues, building supplies, gas, ammo, clothing, special doolollies, and all the trappings (pun intended) that go along with the sport, and that's a pretty fair figure on a 100-pound doe.

Nothing helps erase the aggravation build-up, though, as much as a change of scenery. Come to think of it, when I am enjoying one of these rare escapes, I ask the Lord to smash any lingering anger still in my heart concerning my husband's hunting habit just exactly as I'm squashing the indigenous nuts into smithereens if it happens to be fall. I picture the hunter-orange acorn innards blowing away peacefully in the wind as I walk on down the path.

SCRIPTURE *for* HUNTERS

Genesis 27:3-

"Now then, please take your gear, your quiver and your bow, and go out to the field and hunt game for me."

Proverbs 6:5-

"Deliver yourself like a gazelle from the hunter's hand And like a bird from the hand of the fowler."

Jeremiah 16:16-

"Behold, I am going to send for many fishermen," declares the LORD, "and they will fish for them; and afterwards I will send for many hunters, and they will hunt them from every mountain and every hill and from the clefts of the rocks."

Genesis 10:9-

"He was a mighty hunter before the LORD; therefore it is said, 'Like Nimrod a mighty hunter before the Lord.'"

Dennis Ledbetter's World Famous Venison Backstrap

(That Even People Who Don't Like Deer Meat Will Love)

2 lbs	venison backstrap
2 cups	flour
	Salt
	Pepper
	Garlic powder
	Onion powder
	Tony Cachere's Cajun Seasoning
	Whole or condensed milk
2	eggs
	Peanut or canola oil for frying

- Prepare two pounds or more of backstrap (the tender portion of venison that runs along the backbone) by cutting fresh meat into oblong medallions. Tenderize with a meat cleaver. After pounding each piece, put in a large bowl full of ice. When all meat is tenderized, drain the ice and water. Season meat lightly to taste with salt, pepper, garlic powder, cayenne pepper and/or Tony Cachere's Cajun Seasoning. Put meat in a Ziploc freezer bag with enough whole or condensed milk to cover well. Refrigerate to marinate at least overnight.

Continues

- To cook meat, mix together one teaspoon each salt, pepper, garlic powder, and onion powder in a large bowl or plastic bag for coating. In a separate bowl, beat eggs. Remove venison from refrigerator, and coat each medallion thoroughly with egg, then flour mixture, and set aside.

- Put about two inches of oil in a heavy skillet and heat well while you are coating the first batch. Place coated pieces into skillet until the skillet is full but pieces are not crowded. Adjust oil temperature so the meat won't burn. Medallions will come to the surface when ready to be turned. Brown evenly on both sides, but do not overcook.

- When meat is dark, golden brown, remove from oil and place on paper towels to drain. Set aside each batch in microwave while you continue to cook. When done, heat on low in microwave for a few minutes before serving.

Feeds six.

Love Letter

~ Angie Ledbetter ~

Dear Beloved:

I have so many things that have been on my heart to tell you. I don't know why I've put off writing this for such a long time. Maybe it just takes years of being in a committed relationship before you feel confident enough to put your true feelings down on paper. And it is sort of scary thinking that there will be a permanent record of your most personal feelings, dreams, thoughts, and desires. But it's also a benefit of hanging through the tough times together that you build up a trust that your most cherished loved one would not hurt you by sharing what you have written in private with others. So putting aside any lingering misgivings, I hope you will somehow intuit the deepest meaning of my words.

First, I want to say Thank You for all that you have been to me these many years. You have never, ever failed to support me in my dreams and goals. I know that some of them were foolish endeavors, but you rose above the temptation to make me feel silly or point out that certain aims of mine could only end in heartbreak and loss. You never stopped me when you could have as I tried on different careers and creative pursuits. What a rarity! Even though these things took time away from "us," you let me explore them on my own. I thank you for patiently waiting for me to put you on the top of my priority list. And I realize that I have always been on the very top of yours. If I never acknowledged that, please let me know. I cannot understand how you do not harbor anger and disappointment in me. I am grateful for that, but I can't comprehend it.

Remember the time I thought that I could do without you and that there were probably much better fish in the sea? You patiently waited for me to quit my wandering and wondering, and never withdrew your love from me...even when I didn't deserve it. The hurt I must have caused you was never repaid in kind to me. I thank you for always believing in us and in our relationship, even when I had major doubts. You were a rock. I was a glob of Jell-O. I will try to make up for those years when I withdrew from you and refused your steadfast love. How stupid I was to think that you were smothering me and that I could best be the master of my own ship. I wonder now how it took me so long to realize that a ship moves much more smoothly through calm and rough waters when there are two people manning the oars. I love you for not abandoning me as I did you. Please forgive me for that. I am truly sorry.

What a great helpmate you have been to me! You always seem to know when I am down or when I need an extra helping hand. No chore or request for help goes unanswered. In fact, you often know my needs before I even express them. I hope that I have shared some of this loving thoughtfulness with you, but I know I could have done a better job. I am a much better taker than giver, it seems. How can you stand to be with such a selfish person and still remain in love? Your heart's capacity is truly a miracle. Thank you, dear one, for always lightening my load. Please know that I will try to imitate this quality of yours so that I may one day become a worthy partner to you!

There are so many things I could say, but the more I write, the worse I feel about myself. You have always been joyous when I have succeeded, happy for me when I have done and accomplished things without considering you, and happy to live in the shadow of my greedily outstretched wings. I weep now, thinking of all the times I have let slip by without feeling the same for you. Why was I so blind? I didn't realize that by pulling together and working side by side, we could accomplish so much more! Look how much time I have wasted in our relationship. Can you ever forgive me? How could you sacrifice so much for me when I was willing to give so very little? When I speak these doubts aloud, you only smile, reassure me, and prove that you love me even more. Surely, I am blessed.

Finally, I want to thank you with every fiber of my being for the beautiful children you have given me! That they are growing into fine examples of humanity is a wonderful gift to see. They are taking after you in so many ways and reflect your tender, loving guidance and nurturing. I am so very thankful that they are more like you than me! I cannot adequately express how your filling in for my gaps and mistakes with the kids means so much to me. I pray that they will repay you for all of the love, effort, and time you have invested in them as they become adults, and that they will never wander far from you as their mother did.

Simple words on paper cannot reveal how my heart overflows with love for you, and the bitter regret I have over my past actions and hurtful behavior. I hope I will be able to show you in some measure what your love has meant to me. Please forgive me. Thank you for your love. Your name will remain imprinted on my unworthy heart.

Jesus, my beloved, I love you!

Winter

Timothy, Chapter 6:1-4

"Instruct them to do good, to be rich in good works, to be generous
and ready to share, storing up for themselves the treasure
of a good foundation for the future, so that they may take hold
of that which is life indeed."

A Million Miles Next Door

~ Alaine Benard ~

The winter sun pushes its cheery warmth onto our faces and our joined hands. With prideful excitement, my growing son pulls me to his room. He wants to show off the Saturday cleanup he has accomplished. Not the normal shove-it-all-under-the-bed job-surprisingly, it is truly clean!

I compliment his efforts and hug, pat-pat-pat him gently on the cheek. My fingers linger over the smooth skin as my heart photographs the moment. At five feet in height, he's much taller than most nine-year-olds. Turner is a sturdy, handsome boy, I think with pride. This rare moment I try to hold so tightly. I want a freeze-frame to lock us here, the chubby cheek-last vestige of babyhood-under my hand. Growing up so fast, I wish the mother's wish of stopping time.

My thoughts are replaced by his bubbly voice, "What, when, MOM! Who, where!?" The questions pepper the air as my chatterbox fills the day with his dreams and plans. He names off twenty different possible activities as he spins through the room. Laughingly, I must catch my whirlwind child and restrain him within my grasp. Often he has fallen in such moments to earn a collection of bumps, bruises, and stitches. His twirling speech and body gyrations that so aggravate the world are his ADHD-nature. He suffers much dislike for this reason. Many challenges and heartaches arise from those determined to harness, corral, or stifle the Turner tornado.

But my thoughts are not bogged down by weather analogies or negativities. I am caught up in the positive beginning to our day. Along with setting up for my afternoon ladies' tea, I need to purchase and prepare my party foods. To speed me up, Turner has offered to polish my silverware. He is anxious to get going-to get his video from the store. I cannot stifle a giggle as he asks what the "prissy little forks" are for. He decides that they are the only necessary utensils. I had not realized that my menu consisted of mostly finger foods, and his assessment was going to save us both some time at the store. His power of reasoning and investigation are amazing.

Home from buying the groceries, Turner's focus returns to the video. In a run-on conversation, he describes the action-packed drama of the ninjas he will soon watch. Laughing aloud, I tell him to slow down so I can follow his story. Not slowing down a bit, I catch the sun glinting off his golden head. He's dashing back and forth in front of the window demonstrating martial art kicks and chops. While I arrange tea items, boyish exclamations and whizzing dust motes fill the sun-drenched room.

Chores completed, Turner picks up the movie and flips it through the air. It travels to the ceiling and down again like a heads-or-tails coin toss. The wind pushes the door open in synchronistic movement. Before I can blink, he has spun around three times and skied over to close it.

With hand on doorknob, he freezes. Children's calling voices draw his attention. Car doors slam and more excited squeals are heard. I join my son, thinking unexpected company has arrived. I wonder why my child is so still. Rare are the moments when he is not in full motion. Why has he not bolted out to greet them?

Together we watch a pair of spindly legs sprint up the drive. A boy we have never seen stands before us. In his hand is a gaily-wrapped Harry Potter present. Bows and sparkly glitter wave all around as the gift bearer looks into our house in confusion.

"Uh, ummmm, is this Carter's house?" he asks, quickly averting his eyes from Turner's. His nervous mother is waving at us from behind her steering wheel. My son points across the yard and reassuringly pats the boy on the shoulder. He understands their anxiety. He hollers out to the mom, "It's okay, he's fine, just one house over." He gives her the thumbs up sign and she drives away.

A group of four neighborhood playmates run up the drive next door and join the melee. Water guns squirt mini rainbows into the air. A purple balloon takes flight and drifts above the trees. Turner watches its ascent. His eyes are the only things that move; the rest of my tornado has turned to stone.

I beg God to speed time up so that I do not have this freeze-frame moment. I want the door to shut out the outside world. I want the sparkling day to return.

Slowly, so very slowly, my child pulls his eyes from the dot-sized balloon. His vision focuses on the doorframe as wood meets wood with a soft click. My hot tears are gathering as I watch his hands. The deliberate and careful way they move over the brass knob tell me more than words. His quivering smile and too-bright eyes stop my very breath. The voice inside my hollow heart can only whisper, "Ohh...oh."

I try to tell him with a squeeze that I understand his hurt. His hand responds as he moves away and disappears around the corner to his room. I give him time to grieve and compose himself. At nine, he's at the stage where he thinks he's too old for tears. Alone, I'm free to mourn this new hurt that I'm unable to Band-Aid and kiss away.

Imitating his slow movements, I turn to cutting cucumbers, arranging flowers, and gathering up the silver. The shiny "prissy forks" crush my broken spirit, as I remember our earlier conversation. After a while I go to his room. I want his "taste-tester" skills to remove the bitter taste from our souls. I'll ask him to pause his movie and come help me check the foods. Hopefully, the kung-fu masters have taken his mind away from the birthday party. Maybe a chocolate petit four and some butter mints will help restore our Saturday joy.

In his bed he lies curled beneath his quilts. The unseasonably eighty-degree day has not kept my baby warm. His tear-stained face is turned toward the wall as he pulls in a hitching breath on the way to deeper sleep. I can only smooth his wrinkled covers and pray he finds friendships and boy games in his dream.

Returning to the kitchen, I float the damask tablecloth onto the table's maple surface. The polished tray-laden with pot, creamer, sugar bowl and trinkets-comes next. I set a dainty cup and saucer at my twin sister's place, completing the foursome I've laid out.

Surveying the scene I notice a drooping flower. I pluck it from the crystal bud vase set for my blonde-haired friend. I tug out a folded corner of the vintage needlepoint placemat underneath my own place setting.

I check the fourth guest's spot to make sure it's set perfectly. I concentrate on all her things until china, cloth, and the vintage treasures are flawlessly aligned to my satisfaction. I turn to go, but not before a single tear drips onto the final place setting.

Tenderly, I set the polished "prissy little fork" next to the parchment paper at Carter's mother's place. The sepia words I'd calligraphied on the scroll echoed the truth inside my head: "Breaking bread and sharing laughter over tea with true friends-no better way to celebrate love!"

My heart lifted as I awaited my guests.

Sweet Violet Tea

- Take two and one half ounces of violet leaves, freshly picked. Wash them clean in cold water, place them in a stone jar, and pour over them one pint of boiling water. Secure the lid and let it stand for twelve hours, till the water is green. Then strain off the liquid into a stoppered bottle and the tea is ready for drinking cold. It is essential that the tea should be made fresh every day and kept in a cool place to prevent it turning sour. If any should be left over it should be thrown away. Sweeten generously with honey or sugar. (Taken from www.botanical.com)

MORE TEA TIPS:
Celebrate with friends by brewing a pot of your special-time tea. Add lemon for zing and a dash of spearmint or peppermint oil for excitement.

Wisdom Retreat in the Word:

To erase the bitter taste of swallowing your pride, read how Jesus' humility and forgiveness sustained him from the time he was tormented, crowned with thorns, and finally crucified on the cross. Contemplate his words and attitude while sipping on sweet tea and simple crackers or salty nuts.

Cry No More: Healing *from* Grief

~ *Carol Schwartz* ~

The winter of 1999 found this country girl moving far away to a crowded city. I knew only a couple of people in the new homeland, so I trusted in them when they welcomed me with open arms. I will be eternally grateful to my dear friend Calvin and his mother Bena for their loving welcome.

I became extremely ill shortly after arriving in New Orleans and was forced to spend time in bed recouping, sometimes barely able to breathe and unable to keep even water down. During this time Calvin delivered some of Bena's delicious homemade soup. The kindness this action showed probably helped as much as the soup. Once I could eat, that seemed to help me get my strength back, and I happily returned to work.

But things changed for me after the illness. I had done a lot of praying and meditating during my recovery period, and my faith in a loving God carried me through. What I began to realize while I lay in that sterile first living quarters was how extremely homesick I was, as I found myself crying every day for my California family and friends. Having lived in California for nearly twenty years after a divorce, I missed the lovely view from my living room picture windows of the High Sierra Nevada Mountains and the little high desert town of Ridgecrest nestled at the southern tip of those gorgeous high foothills.

At my old home I could drive within one hour to the base of the highest mountain in the lower forty-eight states and take a nice, long hike and view the colorful autumn flora of gold, brown, rust, beige, red, orange, yellow, and all variations of green. The stroll in the high country (above 9,000 feet) always cleared the cobwebs out of my head. Continuing north for another hour, one hundred forty miles from my doorstep, found me swimming in the relaxing mineral hot springs pool in Bishop.

Bishop always fondly reminded me of the little town in Idaho in which I grew up. Bishop's similarity to Grangeville, Idaho may explain why I loved it so and visited it monthly. The same could be said of Bishop as is advertised about Grangeville: "A rosy glow blankets the little town whose elevation and population meet at around 3,500. Grangeville is a town which enjoys a fascinating history, complete with gold rushes, Indian wars, railroad feuds, and all the colorful lore of the old West."

Autumn was the time of year I enjoyed most in Bishop. Its fragrant smells and fall colors delighted every sensory nerve in my body. It favored cool nights and t-shirt days. People were friendly in Bishop. I didn't know many of them, but when I spoke they returned my hello with a smile. Often I'd go to the bookstore/coffee shop and just chat about the olden days, sort of like people in small towns in Idaho do every day.

Oh, how my heart longed for my native soil in the west and to see my son, Chris, and grandson, Daniel, and hear their laughter. Or to just sit at Casa Java and chitty chat with my friend Marie for hours and hours, and then meet her husband, Bob, and another dear friend, Randy, for dinner. I felt like my soul was dying in the large city of strangers. Folks call it the "Big Easy." I couldn't see much easy about New Orleans. Maybe I missed something.

Oh yes, I faithfully attended mass, although sometimes it was a real effort just to get ready and go, because unless I went with my friend, I knew no one at church. I tried to reach out my hand and smile a sweet hello to folks; sometimes it was warmly returned and sometimes not.

After mass I would go back to my apartment and read or watch TV, and once in a while I'd even get up the energy to drive to Audubon Park and go for a long walk, mostly alone. "No man is an island" is true, and I felt like I was on one by myself, except for my God. Romans 14:7 lets us know that "none of us lives for oneself, and no one dies for oneself."

Sometimes Calvin would join me on Sundays. His company kept the lonely tears at bay, at least for that day. When the weather was nice, we would go to lunch after mass, and then play a few bucks at the local horse races. I wasn't sure whether it was more fun because I wasn't alone anymore, or because we were outdoors in warm sunshine, or because being near the horses made this country gal feel right at home. It was great fun.

Sundays alone were most dreaded. A few Sundays of love and laughter couldn't make up for the majority of them spent alone. Sundays belong to God, for worshiping, relaxing and enjoying times together with those we love-not just living a lonely existence. I prayed so much I ran out of things and people to pray for. I asked God for strength and courage to accept if he wouldn't lead me out of this metropolis.

During Mardi Gras, while others were going crazy celebrating with family and friends, I was alone. I had no one to talk with and was terrified it would always be this way. I had been promised that I would get to ride on one of the floats, but that was just one more broken promise. I had read the book, Broken Promises, Broken Dreams, and now I was living it. How very sad to think I chose to move two thousand miles from my homeland to experience these lessons in life.

I met some lady friends at work, especially a fine Christian, Cathy, and that helped during the week. But Cathy had Al and Charlie, her family, to keep her busy on weekends. Then I met Neila and some of her friends. Neila, a distinguished southern cook, invited me to many a scrumptious dinner.

Restlessness from living in the South never left me. After being there for about eight months, I finally surrendered it all to God. I had no choice, because it felt like I was dying of a broken heart.

Surrendering to God finally gave me some peace of mind and heart, although my soul would not rest. I was not receiving necessary daily soul food. I needed other human beings with whom I felt comfortable enough to share and to care.

It was within a week after having totally surrendered my will to being in New Orleans that I met the first of the Seeds of Faith sisters. She introduced me to an e-mail group of Christian ladies, and that's how I met Angie, Alaine, Deb, and Betty.

Glory be! Hallelujah! It felt like God had sent me some real live angels. My faith began to grow again and I felt alive. My lonely days and nights weren't quite so lonely anymore because of daily communications with these fine new friends.

The healing had begun. God was keeping me in this overpopulated city for a reason, and I just could not figure it out. Maybe I wasn't supposed to know. Knowing God would carry me through the turmoil was enough for the time being; however, I did take action and start applying for jobs west of the Rockies.

Seven months later when I left New Orleans and headed for Boise, Idaho my soul began to heal. I never knew until this experience that a place could make all the difference in the world with its traditions, cultures, and geographic features like mountains, ocean, and daily sunshine.

I would like to thank Calvin for introducing me to some of the lovely old sights of the South. In New Orleans we visited the oldest cathedral in the country, witnessed some Saints football games, grew fond of sipping Café Du Monde coffee with chicory while eating the traditional beignets (scrumptious, homemade fried donuts), walked the lovely grounds of Oak Alley (which were much prettier than any of the beautiful photos depict), and watched the mighty, muddy Mississippi River roll on by. I am grateful for the fond memories.

My soul no longer cries. It is healing from past hurts. This country gal is back in the country, where the mountains are covered with snow in the late fall. I've come home.

GRIEF: HELPFUL HINTS *for* RECOVERING *from* LOSS

- Be aware that you are extremely vulnerable.
- Recognize your loss by putting your grief into words.
- Join a support group that deals with grief.
- Attend a grief workshop or retreat.
- Take care of yourself; eat right, rest, and exercise.
- Try not to take on new or extra responsibilities that will create stress.
- Control the urge to make life-changing decisions.
- If you choose to move far away from friends and family, be aware that geographical areas of our country have different cultures, traditions, values, and beliefs. Ascertain if they fit comfortably with your lifestyle.
- Plan activities that give you something to look forward to and bring you comfort and enjoyment.
- Let your friends and family know what you need from them.
- Learn your workplace's policy on bereavement leave.
- Learn about grief and the grieving process.
- Be attuned as you move through grief.
- Offer help to others in need.
- Share your feelings, thoughts, and memories with someone you trust.
- Recognize unhealthy signs of grieving and take remedial actions.

Italian Minestrone

2 LBS.	LEAN HAMBURGER
6	MEDIUM CARROTS, DICED
2	MEDIUM ONIONS, DICED
4	SMALL POTATOES, DICED
1/2 LB.	FRESH GREEN BEANS
1	SMALL PACKAGE FROZEN PEAS
1	SPRIG OF PARSLEY
3	MEDIUM TOMATOES
2	FRESH CLOVES GARLIC
	SALT, PEPPER, AND OREGANO TO TASTE
16 OZ.	SPAGHETTI, BROKEN INTO SMALL PIECES

- Place all ingredients except spaghetti in large kettle. Cover with water and bring to boil, adding additional water if needed. Add spaghetti; cook until tender. Cures whatever ails ya!

Serves eight to ten.

Changing Horses

~ *Deb Anne Flynt* ~

After a quarter century of moving barges on the river, Carey began to hate his work. He loved being outdoors and keeping odd hours, but he hated the time away from his family. After much deliberation, he announced that he was quitting his job and taking a truck-driving course at a nearby college.

While the other students dreamed of how they would spend spring break, Carey prepared to make his new dream come true. He knew there might be bumpy beginnings, but once he had established a name, he would have more freedom and would see his family more.

His wife Dianne had prayed for guidance, knowing that Carey would not pray. She was not sure he was doing the right thing, because he had made the decision on his own. When she gave it all to God and said, "Jesus, I trust in you," she had peace about what Carey was doing and knew that God would take care of her family.

Their two children, Nathaniel and Carrie, looked forward to traveling with Carey once he was able to take passengers. Nathaniel, the fourteen-year-old said, "It's cool, and he'd better take me with him sometimes!"

Carrie, nine, said she was glad because, "I couldn't go on the boat, but I can go with him on a truck!"

Carey was a good man who said he believed in Jesus, but he did not go to church even when he had the opportunity. He rarely prayed. He did, however, encourage Dianne in her mission work. Certain that he would one day return fully to the Lord, she prayed for him and asked others to do the same.

"He supported the decision that I made without him, to do the Lord's work, so I'll support him in this," she confided to friends. "If there's any way for me to help him, it will be by my actions, not by my words. He won't listen if I try to talk to him about my concern for his soul, but he appreciates my efforts to help others like him. I don't think he understands how far he's strayed from the fold." She was not judging him harshly, and when she talked about him, her eyes revealed only love.

When asked what he thought about Dianne's work, Carey replied, "It's cool," which from him was a compliment. It was also proof that he may not have been as far removed from God's graces as she feared.

As the first day of classes approached, Carey showed little enthusiasm, but that wasn't uncharacteristic of him. They'd been married for sixteen marvelous years, and Dianne knew he was looking forward to the new experience.

Carey graduated and went to work for a good company. He ended up spending more time with his family, as he had hoped. Dianne's mission work led to a new career, and her dreams came true, too. Today she is a published author, still doing God's work.

"When things work out as well as you had hoped and planned, then you have to recognize God's hand in it, and know that it was his plan all along," Dianne tells others. "I thank the Lord every day for his many blessings in our lives."

HOMEWARD

Finally down to the last hundred miles
I envision my children and wife's sweet smiles.
No matter how tired I am at the door,
I'll let the kids grab me and fight to the floor.

Once the playing is done and I'm back on my feet,
My wife will have her chance to greet
The man she has waited for, hours on end.
Now I remember why I married my best friend.

*H*AVENS *and* *H*ARBORS

There may be a place near you where truckers, mariners, and other travelers can stop for a rest in safety, or for a hot meal. The one in our vicinity is supported by area churches. If there is one near you, then volunteer to work there a few hours a week. If it's a non-profit center, like the one near here, they need all the time you can give them.

Consider making a monetary donation to help with the building and supplies. A few hours a week to help someone who may be hundreds of miles from their nearest loved ones would mean much to a tired traveler, and to those who are trying to help them.

It can be very rewarding, as well as immediately satisfying, to know that you are doing something good. Jesus said that whatever you do for one of his people, you do for him-such as when you help the weary find rest.

You never know who might be the next one to stop at one of these centers. It might be someone you know-or at least know of.

MIDSTREAM

Nearly half of his life,
He'd done the same thing
For weeks at a time
Away from his friends

Left wife and loved ones
And children behind
For days and days
Just to tow the line.

He'd thought of it often
And then came the time
He knew he could no longer
Pretend to be blind

To the fact that his children
Were growing up fast
And he wanted to be there.
So he stayed home at last.

He went back to school,
Started over again
Found he didn't get wet
Changing horses midstream.

This one's for that dear man
That I love so much
And for the time that we've missed
And spent out of touch.

This is for courage,
For faith and devotion
And the man that had all that
And followed his notion

To start a new life
With his family at hand
To leave mistress river
And live on dry land.

I thank you dear Lord
For his dream come true.
He would have been soaked
Had it not been for You.

CAREY *and* DIANNE STONE'S FAVORITE MEATLOAF

3-4 LBS.	LEAN GROUND BEEF
2	MEDIUM ONIONS
1 CUP	SALSA
1 CUP	QUICK-COOKING OATS
1	EGG, SLIGHTLY BEATEN
1/2 CUP	INSTANT POTATO FLAKES

- Preheat oven to 350. Mix all ingredients thoroughly. Press into two 8x4 loaf pans. Bake for fifty to sixty minutes. Drain.

Makes two loaves.

Answering the Call

~ Angie Ledbetter ~

This is a true story in which one character remains anonymous simply because I do not know his name, not because I wish to protect his identity.

A friend, my twin, and I were heading for a spiritual retreat and visit with other friends in Texas. We had about eight hours of hard driving still to go that morning. Our chatter naturally turned to our interests-how many pit stops would be a world record for three women making a ten-hour trek; who served the best fast food biscuits; how much fun the gathering would be; how much we all needed a break from our hectic routines; how the power of prayer could uplift your personal situation; family concerns and comparisons; and the like. The hours and road flew by as my left arm toasted near the driver's side window and we listened to Christian music mixed in with some golden oldies from the radio.

Deciding to pull into a burger joint for B&C (bladder and coffee) stop number twelve, we debated the virtues of the chain restaurants that stood on the four corners as we sat at the exit ramp red light. We all pointed to the Jack in the Box and pulled onto the service road running adjacent to it. We'd have to loop around the back to get to the front parking area. Passing beneath a canopy of tree branches, I slowed the van as we approached a surprising scene. There, lying on the ground in tattered clothes with a grimy baseball hat pulled over his face, was a large middle-aged man. Standing sentinel beside him was a grocery store buggy containing his worldly possessions. We crept by slowly so as not to wake him.

Inside, sipping more coffee and stretching our legs, the three of us could not get our thoughts away from the man sleeping outside. We knew instinctively that he was an American veteran with no place to call home. Making our plan, we skipped back to the van excitedly and drove around back again. When we neared him, I rolled down the window said, "We have a little gift for you, and we want you to know that we love you and that you are not forgotten!" He struggled to sit up, but he couldn't stand. To keep him from being embarrassed and trying to lumber over toward us, I tossed him a small note with some money inside and wrapped with the brown, wooden rosary that usually hung from my rearview mirror.

The man smiled, mumbled, "Thank you so much," and began to open the paper. I don't recall exactly what he said, but his eyes were dancing with laughter and he sat a little taller. We asked him to pray for us and drove away with three arms waving from the windows. The rest of our journey was uneventful, but we did get to sample many of the roadside groceries and stores dotting the landscape between Baton Rouge and Austin. Ever so often, one of us would ponder aloud the plight and future of "our veteran" and all those like him, so forgotten and thrown away by society. We have much to atone for in our treatment of the soldiers who've given so much and gotten so little in return.

Our visit, planning sessions, and retreat went well from our cottage beside beautiful Lake Travis. We were privileged to see wild herds of deer running or grazing in family groups in the early morning hours, or after late-night romps. Hawks, beautiful birds of different varieties, rabbits, and even a beautiful gray fox visited with us as we'd have coffee, tea, or cold drinks out on the porch. God gave us all a nice reprieve from the stresses and pressures of our "real lives" back home through our conversations, praying, meeting with other Christians, attending mass together, walking through the scenic surroundings, and sharing delicious meals. My mind turned often to the homeless man beneath the tree, and I prayed that he was not hungry, or suffering in the sudden thunderstorm that we enjoyed from the safety of the cottage.

Rejuvenated and refreshed, we left each other with hugs and prayers to make our return journeys home. Once again, Deb, Alaine, and I boarded the van and began our trip with a safe journey prayer and a recounting of our many blessings.

Hours down the dusty road, we all noticed that it was approaching the three o'clock hour of Jesus' death, so we popped in a borrowed CD of the Divine Mercy Chaplet. This is a rich and powerful prayer devotion, dedicated to calling down Jesus' mercy upon the world and into our individual hearts. We said the ten-minute prayer and gloried in the beautiful music and instrumental sounds for a while longer.

As God would have it, we needed gas and a java break at just about the same juncture where our vet was last seen five days before, which set us all to praying for him and wondering how he was doing. Being closer to a burger joint and gas station on the opposite side of the road this time, we pulled in there instead of the Jack in the Box. At the back end of the parking lot, we caught sight of our vet disappearing down the road! We couldn't believe it was true, but we knew that it was. No coincidence could have put us in the perfect spot at the perfect time to see the person we'd been praying so fervently for! I wheeled the van around and tried to find him. We looped like circling buzzards around the service roads and parking lots trying desperately to find him again. After many rounds and running on gas fumes, we gave up and returned to the gas pump.

About to pull back onto the interstate for home, we spotted our veteran's buggy wedged behind a pole by a trailer lot. Hanging from the cracked handle bar of his buggy was the rosary we'd given him. We vainly called and searched for him. Gathering back at the van, we scraped together a few dollars and wrote him a note saying that we loved him and would always pray for him because God had asked us to. We would be his praying angels.

Saddened by not seeing him again, we went on our way. Talking about the miracle of this impossible double meeting, we wondered if our vet had asked the Lord in prayer something like, "God, I am so lost and lonely. If those ladies are for real, and you love me at all, would you give me a sign? Will you show me in some way that I am important to you?" We then imagined our vet returning to his buggy and finding the note and money once again. I took a photograph of his shopping cart with the rosary proudly dangling from the front. It hangs on my bulletin board as a reminder of the debt we owe to those who serve.

Nearing Louisiana, Deb looked more closely at the notepad we'd used and discovered that it was a variety pack bearing Scriptural quotes for all occasions. She figured out which quote was on the note we'd left for our veteran, and we were all gratified to hear her read on an identical page in the middle of the pad, "Am I my brother's keeper?" (Genesis 4:9)

STEWARDSHIP TIP~ WHAT'S *in* YOUR GROCERY CART?

Take stock of the things you deeply value and see what you would load into your grocery cart should you suddenly become homeless and penniless and all you could keep was what could fit into your buggy. It's a scary thought. I know I have tons of possessions and wouldn't know where to begin to weed out the most precious of them if forced to. Did you remember to put in your Bible, your family photos, your winter coat, or food and water? If you have children or dependents, you would also have to pack in their needed items.

Now think how terrible it must be to only be able to have the things you could push in that cart. And in winter, blankets take up a lot of your buggy's space. The contents are your total sum worth. Even the wheeled container is not really yours. You'd have to take it from a grocery store.

This is the condition in which many of our homeless brothers and sisters find themselves, and it's a particular problem for our veterans. Do what you can to help! Remember that many of our soldiers have lost families, homes, jobs, mental and physical health, and any sense of worth. They carried their wounded and dead friends from the battlefields in the pursuit of freedom for all. Isn't it time we carried them?

Soldier Scripture

Numbers 31:27-

"...and divide the booty between the warriors who went out to battle and all the congregation."

Judges 6:12-

"The angel of the Lord appeared to him and said to him, 'The Lord is with you, O valiant warrior.'"

---

2 Timothy 2:3-

"Suffer hardship with me, as a good soldier of Christ Jesus."

Brother Forgotten

Please forgive me, brother dear
For I have left you shedding tears.
You were loyal and true and brave.
Put to bed in a living grave.

You fought with valor and might
Through many hellish days and nights.
Coming home was much the same.
You shouldered others' share of blame.

I avoid your vacant stare,
Wounded and hurt beyond repair.
One man to you will be just-
A wounded soldier named Jesus.

For More Information on Veterans, Contact the Following Organizations:

Vietnam Veterans

http://www.vietvet.org/

Vietnam Veterans of America (VVA)

8605 Cameron Street, 4th Floor
Silver Spring MD 20910-3710
(301) 585-4000
http://grunt.space.swri.edu/vetorgs.htm

Department of Veterans Affairs

800-827-1000

MARDI GRAS PANCAKES for a CROWD

1 CUP	ALL-PURPOSE FLOUR
2	EGGS
1 1/4 CUPS	MILK
1 TBS	OIL, PLUS MORE FOR FRYING
2 TBS	WATER

- Put flour in a bowl and make a well in the middle. Add the eggs and a little of the milk. Gradually beat the eggs and milk together, incorporating some of the flour to make a smooth, thick batter. Keep pouring the remaining milk until all of the flour is incorporated into a smooth batter. Beat in one tablespoon oil and water. Let batter stand for thirty minutes before cooking.

- Brush a little oil over a non-stick or heavy, flat pancake pan or skillet. Pour a thick layer of batter into the pan, tilting the pan to spread it evenly. Cook over medium heat until the batter is set and the underside is lightly browned. Use a spatula or palette knife to turn the pancake over and cook the other side in the same way. Transfer to a warm plate and cover with a paper towel and continue until all batter is used.

- You can fill with cooked chicken or any dessert or pie filling of your choice. If you are going for the sweet choice, sprinkle liberally with confectioner's sugar.

Pancakes are good to make ahead and freeze up to months in advance. Make sure pancakes are well wrapped and separated with paper towels so they don't dry out. To serve, stack pancakes in ovenproof serving dishes, brush each lightly with a little melted butter, and cover with foil. Set the oven at 200 degrees and reheat for about fifteen minutes. Place hot fillings on warmers or burners and fill pancakes before serving.

Makes fourteen to sixteen pancakes.

A New Chance at Life

~ Carol Schwartz ~

I wasn't "Down and Out in Beverly Hills." I was just down and out-emotionally, mentally, physically, and spiritually bankrupt. The sad thing is I didn't even know it until years later.

I'd just moved from a five-bedroom, two-bath home on the naval base in Portsmouth, New Hampshire to a tiny two-bedroom apartment. The apartment was on the campus of the University of New Hampshire in Durham. It's the area for married students with children. I had two sons who moved with me after a nasty divorce. It felt like moving from luxury to hell, and to make matters worse, my income was barely enough to cover expenses.

The social worker who lived in the apartment downstairs told me to come down out of my ivory palace and that I would soon learn that poverty knows no morals. That one shocked me.

I'd always had a strong sense of right and wrong. My parents and family members had raised me in a church that believed in high morals and the highest standards of living.

What had gone wrong with my life? Here I was divorced with two children to support. I didn't believe in divorce. The Church doesn't believe in divorce.

My problems started when I moved away from God, the Father Almighty. Oh yes, I was still talking to him in church and was actually going to mass about three times a week at the little chapel on campus. So where did I go astray?

I quit listening to God. I walked away from him at some point along the way. I had gotten so busy that I stopped listening to that still small voice inside my heart and soul. My morals slid lower than I ever imagined they could. I'd lost my sense of God and myself, and I was running from some terrible secrets. There was no longer any play or laughter in my life. There was very little love, either.

Sin is truly a separation from God and our fellow human beings. After living in what felt like hell on earth for several years, I left a trail of hurt family and friends. I was divorced from someone I loved and who had loved me very much. I just couldn't make anything work right while living in the disease of alcoholism. Sin is life without the love of God and of mankind. It is the most barren and desolate place on earth.

Then I experienced God's great gift of love, an answered prayer. On January 31,1983, God lifted my feet out of the muck and put them on solid ground, his way.

I was driving home from work one evening, and the thought came to me that I didn't want to live the way I was living anymore. I wasn't sure what to do, so I prayed to God for help.

The very next day God answered that simple, soulful prayer. God introduced me to Marie at work. She is an angel on earth and a dear, sweet friend. She has shown me by her loving example how to live a God-filled life. With her friendship and guidance over the past nineteen years, I'm learning a better way to live.

I wish I could say I went back to church on a regular basis right away; however, that took almost another three years. At first I would sit in church and all I could do was cry tears of remorse all through the service. So I'd wait another few months and try it again. Eventually through my friend's love I was able to see that maybe I was a little bit loveable and that God could forgive me.

I had earned bachelor's and master's degrees along the way, which opened some professional doors for a new way of life. Degrees alone did not fill the empty hole in my soul. I needed more. I needed God to take over and run my life.

I had moved to California to create a life. My dear friends there showed me the way, the truth, and the life. It turned out to be a whole new way of life. They taught me about love by loving me. They taught me about truth and trust by being truthful and trustworthy. Most important, they taught me about a loving God who forgives.

As taught us by Jesus, the greatest gifts we can give are our love, showing love for God, and sharing our love with others. For nineteen years now I've tried to pay back by giving to others the love of God that was so freely given to me. It's free and it costs me everything. This is the paradox of God's love.

He commands that we follow his will and gives us the choice to do otherwise. He commands that we love our neighbor as ourselves, and only by loving ourselves can we love our neighbor.

God truly leads my life today, one day at a time. My life by all outside appearances is one of social success. I am not at the top of the wealth ladder, but I am far from the bottom. The Lord promises to lead us to success, so long as we remain open to living life his way.

After thirty-six years of wandering all over the fifty states, I am returning to the beautiful mountains of the homeland I love. Idaho is God's country, I learned growing up in Grangeville. It is the place where the skies are bright blue and the lakes and rivers are crystal clear and pristine.

I spent some time traveling in Idaho, Washington, and Oregon between 1979 and 1981 doing work for the Department of Energy. Now I get to do it again, working and living in Boise and traveling the southern portions of the state and other beautiful mountainous country.

I will be near family and friends to do work that I love and enjoy doing. What a blessing! What a gift from God in a simple answer to prayers asking for his will for my life and the power to carry it out.

When I turned my will and my life over to God's care, I experienced the promise of Luke 12:29-31, in which God tells us "Do not keep striving for what you are to eat and what you are to drink, and do not keep worrying. Instead strive for His kingdom, and these things will be given to you as well."

My life has totally changed since God lifted me out of the muck a little over nineteen years ago. It is a miracle that he took my lost soul and transformed me into a successful example of what only he can do. He promises in his word to do just that. Praise the Lord for an answered prayer!

REFLECTIONS

In Paul's letter to the Ephesians,
Chapter 4 verses 22-23, he tells us that Jesus
taught about putting away our former life
and our old self to be renewed in the spirit of
our minds according to the likeness of God.

PASSION FRUIT PUNCH

COMBINE:

4 CUPS	WATER
2-4 CUPS	SUGAR

- Boil this syrup for five minutes.

COMBINE:

2 QTS.	HULLED AND WASHED STRAWBERRIES
1 CUP	SLICED FRESH (OR CANNED) PINEAPPLE
1 CUP	MIXED FRUIT JUICE (PINEAPPLE, APRICOT, RASPBERRY, OR YOUR FAVORITE)
	JUICE OF 1-2 LARGE ORANGES
	JUICE OF 1-2 LARGE LEMONS

- Add the chilled syrup to the combined fruit.

JUST BEFORE SERVING ADD:

2-3 QTS.	CARBONATED WATER
3 CUPS	CRUSHED/CUBED ICE

- Unless you prefer a minimum amount of sugar, add one half-gallon of vanilla ice cream or pistachio nut ice cream.

Feather

~ Deb Anne Flynt ~

An ancient stranger came into our camp one night. The next morning I found him looking far up into the sky. I stopped and gazed up with him until I found what he saw.

A feather was floating down on the breeze, twirling and sailing as it came.

I asked him, "How does a feather find the wind?"

"It does not. The bird finds the wind and the wind finds the feather."

I thought of the old stories. "Then it has always been so?" I asked.

"Yes, but it will not always be this way."

"How can that be, Old One?"

"The young bird cannot fly because he does not have his feathers, but he eats the locust that does fly. He eats because he is provided for by those with feathers."

"Because they must?" I ventured.

"Because they care if the young survive until they have feathers and can ride the winds. The father and mother birds would still live, even if they did not feed the young ones. They do not need them, but they care that there will always be birds."

The feather fluttered and spun as we watched it fall. The old grandfather reached out and plucked it from the air. He asked me, "Do you understand?" I nodded slowly, uncertainly. "Now you can fly, too," he said as he handed me the feather.

I looked into his eyes for a moment. Though his face was wrinkled with age and sun, his eyes were clear. Then I understood, and I accepted the feather.

As soon as I took the feather from him, the old one transformed into a great eagle. He found the breeze and took flight. He circled upward as if greeting each of the four winds over and over, then he flew into the sun and disappeared from my sight.

I twirled the feather between my fingers. It created a small breeze as it spun. Old One had shown me my feathers. I would someday fly too. "He will shield you with His wings. He will shelter you with His feathers." (Psalm 91:4)

SEASONS of my SOUL

In the garden of my mother's womb, the Lord planted my soul, blessing the seed that was to become who I am, and my winter ended.

In the months leading to my birth, the Lord sowed many crosses. He left me here with instructions planted in my heart. As I was wrapped in a warm blanket and suckled my mother's breast for the first time, I felt spring upon my cheek. My soul carefully tended the crosses, though I knew not what they were, nor their reason for being. So little did I yet understand.

In my twelfth year, I passed into summer. I began to realize what the garden was, and that these crosses were to be borne by me. I began to lament my garden, but I still never ceased to care for it, for so far as I knew, it was still my sole purpose in life. "When comes the harvest, O Lord? I cannot bear so many crosses alone!"

My summer passed slowly and I began to understand that I would never be expected to carry the burden of my harvest by myself. Very soon after that, some of the crosses bloomed names: materialism, avarice, envy, pride, egoism, malice, doubt, apathy, sloth, and others, some I thought nearly the same. "Lord, must I carry all these alone? I do not want this lot! Will you not take them from me?"

With that, the sky darkened and a storm of hail burst forth. All the crosses in that garden were destroyed. All but one. There, in the center of the waste of my garden, stood the smallest cross-which I had neglected for lack of seeing it beyond the others. A gentle rain began to fall, washing away all the fragments of those crosses I had refused to bear. I stood in the cleansing rain, my mouth open upward to catch a cool drink. The rain tasted like wine and my thirst was immediately satisfied.

I walked over to the small cross to read what name it bore. The placard said what I knew it would-I-N-R-I, but no inch of that cross was left uncovered by words pounded and scraped into the wood by the hailstones. I began to read.

MERCY,
COMPASSION,
LOVE,
FAITH,
HOPE,

PATIENCE,
TOLERANCE,
EMPATHY...

His voice broke through my reverie. "My burden is light," said my Lord. The cross became feathers that fell to the ground, turning into seeds. I gathered several up and gave them to friends.

One was courage, which I planted in the garden of a mother who had just lost a son.

One was prayer, which I handed to a writer of God's love, and we nurtured it together.

One was faith, which I gave to a new Christian, and we spoke of our Lord's mighty works.

One was hope, which I sent on the wind to a friend who was battling cancer.

One was strength, which I passed to a child who was teased for praying in public.

One was love, which I shared with you.

One was peace. This one kept and made into a pen, with which I wrote this for you.

*P*RAYERS *are* *F*EATHERS

Of eagles who soar,
fearless,
above the wild wind.

Of angels who stand,
head bowed,
in the presence of God.

Of swallows who fly
homeward
to nest near the tabernacle

Of songbirds who reach
with ancient wisdom
into our hearts
and rejoice or weep
with the Spirit
when words fail.

~ Rose Bluefeather

Hummingbird Cake

3 CUPS	PLAIN FLOUR
2 CUPS	SUGAR
1 TSP	BAKING SODA
1 TSP	SALT
1 TSP	CINNAMON
1	18-OZ CAN CRUSHED PINEAPPLE WITH JUICE
1 1/2 TSP	VANILLA EXTRACT
1 CUP	CHOPPED PECANS
2 CUPS	CHOPPED BANANAS
1 CUP	VEGETABLE OIL
3	EGGS, SLIGHTLY BEATEN

- Preheat oven to 350 degrees. Grease and flour three nine-inch round cake pans. Combine first five (dry) ingredients in a large mixing bowl. Add eggs and oil, stirring with a spoon just until moist. Stir in vanilla, pineapple, pecans, and bananas. Batter will be thick. Spoon into pans and bake for twenty-five to thirty minutes. Cool completely.

Cream Cheese Icing:

1/2 CUP	FINELY CHOPPED PECANS
1/2 CUP	BUTTER, SOFTENED
1 TSP	VANILLA EXTRACT
1	8-OUNCE BLOCK CREAM CHEESE, SOFTENED
1	16-OUNCE BOX POWDERED SUGAR

- Combine cream cheese and butter. Beat until smooth. Stir in vanilla. Add powdered sugar and beat until fluffy and light. Spread icing between layers and around sides of cake. Sprinkle top with pecans.

NESTING

~ *Angie Ledbetter* ~

The circle of life is nicely reflected in our nesting from birth to death. From a warm, protected nest we begin in our mothers' wombs, and to the earth's womb we return one day. In between the two, life provides most of us with opportunities to live in different nests. We spend our growing up years in the nest our parents built, where we are taught the skills we'll need for survival on our own. If blessed, we have good parents who provide us with more than the basic human needs. It's these "extra" gifts of gospel values, a good work ethic, caring for our fellow human beings, a sense of responsibility, a view to the truly important things in life, maybe a sense of humor, and awe at the good things God always offers us that we take with us to all future nests.

When we fly from our familial nest in search of adulthood, our first solo home is probably filled with a hodgepodge of hand-me-down furnishings and a variety of roommates. The trials and errors of living with our own choices and decisions fill our time in this nest. Our creativity has an opportunity to blossom as we are also faced with the realities and challenges of how to keep our bathrooms stocked with toilet paper and our checkbooks with a few dollars.

Here, we have the freedom to soar freely without parental or spousal supervision or restrictions. The lessons we learn-about not studying enough at school, or working hard enough at work, or partying too much, or being lazy-give us practical experience for the years ahead. Our solo nest is a proofing ground for a better future, if we are smart enough to learn from our mistakes. I especially learned the value of providing for an emergency by always keeping a nest egg hidden from myself.

More than likely, we've kept the spiritual and emotional gifts inherited from our parents, teachers, and mentors packed away, but not forgotten. These will come in mighty handy in our next home nest. Our first fully adult home will likely be our married home, a place where these ancestral gifts will be unpacked, set out for others to see and admire, and shared with our own babies.

In this nest, we learn to share responsibilities and to make sacrifices for the other occupants of our nest if we are mature. If we have not grown up, then this nest will also be a place where our immature egos seek fulfillment in destructive ways. The family nest we create is a reflection of our past lives now joined as one to provide for our offspring.

Feathering this nest is an awesome chore, as the blending of personalities and temperaments often clash. Far from easy, self-fulfilling, and pleasing, many seasons in our home nest are filled with the clashing of individual dreams and desires. Having the power of prayer, the Word, spiritual reading, devotions, and access to the sacraments has helped me weather these times. As the nest-builders have always known, with the changing of the seasons, new conditions and circumstances arrive. It's our ability to hang in and wait for a new cycle that gets us through the bad times and looking forward to the good.

Perfect relationships and families do exist, but only in fantasy romance novels and bad movies. In reality, we put a lot of grueling work into making our nests sound and peaceful, and eventually we are rewarded to see the fruition of that work. It is never easy to see our childhood dreams and plans wing away as they are replaced by the new goals life provides. If we look with a bird's-eye view, though, instead of at the short-term or immediate picture, that which is yet to come will gratify us.

In my own first family nest of seventeen years, there were times of great joy and hope, but also just as many struggles that accompany making a marriage commitment work in the midst of raising three steppingstone children. Storms and high winds have threatened to blow my nest to the ground, but through prayer and sheer determination, and an eye on the goal, it remains secure in God's tree of life.

This nest is filled with the sound of our parents' and grandparents' wise words and lines of advice issuing forth from our own mouths. These once-detested sayings and reasons for denying our childish wants and wishes are now part of our daily dialogue with our own children. The boxes they have given us have all been unpacked and are in full use in our family nest. I thank God daily for our parents' unselfish and kind gifts. They comfort me in mid-life and benefit my young family.

Many opportunities to help feather others' nests have been given me as we've lived almost two decades in our comfortable, worn nest. At this stage of life, many of us will be called on to help those around us. Maybe we will aid an elderly relative in his/her transition to the final nest of a small apartment, to live with another relative, or into a nursing home. Some of us help younger family members starting out on their own to furnish their first solo nest. If we're alert and open to such, we find opportunities to share in ministry, youth, or community volunteer work. Our family nests become a center of abundant activity like the busy martin house in my backyard. In these ways, we can bless others in need by giving them the raw materials needed to build a small, comfortable nest.

My family nest, a small, fifty-year-old, cottage-style house on piers, has been lovingly renovated and expanded to fit our growing family's needs. It sits on a pretty corner lot full of beautiful, mature magnolia and oak trees. There are a couple of satsuma trees that have shared their fruits with us over the years. It is not fancy, but homey and comfortable, surrounded by good neighbors and good memories.

But our city is expanding and our street was recently expanded to four lanes to make traffic flow more smoothly to the new mall beyond the interstate. Neighbors were displaced and moved away. Most of our front yard is gone, and where our mailbox once stood is now the middle of the new boulevard.

Unhappy about this progress, and uneasy about what would happen to us now that we were a stranded island on the fringes of the new neighborhood demarcations, I questioned the wisdom of our decision to "fight city hall." Would refusing the city's offer to buy us out at what they considered to be fair market value lead to bigger problems? A year of heavy construction and the attendant headaches followed as our driveway was moved to the side street. We detested the close traffic and feared for the kids' safety.

Praying in my favorite chapel and wherever my daily routine found me, a solution finally dawned on me. There was an old and respected devotion at my disposal, a powerful novena that had worked for every person I'd known who'd tried it, including my Baptist mom! I'd call on faithful St. Joseph, put the matter in his hands, and rest easy. St. Joseph is the patron saint of real estate transactions, homes, and family finances-having been charged with those responsibilities as an earthly parent to Jesus. He always kept his little family from harm and found the perfect place for them when danger lurked or mad rulers pursued. Yes, St. Joe would figure the situation out, and I'd ask him daily to bring my request to Jesus' feet as I prayed with him.

The idea behind a novena (from the Latin word for nine) is that you agree to pray for an intention for nine hours, days, or months until it is answered one way or another. You put your faith and devotion into your prayer request and seek the aid of a certain saint. It's similar to asking your Christian friends to pray with and for you over a matter. It's not a magic incantation or superstition, just an agreement to pray without ceasing.

This particular "real estate novena" involves purchasing a small statue of the saint, repeating a short daily prayer, and, as some advise, burying the figurine in a plastic bag in front of the property you need help buying, selling, or renting. When the sale or desired transaction takes place, you unearth the statue and put it in a place of honor in your home. So, all of this I did, and I refused to worry or second-guess what would happen to our nest.

As winter came, my family was busy in its usual pursuit of activities and work. We prayed at meals and bedtime over our future, but we didn't spend time speculating on possible scenarios. Within days of beginning the novena, we were approached by a realtor/developer who wanted to buy our property at commercial rates. I didn't get overexcited, but I trusted that the final outcome would be right for us.

Back-and-forth dealings and negotiations began, along with offers, counteroffers, calling-it-quits, and then renegotiations. Without the comfort of my nest novena devotion, I'd have probably gone bonkers through those months. The last time we signed sales agreement papers with the buyers, we told them that this was it, and if it didn't work out, all deals were off. We also felt obliged to help our dear friend and widow neighbor adjacent to our backyard not get hurt by the deal. She wanted to sell too, but she wanted a fair price. My husband and I made sure that we stood in her stead during the negotiations and gave a portion of our proceeds to make the offer more fair for Mrs. Ethyl.

In all, the sale worked out, and we faced the prospect of locating a new nest after all those years. It burdened my heart that our little red schoolhouse cottage would be bulldozed down at some point, so I quickly added an intention to my thanksgiving prayers for it to live on in some form.

Not surprising, God led us to the perfect home! It's in our same neighborhood, which we love and didn't want to move from, and it is exactly what we would've built ourselves-minus the pains of actually having to live through the building period. It is beautiful, yet warm. Our nest is spacious, and I have the home office I've long prayed for. In essence, it is what I have dreamed of owning, without ever thinking it would actually happen. Yes, through St. Joseph's intercession and the prayers of many, the Good Lord found us a nest beyond compare in which to finish the rearing of our family. And we are thankful.

I have to adjust to the new surroundings, and I do at times feel an overwhelming sense of unworthiness at being placed in such a palace, something akin to "Winner's Guilt." There are so many people close to me who are much more deserving and/or in need. But I'll work to make this nest feel like my own and continue to pray for and to help others reach for similar dreams. All the while, I won't forget to thank the Builder of all nests.

Birdbrain Lessons

Our feathered friends can teach us much. Think of the common sayings that pertain to birds and nests. How do they reflect things in your own life? Also, picture the activity and nature of birds. What can you learn from them? Here are a few thoughts you might want to add to.

- Feathering your nest
- Nest egg
- Don't put all your eggs in one basket
- Empty nest syndrome
- Birds of a feather flock together
- It's hard to soar with eagles when you're surrounded by turkeys
- Birds are great natural recyclers. They take our trash and raw materials from God's bounty and build lovely and secure homes with them.
- Our nests are a reflection of what we get out of the world around us.

SCRIPTURES *for the* BIRDS

Numbers 24:21-

"And he looked at the Kenite, and took up his discourse and aid, 'Your dwelling place is enduring, And your nest is set in the cliff.'"

Deuteronomy 32:11-

"Like an eagle that stirs up its nest, that hovers over its young, He spread His wings and caught them, He carried them on His pinions."

Job 29:18-

"Then I thought, 'I shall die in my nest, and I shall multiply my days as the sand.'"

Psalm 84:3-

"The bird also has found a house, and the swallow a nest for herself, where she may lay her young, Even Your altars, O Lord of hosts, My King and my God."

Proverbs 27:8-

"Like a bird that wanders from her nest, so is a man who wanders from his home."

Matthew 6:26-

"Look at the birds of the air, that they do not sow, nor reap nor gather into barns, and yet your heavenly Father feeds them. Are you not worth much more than they?"

Matthew 8:20-

"Jesus said to him, 'The foxes have holes and the birds of the air have nests, but the Son of Man has nowhere to lay His head.'"

Luke 13:19-

"It is like a mustard seed, which man took and threw into his own garden; and it grew and became a tree, and the birds of the air nested in its branches."

GROWING ROOTS

Had an old neighbor when I was growing up named Doctor Gibbs. He didn't look like any doctor I'd ever known. Every time I saw him, he was wearing denim overalls and a straw hat, the front brim of which was green sunglass plastic. He smiled a lot, a smile that matched his hat-old and crinkly and well-worn. He never yelled at us for playing in his yard. I remember him as someone who was a lot nicer than circumstances warranted.

When Doctor Gibbs wasn't saving lives, he was planting trees. His house sat on ten acres, and his life-goal was to make it a forest. The good doctor had some interesting theories concerning plant husbandry. He came from the "No pain, no gain" school of horticulture. He never watered his new trees, which flew in the face of conventional wisdom. Once I asked him why. He said that watering plants spoiled them, each successive tree generation will grow weaker and weaker. So you have to make things rough on them and weed out the weenie trees early on.

He talked about how watering trees made for shallow roots, and how trees that weren't watered had to grow deep roots in search of moisture. I took him to mean that deep roots were to be treasured.

So he never watered his trees. He'd plant an oak and, instead of watering it every morning, he'd beat it with a rolled-up newspaper. Smack! Slap! Pow! I asked him why he did that, and he said it was to get the tree's attention.

Doctor Gibbs went to glory a couple of years after I left home. Every now and again, I walk by his house and look at the trees that I'd watched him plant some twenty-five years ago. They're granite strong now-big and robust. Those trees wake up in the morning and beat their chests and drink their coffee black.

I planted a couple of trees a few years back. Carried water to them for a solid summer. Sprayed them. Prayed over them. The whole nine yards. Two years of coddling has resulted in trees that expect to be waited on hand and foot. Whenever a cold wind blows in, they tremble and chatter their branches. Sissy trees.

Funny thing about those trees of Dr. Gibbs. Adversity and deprivation seemed to benefit them in ways comfort and ease never could.

Every night before I go to bed, I go check on my two sons. I stand over them and watch their little bodies, the rising and falling of life within. I often pray for them. Mostly I pray that their lives will be easy. "Lord, spare them from hardship." But lately I've been thinking that it's time to change my prayer.

Has to do with the inevitability of cold winds that hit us at the core. I know my children are going to encounter hardship, and my praying they won't is naïve. There's always a cold wind blowing somewhere.

So, I'm changing my eventide prayer. Because life is tough, whether we want it to be or not. Instead, I'm going to pray that my sons' roots grow deep, so they can draw strength from the hidden sources of the eternal God.

Too many times we pray for ease, but that's a prayer seldom met. What we need to do is pray for roots that reach deep into the Eternal, so when the rains fall and the winds blow, we won't be swept asunder.

(From Front Porch Tales, Philip Gulley, HarperSanFrancisco. Used with author's permission.)

Gittin' the Best Present: a Biker's Christmas Tale

~ Alaine Benard ~

The news crews arrive to capture our legendary takeoff. Too many cops have positioned themselves around the perimeter of our group. Navy polyester uniforms appear to bristle at all the head-to-toe black leather. Drizzly December rain keeps sparks and friction fires from igniting the opposing fabrics.

Word has spread that certain outlaw gangs-the Bandits, Skulls, the Red Riders, and Sons, are riding today. "In-Laws" (the new breed of doctor/real estate/lawyer motorcyclists) are conspicuously absent. Their shiny new DynaGlides and Fat Boys with electric starts are parked up in fancy, dry garages while the owners make excuses about prior commitments. Throttled up and ready to party are one hundred forty-eight assorted Pan Heads, Shovels, and Choppers, none newer than a couple of early '90's.

At ten o'clock sharp, we mount our steel horses. The air fills with the thundering of a hundred beasts being whipped into action by their masters' heavy boot. Excited tension burns off some of the gray mist. I become the lightning of the chrome and the vibration of the thunder when we hit the trail.

We charge the road for our twenty-mile trek. Our leader is a three hundred-pound Santa-suited biker. He's pulling an elf in his sidecar-a truly menacing, Twilight Zone vision. With cameras rolling and nervous police in pursuit, we drive the terrified cars to the shoulder of the blacktop. I see shocked mouths open and wrinkled hands cover hearts as we gallop past. My spirit soars ahead to the end of our ride!

The downtown inner city is not a pretty place. Trash and hopelessness litter the alleyways. We arrive at our destination, a seventy-year-old elementary school surrounded by razor wire. It is a modern day Bethlehem, but with plenty of room at the inn. This is the spot for our annual Christmas blowout.

I take off my helmet and shades as curious urchins creep out to get a look at what has descended upon their turf. They are shy in their tattered hand-me-down clothes. The older ones pretend not to be afraid of us and make their way toward the bikes. They are fascinated by all the hair and leather as they ask questions about our Scoots. Opinions and tentative friendships began to form.

When the last kickstand is down, we follow Santa through the broken gym door. Inside are forty children running wild with over-excitement and red Kool-Aid. The few parents present, mostly moms, offer us meager smiles before they retire to the shadowy back wall to gawk. Their embarrassment, fear, and pride are palpable.

Spider has caused considerable commotion in the hall. He has kicked in the bathroom lock because his new buddy, T'yrelle, needs to use the facilities.

"Why the hell are these doors locked?" he bellows in outrage.

Tempers flair as someone else curses the fact that there is no heat in the building. Sergeant Boudreaux is having a talk with the hotheaded Brothers and giving instructions on our expected behavior. Santa grabs the mike to squelch the brewing trouble. Time to get things kicked off.

At last month's Poker Run, we'd each drawn a name of one of these children. When our child's name is called, we hold up a hand and form a circle around him or her. Five of us "win" a scruffy blonde boy with a knife scar running from eyelid to mouth. We tell Dakota our names, which he stutteringly repeats. Earnestly, he high-fives the big men and lightly shakes my hand. He is bright and street-savvy. By the way he gives me the once-over, I can tell he has seen too much for his five and a half years. The children sit in the center of their new tribe, and the event we've been waiting for finally begins!

Joy beams forth as Dakota selects the first gift from his stash. Carefully he removes Preacher's brown bag wrappings and finds a pink stuffed pig, dressed in a tiny biker outfit. He squeals in delight and hugs Hoggy to his chest. Dakota's loot grows as he piles up a radio-operated truck, baseball glove, H-D shirt and cap, Junior Monopoly, chemistry set, books, and a pair of boots. Someone has taught him to go from largest to smallest or that "good things come in small packages," or maybe he just loves shiny paper, because he has saved my tiny, glittery box for last. He holds it tightly and momentarily focuses his attention on his friends' intermittent yells and whoops.

With the finesse of a surgeon, he creases and folds the silver foil, adding it to his neat pile. He is keeping it for future use, he tells us. He will wrap his school drawing for Momma in the red piece.

"Momma likes bright colors," he says quietly.

We bikers smile proudly over his head at his thrifty thoughtfulness. He opens the velvet box to discover a small Bible. Lifting the Book's cover, he spies the sterling chain and crucifix hidden in a cutout compartment. Gingerly pulling it out, he holds it to the light and watches it twinkle.

Suddenly, a frown pushes his pleasure away and his mouth trembles with emotion. Worriedly, he asks me if it can only be worn for church. I gather him in my lap and assure him that he may put it on and wear it forever.

"It is to remind you that Jesus is always with you," I whisper. As if for confirmation, he asks Spider if this is the truth. "Yes, son, it is. The Lord will never leave your side," came the deep baritone answer.

Dakota asks if he can say a prayer. We tighten our ring, join arms, and bow our heads.

Shakily, our little man prays, "Thank you, Good Jesus, for all this cool stuff! Thank you for my friends, I even like Spider. God Bless my Momma, my Grandma, my doggie who ran away and all the bikers in the world. AMEN!...Oh...and thank you for gittin' me the best present outta everybody here!"

One by one, we kneel down so Dakota can climb up and share the tightest, heartfelt hugs his little arms are capable of. He gently wipes the tears from our faces. He kisses me on my cheek and says I love you, with his wise, old man eyes. We weep openly, as do all the outlaws in the room. We are not ashamed. We are Spirit-filled and knocked over by our feelings. None of the hardened, war-torn vets and outlaws try to hide the emotions. We simply let them go. Society's "biker trash," children, and cops alike are blessed with God's grace in this dingy place.

It is hard to leave. No one wants to break the spell. Reluctantly, we gather up our gear and load up. Sergeant B. and his men are slapping backs and making plans to join us back at the shop. They will sign up for next year's Toys for Tots run. Spider and his brotherhood are getting school board phone numbers so they can do some volunteer work around the campus. They promise future rides to their new sons and daughters of the heart.

I stuff my auburn ponytail under my helmet and thank Dakota for the present. He thinks I am referring to his sweet kiss. We hold hands until the bike's motion pulls us apart.

Looking over my shoulder, I see him with one hand extended in statue wave, the other clutching his cross through torn t-shirt. With the wind beating its wings over me, I scream out, "Merry Christmas!"

No, dear Dakota, you did not "git the best present of everybody." You gave us another year's worth of love, joy, and hope. You gifted us with restored faith.

BIKERS' PRAYER

~ *Alaine Benard* ~

Mighty Eagle Father
Be the leader of my flight
Spread your powerful feathers
And share your faultless sight

Let us ride together upon
Freedom's swiftest winds
Shield all sisters and my brothers
Guard these faithful friends

When we reach the final mile
Return us safely home
To honor your Spirit and our
Own two wings of chrome

Homemade Holiday Wine Cooler

5 oz.	alcohol-free white wine
	Soda
	Cranberry juice
	Ice

- Pour wine over ice. Splash soda to almost fill glass. Float cranberry juice on top. Garnish with a twist.

Break bread with new or old friends. What better centerpiece for your evening of fellowship and prayer? Keep things simple and focused on the Lord. You can even include a table for children with their own bread and wine to share while they color pictures of what they think Jesus wants them to do.

Modern Drummer Boy

~ *Angie Ledbetter* ~

Tony May constantly got into trouble at school, during Scout meetings, and in general, wherever he went. It's not that he tried to make waves or cause problems; it just seemed to follow him like a shadow.

While others sometimes walked to the beat of a different drummer, Tony was the drummer, and he banged the eight-piece drum set in loud, offbeat non-rhythms.

"Tony, go see Ms. Cavanaugh!" was the phrase the boy heard most often during the school day. Ms. Cavanaugh, the principal, had quit listening to his explanations and now only tried to find exactly the right punishment "key" to close young Tony's "lock."

"Mom, I don't know why I get sent to the office so much!" the youngster told his mother as she sat wringing a piece of damp tissue.

"Yesterday I was just trying to help Mallory pick up her books and I stepped on one by accident. She ran to tattle to the duty teacher, and Mrs. Ropollo wound up thinking I'd knocked all her stuff out of her hands," Tony explained.

Mrs. May squeezed her temples as a tear slid down her face. Her heart broke daily for her young son. "Oh, Tony, I wish everyone could see the beautiful person you are inside," she whispered, patting his head.

"Mom, it's okay. Don't cry, please. I'm happy and a lot of people like me and Ms. Cavanaugh is nice." Tony grabbed his basketball and headed off to shoot hoops.

Marion May shook her head in amazement. Her son never held grudges and didn't see the negatives that surrounded him. Tony just wanted to keep busy and have fun. Fights, disagreements, and personal troubles rolled off him.

Tony's mom smiled as she watched him through the window, and she thought once again, He's a gift to the world. They just don't know it yet.

The counselors and doctors had assured Marion that Tony was in perfect health. The ten-year-old, in fact, had tested in the genius IQ level. The combination of youth, a high-geared mind, and attention deficit hyperactivity disorder (ADHD) all worked together to his disadvantage.

But what they didn't know or couldn't diagnose was that Tony had a heart of gold. With old-fashioned discipline, lots of love, encouragement to maintain his straight-A grades, and a full schedule of activities, Marion prayed that her son's self-esteem would not be damaged by his peers' and authority figures' constant disapproval and cutting remarks.

Tony loved helping the old folks in his neighborhood by raking their yards, bringing in their newspapers, or doing whatever he could to make their day a little brighter. He also had a way with babies and young children. Tony was drawn to people with disabilities, too, and he bent over backward to help them. He didn't see color, age, deformity, or dividing differences in people.

Tony didn't even seem to mind his classmates' cruel teasing for long. He only felt down on himself for still sleeping with the small swatch of cloth that remained from his baby blanket.

"Nanny, I think it's time for me to give up my bobadee," he told me one December day.

"Really, baby? I thought you liked to have it when you went to bed," I said. He'd spent the night with his cousins at my house and we were playing board games.

"Yeah, I do love it, but Kyle and some of the guys at school said only babies sleep with blankets or stuffed animals," he grinned in his lopsided way.

"Well, Tony, we both know not to listen to what other people say," I reminded him.

"Yeah, I know, but this time, maybe they're right," he said.

The worn, striped cotton square had given him comfort and soaked up many a tear, but maybe this was something he needed to do for himself. I discussed it with Marion, and we decided that he'd asked for my help instead of hers as a safeguard. If she'd discarded it, maybe he'd always wonder if it was still somewhere around the house.

As Christmas approached, we had unusually cold weather in our Gulf Coast town. Temperatures dropped below freezing, and we were called often to cook meals for the men's shelter to help with the extra crowd. Tony was always ready to help serve spaghetti, pour drinks, or just to visit with "the guys," as he called the men.

Driving home from a meal serving session, Tony reminded me, "Nanny, don't forget about my bobadee. I've thought about it all week like you told me to, and I'm still ready to give it up."

I looked in my rearview mirror. He and my son, Josh, were jostling and whacking one another in fun as they planned what they'd do while Tony spent the night.

"Okay, but what do you want to do with it?" I asked.

I drove on toward home, pointing out the unusual icicles hanging from eaves and branches, and hoping my van's heater would soon warm us up.

"I wish I could give it to Baby Jesus. It's so cold outside, and he must be freezing!" Tony said as we passed a huge church with an outdoor manger scene set up out front.

I smiled at his sweet idea. At the next stoplight, I thought what a perfect solution that would be. Tony would be sharing his most prized possession with the infant Jesus. I couldn't think of a happier answer for my nephew's wish to give up his own babyhood.

I made the block and headed back to the church, talking to Tony about his decision.

"Are you sure that this is what you want to do? 'Cause you know, once we give something to the Lord, we don't ever take it back," I quizzed him.

"Oh, yes! I think he really needs it more than I do. Anyway, it's almost his birthday and I don't have anything else to give him," Tony said with finality.

I wiped my misty eyes before the boys could see and pulled up along the curb near the huge creche. There stood a proud Joseph guarding the baby amidst the marble barn animals in the skimpy wooden structure. A beautiful Mother Mary bent slightly over the baby with a smile as his arms reached up to her from the small, hay-filled trough.

"Boys, say a prayer that my old arm can throw Tony's blanket up over that fence, okay?" I said, wadding it up into a small ball.

Both boys giggled and mumbled prayers. I prayed along with them, "Lord, please deliver this package for me."

I rolled down my window, hoping my weaker left arm would do the job. Saying a final quick prayer, I lobbed the fabric ball as hard as I could.

It seemed to hang in the air about two feet short of its target as my heart fell and my eyes closed. There would be no retrieving it for a second shot once it went over the fence.

"Nanny, look!" Tony screeched. I opened my eyes as a gust of wind picked up the material and seemed to guide it into a tiny, outstretched hand.

We hooted with joy as Tony's precious gift draped down over the Christmas Infant, and we drove away, smiling like fools. The boys relived the moment over and over, adding imaginary details and exaggerations to our adventure.

My Christmas had come early that year and I said a silent prayer of thanksgiving. I couldn't wait to call Marion to share with her about Tony's inspired gift.

Almost home, I turned on the radio and the three of us joined in singing "The Little Drummer Boy." Only I found new significance in the song's lyrics and the plight of the young instrument player who first offered the Lord his gift of drum playing.

LAYETTE *for* BABY JESUS

1ST DAY: CRIB

I'll do very well in all that I do.

2ND DAY: CRIB MATTRESS

Do all assignments neatly.

3RD DAY: BUMPER PAD

Skip desserts.

4TH DAY: MATTRESS PAD

Say many times, "Come, Jesus, and make your home in me."

5TH DAY: BOTTOM SHEET

No snacks today. Go to church.

6TH DAY: TOP SHEET

Sit and stand straight all day (good posture).

7TH DAY: BLANKETS

No TV today.

8TH DAY: PILLOW

Sleep without a pillow tonight. Say extra prayers.

9TH DAY: QUILT

Give allowance or donation to the poor.

10TH DAY: DIAPERS

Listen well all day and do your lessons without argument, or do your work with a good attitude.

11th Day: Undershirts
Say "Thank You," "I Love You" and other nice things to your loved ones.

12th Day: Sleepers
Give your room a good cleaning.

13th Day: Booties, Socks
Give closets a good cleaning.

14th Day: Sweater
Do something nice that will please someone.

15th Day: Bonnet
Share toys willingly with your sisters, brothers, and friends, or share your time and talents.

16th Day: Towels
Help Mom clean the bathroom, or do laundry.

17th Day: Baby Shampoo, Soap
Tell Jesus you're sorry if you did something wrong or say the "Act of Contrition."

18th Day: Baby Lotion, Oil
Do a chore for someone.

19th Day: Baby Powder
Do all your work without complaining.

20th Day: Baby Bottle
Pray as a family.

Continues

21ST DAY: RATTLE
Play with a baby or youngster to help a mom.

22ND DAY: BABY CAR SEAT
Run errands for someone.

23RD DAY: PACIFIER
Watch the words that you say.

24TH DAY: BABY SNOWSUIT
Help someone. Go to church.

25TH DAY: CARRIAGE
Find some quiet time to talk to Jesus alone and thank him for all your wonderful blessings.

26TH DAY: TEDDY BEAR
Visit an elderly or shut-in person.

27TH DAY: NIGHT LIGHT
Read the Christmas story from the Bible.

28TH DAY:
Your own personal gift to Jesus.

(THANKS TO FRIEND, PAULA CAPAK)

Authentic Louisiana Gumbo

Gumbo is a staple food of Cajun people, and the rich stew's aroma fills many a home during the "gumbo weather" season of autumn. Hunters and fishermen bring home their catch to add to the bubbling pot. Genuine gumbos vary from region to region, but most start with a basic roux, okra (or filé powder, which is ground sassafras leaves), and a good imagination! So, as Cajun cooks say, "First, you make a roux..."

Roux:

- The fat you choose in making your roux may be shortening, oil, butter, lard, or meat/bacon drippings. Mix fat with an equal amount of flour. One-half cup of each makes a nice amount. You can store excess in refrigerator.

- Melt fat in a heavy black skillet. (Using an iron skillet that's been seasoned through many cookings always works best.) When fat is warm and fluid, sprinkle in flour a little at a time. Stir constantly until brown, usually about twenty to thirty minutes. Remove from heat immediately or add other ingredients your recipe calls for. It is important that the roux is not allowed to burn even in the slightest, as your gumbo will carry a bitter taste.

Gumbo Ya Ya:

1	5-pound roasting chicken, cut up
	Salt, cayenne pepper,
	and garlic powder to taste
2 1/2 cups	flour

Continues

1 CUP	VEGETABLE OIL
2 CUPS	COARSELY CHOPPED ONIONS
1 1/2 CUPS	CHOPPED CELERY
2 CUPS	GREEN BELL PEPPER, COARSELY CHOPPED
6 CUPS	CHICKEN BROTH
1 1/2 TSP	FRESH GARLIC, MINCED
1 LB.	ANDOUILLE SAUSAGE, FINELY DICED (OR SPICY SAUSAGE SUCH AS KIELBASA)
4 CUPS	HOT COOKED RICE

- Cut chicken breasts in half crosswise to get a total of ten pieces of chicken. Season with salt, cayenne pepper, and garlic powder and let stand at room temperature for thirty minutes. Measure flour into a large paper bag. Add chicken pieces and shake until well-coated. Remove chicken and reserve the flour.

- In a large skillet, brown chicken in very hot oil, remove, and set aside. Stir oil remaining in the skillet with a wire whisk to loosen any brown particles remaining in the bottom of the pan. Whisk in one cup of the remaining flour and stir constantly until the mixture of oil and flour (the roux) becomes dark brown (do not burn!). Remove from heat; add onions, celery, and bell pepper, stirring constantly until vegetables are tender.

- Transfer roux and vegetables to a large, heavy saucepan. Add stock to roux and vegetables and bring to a boil, stirring. Lower heat to a quick simmer and add garlic, sausage, and chicken. Continue cooking, covered, until the chicken is tender, approximately two hours. Adjust seasonings and serve in bowls over the cooked rice.

Serves ten. C'est si bon! (It's so good!)

Popcorn and Pride

~ Alaine Benard ~

The day after Christmas found me begrudgingly keeping my promise to take my son to a movie while he was on holiday from school. His talkative excitement wore on my frayed nerve-the last one. After five minutes of his rapid gunfire speech, I thought I would lose my mind. I requested that he remain quiet until we reached the theater.

I explained that after the grueling weekend, I could not bear to hear him rattle on another second. "Be quiet or we are going home!" was my actual remark.

In the silence of the truck, I replayed the events of our annual holiday get-together. It had been a total disaster. That was not the shared opinion of the attendees, who thoroughly enjoyed the event, but was my opinion alone. For months I had planned the family camp-out, made the arrangements, and done all of the work. I took care of every detail for our group of fifty, down to the last recipe and provision.

Several members had to be called, recalled and begged for head counts and other information. As I was getting ready to drive to the campground, one relative phoned to say that seven extra friends would be joining us. That was a precursor of things to come.

One family member arrived with three bags of chips instead of her assigned rolls of toilet paper, not at all concerned about how fifty people were going to survive on one roll of Charmin. Rain, ill-mannered children, forgotten food, extra guests, and preteens allowed to stay awake in the common bunkroom until 3:00 a.m., pulled my composure over the cheese grater.

These and other unhappy memories replayed in my mind as I stood in line at the crowded theater waiting for popcorn and drinks. My son had been sent off to find seats.

Standing in the concession line for more than thirty minutes and missing part of the movie gave me more time to mentally rehash all the disappointing, irresponsible, and commitment-breaking campers. By the time I reached the counter, my hands were shaking with pent-up rage.

I called for the manager. I reamed him out like nobody's business for the ridiculous delay and understaffing on a busy holiday movie night. I ranted and spewed out my venom until my refreshments were handed over. Muttering, I stomped off to locate my child. I slammed the stuff into his lap and sarcastically said I hoped he enjoyed it after all the trouble.

I was convinced of the righteousness of my indignation until halfway through The Grinch (how appropriate!). My son, way past the hand-holding age, reached over and squeezed mine with all the love he could muster. In that instant, my heart flooded with shame over my behavior. I had attacked an innocent man and worried my son because of my own frustrations.

Tears filled my eyes as a vision of the manager's face flashed before me. In slow motion I saw him leave his chore and run to the counter to speak to me. He was sweating so profusely that rivulets were streaming down his chubby baby face, causing his glasses to slide down his nose. This hardworking, obese young man was obviously suffering untold stress from the angry customers he faced. I had never even slowed my rant to consider his feelings.

He apologized sincerely and took all the blame upon himself, saying how truly sorry he was for the delays because they were indeed his fault.

I was overcome with remorse when I recalled his innocent eyes and demeanor, so very much like Jesus' own must have been at his crucifixion. I could hardly bear the comparison of myself to the angry, persecuting mob that Christ faced. The first few kernels of popcorn stuck in my throat, preventing me from eating any more.

At the movie's end, I swallowed my pride and asked to see the manager again. Surprisingly, he did not hide from me but came forward politely to see what I wanted. I asked him for his forgiveness, explaining how very wrong I had been to take my anger out on him. I assured him that I knew he was doing his best in a short-handed situation. I reached out to hold his hand as my son had reached for mine. He bowed his head, but not before I saw a tear roll down his cheek.

He said, "Oh, Ma'am, there's nothing for you to apologize for. I did not do my job well and I ask you for your forgiveness. The blame is entirely mine." He continued by saying, "I cannot tell you what it means for you to come and talk to me."

Driving away from the theater, my son thanked me for the best movie trip he'd ever had. I asked him if he wanted to stop and get ice cream, but he declined. I stared in shock as he added that he would rather say a prayer with me. My soul soared as I nodded in agreement. Together we offered up the manager's personal intentions. We asked Our Lord and Our Lady to bless him and keep him tucked closely between them all his days of working with the public. We asked that he be graced by a special treat for his loving and gentle heart.

DRINK

O Forgiving Chalice
Sweet covenant of
Redemption's Love
Wine transformed
Into Sacred Blood
Wondrous Cup
Shed for all
To share
One
hope
Life
deed
Word
Sacramental Miracle

Terrific Three Grain Bread

1/2 CUP	ROLLED OATS
2 TBS	MILK
1 CUP	BREAD FLOUR
2 TSP	BROWN SUGAR
1 TSP	ACTIVE DRY YEAST
3/4 CUP	MILK
1 1/2 TSP	SHORTENING
2/3 CUP	WHOLE WHEAT FLOUR
1/2 TSP	SALT

- Preheat the oven to 350 degrees. Spread the barley and oats in a shallow baking pan. Bake for fifteen minutes, stirring every five minutes. Let the barley and oatmeal cool to room temperature. Place the barley and oatmeal in a blender and blend until the mixture is the consistency of flour. Add all of the ingredients to the bread machine as directed by the manufacturer. Do not use quick cooking barley or oats. You may use 3/4 cup plus two tablespoons water and three tablespoons dry milk as a substitution for the milk.

This hearty bread compliments any meal. Try drizzling with honey for reheating and enjoying.

Why not invite the wedding officiator to break bread with you at your next family meal?

PRAYERS of the HEART

~ *Deb Anne Flynt* ~

Some might call them circumstances or coincidences, but I have no doubt that God set me up for miracles. I'm only aware of some of the arrangements, but it's enough to thoroughly convince me that I'm not lucky-I'm blessed.

I remember the day I first met Marie and her family. Her dad had just been transferred to my hometown. Since he was working closely with my dad, they naturally talked about their families. They decided that we should all meet, so one warm southern morning Daddy loaded us up and took us to the Smalls'. We all became friends, and I was thrilled when they moved into town and Marie started going to my school. We soon became best friends.

We remained best friends throughout high school, and her family considered me one of their own. After graduation, Marie went to a local college, and I went to one 300 miles away. We only saw each other during summer and Christmas, but our friendship endured the tests of time and distance. When she graduated, she moved back to our small town, and I transferred to a university that was still far from home. After my one-semester stint there, I decided to stay in my apartment across from campus instead of moving home. Then one day I got a strange visit.

A man pulled into the parking lot beneath the open window of my apartment. He began yelling up at me, asking for directions. He asked if I knew a friend of his-me! With forced calm, I asked who was looking for "her." Suddenly, Marie sprang from the passenger-side door and ran upstairs, laughing and crying all the way! By the time I opened the door, I was in tears, too.

We didn't write much, and she had kept it a secret, but this was her new husband, Mick. No wonder the man considered me a friend. Before she left, she told me that they were living about thirty miles away from me. Finally we would be able to spend time together again. I couldn't believe that this far from home, we were reunited.

A few weeks later, I was robbed. I didn't want to move back in with my parents, but I was living check-to-check and my August rent money was gone. I was considering my options when an unlikely idea struck. I gathered my courage and made a phone call. Marie and Mick said yes, I could stay with them for a while. That Saturday night, I moved to Columbia. Marie and I talked nonstop the whole trip. She told me about a friend she wanted me to meet, but I was not anxious to see anyone-especially men.

While I was unpacking, someone came to the door, and Marie and Mick asked me to get it. There stood a guy who, judging by his expression, was probably the friend they wanted me to meet. It was not love at first sight. As we sat and talked, though, it became obvious that Gary and I would be friends. In December of that same year he took me to New Orleans. Although it was a year before we would admit it to each other, it was then that we fell in love.

Because jobs were so difficult to find and keep during the recession, I finally had to move back in with my parents. Every few weeks I would make the trip to Columbia to see Marie and Mick, and of course Gary, who usually drove me home. It was during one of these trips home that I decided I had to tell him an awful truth.

"Gary, I know we haven't talked about marriage or anything, and I'm not trying to now, but I have to tell you something important before we grow any closer to each other." I drew a deep breath knowing that if I hadn't just destroyed the relationship, I was probably about to. "I can't have children. If you want a family, I'm sorry, but I can't give you one." We hadn't yet expressed our feelings to each other, and this was his chance to get out before he got hurt.

He looked at me and said, "We'll cross that bridge when we come to it. Besides, we can try to adopt." That was when I realized that he loved me.

Two years after we met, he asked me to marry him. A year later I did. Marie was my matron of honor. Gary and I were so happy. One day we were driving home from a visit to my parents' house, and we began talking about a family of our own. We weren't planning, praying, or complaining. We were just talking about what it would be like if we were able to have kids.

First we would have a little boy. He'd be as strong as his dad and as handsome. He would, of course, be a genius. He would have a loving heart, because we would love him so much. When he turned four or five and started school, we would have our daughter. She would be sweet and delicate-a little flower. Her big brother would always be there for her-to look after her and take up for her. Naturally, she would also be a genius. That's what we decided we'd want, if we could have a family. We kept our bittersweet dream in our hearts. We didn't feel deprived. It was just a fantasy we visited sometimes.

I was working at a Mexican restaurant at that time, and I gained an inch or two across my waist as well as a stomach bug from a customer. I took a few days off to get rid of it. Slowly an idea began forming at the back of my mind. I didn't have any reason to suspect that it was true, but the idea persisted. I gave in to it and bought a pregnancy test. The next morning, as usual, I kissed Gary good-bye and sent him to work.

Of course I knew what the result would be, but I wanted to be sure the next time that little idea came around. I took the test and all the pertinent paperwork upstairs, where I waited for the results on our bed beneath an east-facing window. I watched the contents of the tube refuse to change to gray, and then I began reading the enclosed papers again. The sun was rising behind me, and I compared the tube to the chart. Naturally, it was negative, but the time wasn't up, so I just sat there on my bed waiting to confirm my doubts.

The brightening light behind me gave the illusion that the liquid in the vial was getting paler. I watched this for a while, occupying my mind with the trick of the light to avoid the inevitable disappointment. I don't how long I did that before it occurred to me that the fluid was practically clear. If it had been positive, it would have turned gray; if negative, it wouldn't change color at all. I picked up the chart again to find out what this meant. In fine print in one corner at the bottom, as if it weren't important, that in a small percentage of women the fluid would become clear. This result was positive.

Okay...

WAIT! WHAT? POSITIVE? No, I must have misunderstood. I read it again-three or four times. It didn't change. It said the same thing every time.

I think I might have shrieked, hollered, yelled out, or screamed, or all of it. I know I cried. As soon as I could, I got to the health department, and they did another test. Yep. I was pregnant. Yesssssss! Wow. Me-a mom! Thank you, Lord, thank you!

When that one was a hearty two-year-old, I became pregnant again. These twins reached heaven before they were born. I went to an ob-gyn to find out why, and he admitted that it took a miracle for me to have gotten pregnant-ever. Unfortunately, even if I did somehow get pregnant again, it would be nearly impossible for the baby to survive much past the first trimester. If, he told me, I did conceive, "come back and we'll take the best care of mom and baby that we can." One year later, I had another miracle happen. Naturally, I went back to the same doctor. Nine months later, our delicate little flower was born.

I learned a very important lesson through my children. I already knew how to pray, and I knew that my prayers were heard and answered. What I didn't already know is that God also listens to the prayers of a loving and faithful heart, even when they aren't intentional.

Through this miracle, God has given me the opportunity to share hope with many women who have been given the heartbreaking news that they will never be mothers. I always enjoy sharing my story of God's love, and how miracles can happen to anyone, anytime.

"So faith, hope, and love remain, these three; but the greatest of these is love." (1 Corinthians 13:13)

Small Things Appreciated Big-Time

Not too very long ago, giving birth meant a two-week hospital stay. Things sure have changed! My daughter was born in the afternoon, and we went home the next day. Of course, this meant that I wouldn't be able to do many of the things that needed to be done when we got there. I remember one particular thing that my doctor forbade me to do, besides the obvious stuff. Naturally, this was the thing that I most wanted done when I got home. He told me not to sweep for several days. I don't remember how long it was before I was allowed to sweep, vacuum, or mop; but it bothered me that it wasn't done.

I'd have appreciated it so much if someone had simply picked up a broom and swept my floor. I wouldn't ask anyone to do it, but I would have been very grateful if they'd volunteered.

Neighbors brought food, and family brought gifts, but nobody changed my sheets or scrubbed my bathtub. These are things I could not do. Somebody chauffeured me around until the doctor said I was okay to drive, and others took wet clothes from the washer and put them in the dryer for me. I wasn't allowed to lift anything heavier than my baby. I wasn't even supposed to move a gallon of milk from the fridge to the countertop and back.

Since new moms' hospital stays are so short now, help one do the things she isn't allowed. Clean her floors. Put away her groceries. Help her with the laundry. These normal jobs are too big for her, but not as big as her gratitude for helping her get them done!

Mourning Sickness

Familiar feeling,
Leaning over, wretched retching.
My stomach reels, but my heart soars.
Once again I wait.

I reach down, pat my distended belly,
knowing there's much to be done
to prepare for the stranger.
Small wonder, this person already.

They spill my blood for a test,
to tell me what I already know.
I am joyful and expectant.
Radiant, glowing.

They tell me to wait. I am already waiting.
They come back, not smiling...
I'm sorry. You were pregnant,
but there's nothing we can do...
Yes. Cry with me.

OH, WHEN *the* SAINTS COME MARCHIN' IN...

...to the Superdome, I know it's time for me to have some chips and dip ready. It's football time. We have favorite snacks just for the games, and it's a family event. We all watch together, hoping every season that "maybe this will be the year" the New Orleans Saints make it to the Super Bowl! Go, team, go! Or as they say in Louisiana, "GEAUX!"

ANGEL-ED EGGS
(NAMED BY CAITLIN):

12	EGGS, HARD-BOILED
1/2 CUP	MAYONNAISE
1/4 CUP	SWEET PICKLE CUBES OR RELISH
1 TSP	MUSTARD
6	OLIVES
	(GREEN, STUFFED WITH PIMENTO), CUT IN HALF
	SALT AND PEPPER TO TASTE
	PAPRIKA

- Peel eggs and cut in half lengthwise. Remove yolks and mash with a fork in a small mixing bowl. Add mayonnaise, relish, mustard, and salt and pepper. Mix well and spoon into egg halves. Sprinkle with paprika and top each one with an olive half. (Add a small can of deviled ham for more taste, but don't tell Caitlin I said so.)

Gooey Easy Cheesy Dip
(For Saints games and the post-season):

2 cans	cheese soup
	(condensed soup such as Campbell's*)
1 can	diced tomatoes with peppers
	(such as Ro-Tel*)
1/2 cup	shredded mozzarella cheese
1/4 cup	shredded cheddar cheese
1/4 cup	jalapeño pepper, finely chopped
1/4 cup	milk

- Empty both cans of soup into a medium-large saucepan. Heat on medium, stirring frequently, until smooth. Add tomatoes with about half the juice from the can. (Reserve other half.) Stir until smooth. Add chopped jalapeño and both cheeses. Stir constantly until near boiling. If necessary, drain the grease from the cheddar off.

- Reduce heat slightly, keep stirring, and alternately add juice and milk a smidgen at a time until you reach the desired consistency. Remember that this is cheesy, so it will stiffen a bit as it cools. Serve hot with tortilla chips, and eat carefully.

* Use cans that are about ten to twelve ounces. Any brands will do, but be sure soup is condensed, and that the tomatoes have the peppers with them-or if you can't find them, use extra jalapeños and a can of regular diced tomatoes.

A DEVOTED MOTHER

~ *Carol Schwartz* ~

"I choose the poverty of our poor people. But I am grateful to receive (the Nobel) in the name of the hungry, the naked, the homeless, of the crippled, of the blind, of the lepers, of all those people who feel unwanted, unloved, uncared-for throughout society, people that have become a burden to the society and are shunned by everyone."

- Mother Teresa of Calcutta, India

What kind of person would choose to give seventy years of her life living with and mothering the poor, the sick, and the dying? She was not an outcast in society. She had a good education including medical training, was from a respectable family, and was a little shy growing up but popular among her many friends.

At a young girl's age she knew she was meant to serve God; she told her mother that she didn't know how she was going to do it, but she would serve him. In 1946, when she was traveling on a noisy train in the Himalayas, God spoke to her.

In her own words she said, "I was sure that this was the voice of God. I was sure that he was calling me. The message was clear: I must leave the convent to help the poor by going to live among them. I understood what I needed to do, but I did not know how to go about it." She chose to leave the protection of the convent at age thirty-eight. She went alone to work in the slums of India and thus began the Missionaries of Charity.

If you look back during that time, the 1950's, it was not a popular thing for a woman to go unaccompanied out of her parents' home into the world, let alone to live among the outcasts of society. Two years later she opened a home for abandoned children, the dying, lepers, and alcoholics/addicts. In the next twenty years of her life she opened many homes around the world for the "poorest of the poor." Surely people must have thought she had lost her mind. In fact, the first time she asked to be relieved of her sister duties, she was denied.

One characteristic of Mother Teresa was her persistence. When she wanted something, she didn't care what others thought, and she went for it. She won out every time and got what she asked for. Surely she had the Almighty, all-powerful God on her side. Her caring for the poor spread to fifty Indian cities and thirty countries, including the United States, South America, Italy, England, Ireland, Africa, and Australia to name a few. There are four hundred fifty monasteries in the world that have joined in spiritual cooperation with Mother Teresa's work of serving the "poorest of the poor." She influenced the beginning of the Missionary Brothers of Charity, an organization serving the homeless, alcoholics, drug addicts, and abandoned elderly people.

A second characteristic of Mother Teresa was her willingness to give, expecting nothing in return. "It is in the giving that we receive and I have always received more than I have given," she said. Because she gave her all, it is hard to imagine that she received more than she gave. She expressed her manner of living when she said, "We need poverty if we are to live free, both materially and spiritually." Poverty, obedience, and discipline were her watchwords.

This woman of God, standing all of five feet tall, was surely one of the most open-minded, willing, devoted, and courageous women of all time. She was willing to die for her children, the "poorest of the poor."

What a challenge this would be for any human being who claims to love God-to carry out such a task. "Strength is needed and unlimited courage; and this is obtained by the fruit of prayer." Prayer, meditation, and adoration were her daily foods, and played an important role in Mother Teresa's life and spiritual growth. To listen to her, her life was "full of good fortune and happiness."

Watching my two sons, Chris and Matt, grow up and go through their own struggles with life, it is natural to see how a parent loves so unconditionally. The joy of being involved in their lives with five grandchildren is one of life's greatest blessings.

If you are a loving parent and have given many things and much of yourself to your children, you have an inkling of the love and devotion of this woman.

Mother Teresa was one tiny soul who lived her life totally devoted to God until she died on September 5, 1997. She has been likened to Jesus' parable of the mustard seed found in Matthew 13:32-32,

"It is the smallest of all seeds, but once it has been planted, it grows and becomes the largest plant in the garden, and eventually turns into a tree which offers its branches to the birds of the air, which come and build their nests in it."

Scriptures *to* Live By

Matthew 6:33-

"Strive first for the kingdom of God and his righteousness,
all these things will be given to you as well."

James 1:5-6-

"Ask God, who gives to all generously-and it will be given you.
But ask in faith, never doubting."

Ephesians 4:32-

"Be kind to one another, tenderhearted, forgiving one another;
as God in Christ has forgiven you."

Romans 1:11-12-

"For I am longing to see you so that I may share with you some
spiritual gift to strengthen you-or rather so that we may be
mutually encouraged by each other's faith, both yours and mine."

Mary Untersinger's Famous Potato Soup

When I was recovering from illness, my dear friend Mary made some of her homemade soup and delivered it to me. There is none better! We worked together in Ridgecrest, California, and Mary always went above and beyond the call of duty in friendship and at work.

3-5 lbs	potatoes
1	bunch celery (leaves and all), chopped
1	large onion
	Garlic powder
1	stick butter or margarine
1	8-oz block cream cheese
4 oz	sour cream

- Cook the above ingredients until tender and mashable. Drain excess water and replace with milk, then mash to your desired thickness. It is best to mash with hand masher so you can have some chunks of veggies.

- Add garlic powder to taste. Add one stick butter or margarine. Add cream cheese and sour cream. Mash until creamy. Add salt and pepper if desired. Enjoy!

For All Seasons

The Sacraments: Signposts of Grace on Life's Journey

~ Angie Ledbetter ~

The seven sacraments hold the power to turn our lives from a simple walk to a vibrant, multi-dimensional journey. Christianity has become somewhat divided by a lack of understanding of the essential meaning of these floodgates of grace, because many do not believe in their power or understand their true significance. I've been blessed to see them work in my life. They are the power that propels us to praise God and to continually renew our love for and devotion to him.Our destiny as children of the Lord is to return to him in eternity when our lives here are finished. God became man to help the human race in that pursuit. With Jesus as our model, we have the challenge of using our free will to help get us home. The bounty of his sanctifying grace can help us in battles with our free will thinking and our human-driven urges to do other than what he would have us do. The sacraments are the "Master Card" that we shouldn't leave home without. Each of these seven channels of his grace has a special way of offering us help.

In seeking a better understanding of the role of the sacraments in a Christian's journey, I turned to Father Jeff Bayhi. Father Jeff is the vocations director of the East Baton Rouge Diocese, pastor of St. Agnes Catholic Church, chairman of Metanoia, Inc. (building facilities and programs for youth), spiritual director, immediate past state chaplain of the Catholic Daughters of the Americas, and an active participant and leader in many other ministries and good works. This information is largely what I learned from our conversation during a recent luncheon date. Father Jeff claims some Middle Eastern heritage and loves Greek/Lebanese food, so we ate and talked at one of his favorite restaurants.

To obtain more information on Metanoia Inc., email Metanoia98@cs.com. Father Bayhi's Way of the Cross CD/tape with Aaron

Neville can be ordered through this address also. All profits go to defray the costs of the retreat and youth center. This tape is responsible for bringing many hurting souls onto Jesus' loving path and is an invaluable contemplative tool.

Baptism

"I baptize thee in the name of the Father, the Son, and the Holy Spirit."

- Trinitarian Baptism, Matthew 28:19

Through baptism, we receive our first share of God's divinity. We literally take Christ's promise of life to our souls in the words he spoke to Nicodemus: "Unless you are reborn of water and the Holy Spirit, you shall not reach the kingdom of heaven." We accomplish this at baptism with the wonderful symbolism of washing to show interior purification. The sight of a newborn baby getting his very first bath is poignant and powerful, and I imagine it is comparable to how our souls look to the Lord on the day of our baptisms.

There are two aspects of baptism explained in Scripture: "Go therefore and baptize all nations," and "teach them to carry out what I've commanded you."

Baptism is a beautiful ceremony. Parents especially need to study the true meaning of the sacrament and realize that baptism is much more than an "after birth thought." The ceremony pales in comparison to the reality of what is taking place. Ordained priests go through a rite of consecration in which their hands are anointed by the oil of sacred chrism to perform baptisms. This is the same oil that is used to baptize the uninitiated. Baptism opens us to the priesthood of Jesus Christ.

We are called to be active, not passive, in the practice of faith. In baptism, we become part of the Body of Christ and begin our journey to be Christ's presence in the world. Baptism initiates this grace in us and validates the reason that Jesus came to us as man. Washing away original sin and making us clean and new for our journey are just two of a multifaceted cleansing ritual held in this first and beautiful sacrament.

PENANCE AND HOLY COMMUNION

"...may God give you pardon and peace, and I absolve you from your sins in the name of the Father, and of the Son, and of the Holy Spirit."
"This is my Body which was given up for you."

- CATHOLIC RUBRICS, FORMULA OF ABSOLUTION AT RECONCILIATION

After the Lord told us that we need baptism to ignite the life of grace in our souls, we were shown how to keep this life within us alive through the reception of his most holy nourishment. Our physical bodies are born from water at that first gasp of air, and then we must have food to stay alive. Our spiritual bodies need the same things. To his amazed followers, Jesus said, "Unless you eat the flesh of the Son of Man and drink his blood, you shall not have life in you." Just like "real" food, the Eucharist fuels and strengthens our spiritual machines.

Through the beautiful sacrament of penance, also called reconciliation and confession, we are given the means of receiving forgiveness when we fall away from the Lord's friendship through sin. The grace that flows to us from Christ is immense when we take the opportunity to reconcile ourselves to our neighbors, friends, community, and Christ through reception of this powerful healing agent. God generously gave us a prescription to cure our souls of the ailment and stain of sin. Confession also works to heal other areas of our lives.

Psychologists and therapists are beginning to correlate the increase in patients' emotional and mental problems with the fact that many lack a clear-cut understanding of sin and guilt. Hurting people are left with bad feelings, hollowness, and worse because they have not been taught to seek reconciliation with others and/or that guilt is a good compass for our souls-not something to get rid of at all costs by ignoring, transferring, or blaming.

Thankfully, the sacrament of confession allows followers a healing cure given to us by Jesus on the night of Easter Sunday. Like all good children, we should want to come to the table clean and presentable.

Many years ago, Gandhi said to the many hungry people gathered around him that God couldn't have come in any other form other than bread. This basic food is available to all, as is Christ himself. At the Last Supper, God said that we were promised by the power of the Holy Spirit that ordinary bread and wine would become the true Body and Blood of Jesus Christ. He chose the most ordinary items for our benefit.

This is amazing, because we will spend countless dollars to get the right prescriptions, self-help books, or therapy, and then finally fall to our knees and say, "What in God's name am I gonna do?" This should be our first resort always. Turn to God when in need, and go from there. We are given sanctifying grace, the promise of salvation, and eternal life through this sacrament of communion. When we open up to it, it is our daily reminder to live holy lives.

Father Jeff shared a lesson that a fifteen-year-old boy taught him. "I was a young seminarian living in a subdivision. I was trying to help this boy with a drug problem and befriended the family. His brother was a gangly thirteen-year-old, and I got close to him, too. The brother on drugs was missing for months, then one day I heard a horn blowing in the driveway. I thought, What is this, a curb-service church? The kid brother was proud of his new driver's license and had come to show me. I told him to be careful as he drove away.

"Hours later I got a call from the sheriff's office to go to the emergency room to be with this family. I thought it was surely about the son on drugs. But it was Glen, the new driver. He had missed a curve and hit a light pole, which fell and hit him in the head. His neck was broken. The neurosurgeon said that if Glen lived, the spinal cord injury would make him a quadriplegic for life. The older brother came to the hospital. He hadn't spoken to his father in a very long time.

"We had a prayer vigil for seventy-two hours to see if Glen would breathe on his own. He was strapped into a halo on a wheel bed. I did the cheerleading routine, but I was broken for him. I had to tell him that he was a cripple and we both shed many tears.

"Glen said, 'I don't want to be a cripple. But if Dad and Carl stay close, it's worth it.'

"The family is still together. Carl married and has a family and is very active in ministry work. This is the Eucharist, the sacrifice of love."

Through confession, God truly forgives us so that we can start over again. Scripture is clear on this, but people often say, "It's between me and God." I don't take on God that way, saying, "Hey Big Boy, give me some more."

We need to realize that our sins are against God and also one another. It's not magic, but it IS the Holy Spirit that works when we desire a change in our heart.

Father Jeff said, "A therapist I know well told me, 'I charge $150 an hour to give out a pill, and you do it for free.' We both know that pain and separation from God draws people to confession and resolution. That is at the root of so many people's hurt, and this sorrow is helping to bring them back to God if they let it. As a priest, reconciliation gives me the opportunity to help them take steps back to God.

"I had only been a priest for six months when an old woman came to confession. I knew she was old because I heard her shuffling feet as she approached. It had been sixty-one years since her last confession because she had had an abortion when she was twenty-one. This eighty-two-year-old fell to the floor, and I was able to take her in my arms. I was so angry that someone had told her that she would go to hell and was doomed. But I was grateful to tell her that God wills and wants us to come home to him! That was a blessing to me.

"God heals us of confusion and pain if we let him. He loves us all so much."

CONFIRMATION

"...and give them new life.
Send your Holy Spirit upon them
to be their helper and guide.
Give them wisdom and understanding,
the spirit of right judgment and courage,
the spirit of knowledge and reverence."

- RITE OF CONFIRMATION, AS READS IN THE CATECHISM

Jesus lets us know in the Gospels that his followers would need to have our faith strengthened. This is one of the graces given to us at confirmation.

We make firm our decision to be Christ-like and to go out into the world and live his message under a seal of approval from him. Confirmation perfects our baptismal grace and allows the Holy Spirit to root us deeply in the divinity of the Lord. The sacrament of confirmation is also a bridging from childhood to our adult journey. We move from our parents' guardianship over our morality into our own understanding and decision-making.

Father Jeff explained, "This sacrament is about choice. Young people begin to embrace and live out their lives on the same track that their family has instilled. Being a soldier of Christ is one way of describing one who has been confirmed, but that is not to say that the young adult is on some 'G.I. Jesus' routine. It is a realization that we cannot make it without God. People come to this realization at different times, not necessarily connected with their age.

"The Jewish faith has a similar rite in the bar mitzvah, which makes the celebration of our sacrament pale in comparison. There is something awesome about a fifteen-year-old boy leading the prayers of his people in Hebrew.

"It really fries me to hear parents say, 'Well, at least they're in church.' (Referring to their teens being at mass.) Compare these same parents when it comes time for sports, and there's a huge chasm.

"They are enthusiastic and dedicated to these athletic events, practices, equipment, games, and tournaments that take up days at a time. They are displaying to their children what is important to them. Kids are smart, and they know that adults vote with their wallets and their watches!"

Holy Orders

"...Our Lord Jesus Christ, ...by your gracious word, ...You established rulers and priests and did not leave your sanctuary without ministers to serve you..."

- Rubrics for Ordination Rite, Order of Bishops

Jesus gave his disciples the grace to continue his ministry in his name. The Bible shows that he clearly intended for his work to be carried forth for the benefit of others. At the Last Supper, Jesus instituted the priesthood and established the sacrament of Holy Eucharist. Both serve as reminders and nourish our needs in different ways.

Father Jeff added, "Being a priest is an opportunity to be Christ to the world. In seminary, there was a Cuban fellow named Pedro a few years ahead of me in the studies. I was blessed to serve at his first Mass.

"He told me, 'I am ready to die now. To be given the opportunity to do what Jesus did—to turn ordinary bread and wine into the Body, Blood, Soul, and Divinity—I am ready now.'

"Being a priest, pastor, or religious is an absolute gift from God. If it's 'all about me,' then a person cannot serve in those capacities. It's only by allowing him to work through you that you become awesome.

"My gifts have been multiplied. I don't have time to be lonely. I have many 'wives and children' (in my flock) to care for, and who care for me. If people knew the sacramental gifts available to us, we would all be glowing in his love.

"God owes us nothing for our service in any capacity to him. Expectations turn our relationships with God sour. But when we are open to giving instead of getting, the blessings flow.

"When we say 'Yes' to God, we must do so in humble gratitude, and then if we let him do the work, the sacrifices become only blessings. All of our gifts and talents come only from him. Living in this way brings us many opportunities.

"People come to me because they want me to see their soul and help heal it. That is an unbelievable gift from God when you think about it. The sacrifices of priests/pastors are much like those of parents. The small sacrifices are part of any committed, vowed life."

Holy Matrimony

"May the Lord who began His divine miracles at the wedding of Cana of Galilee, bless you in your new life."

- Rubrics of Orthodox Wedding Vows

Christ gives us instructions in Scripture and the Ten Commandments about the importance of a monogamous marriage relationship. So that we could thrive and make the institution one of holy vows for the duration of our lives, Christ put great importance on the fact that we should leave our parents and cleave to our spouse, let no man or entity drive our unions asunder, and remain faithful to one another.

A sacramental and covenantal marriage with God as the third party in the relationship helps inoculate our vows from the forces that try to break them up. With the grace given to our marriages through this sacrament, we stand a much better chance of making it through the rough times and sacrifices that any committed relationship takes. We need to study and understand this sacrament more fully to reverse the breakdown of the family trend that has plagued us over the last few decades.

Part of the vow that many couples take on their wedding day says that we promise to remain together "for better or worse." Our current definition of that phrase has come to mean, "until I need to fulfill myself more," or "until you start to aggravate me," or "you're not doing your share in this marriage so I think I'll look elsewhere."

The old saying needs to be dusted off and placed in a prominent place in our homes: "The family that prays together, stays together." Father Jeff says, "In John's Gospel we are told by Jesus to love one another as 'I have loved you.' This is the heart of the sacrament of matrimony. It is not merely a legal contract, but the law of God, which is more binding than any civil law. Comparing marriage to a contract is like saying that bussing will achieve racial equality. The quality and intent has to come from within.

"The young today are greatly challenged to find any sense of permanency, because many grow up in broken homes and marriages. They are also inundated with the mass media message that everything should be a convenience and not necessarily a conviction. They look at marriage like a warm-up lap to some other event. It's become a 'McWorld' of instant fulfillment, an age of materialism producing generations of 'unmarriables.'

"Kids think that they must be entertained and happy 24-7. Every day should be Christmas. And parents have fallen into the best friend syndrome. They are not parents, and their children do no wrong. It is the teacher, the school, the coach, and the arresting officer that are wrong. Another problem besides over-indulgence is that kids get married too young many times when they are really in heat, not in love. They haven't a clue that marriage is the ultimate sacrifice.

"I remember hearing that a kid was on trial in Florida for killing his teacher. The local news interviewed the grandmother and she said, 'We gave that kid everything he ever wanted. I just don't understand.'

ANOINTING OF THE SICK

"Through this holy unction and His own most tender mercy may the Lord pardon thee..."

- RUBRICS FOR ADMINISTRATION OF LAST RITES

This sacrament is given to our earthly bodies as we approach our final days on earth. We are given a mighty gift to help us enter eternity in the confidence of God's Divine Mercy. Facing death is traumatic and this sacrament gives us extraordinary assistance from God. Also called the last rites, it is the last of the seven sacramental gifts from our Savior.

Father Jeff related, "I was in Calcutta with Mother Teresa and had asked to work in her home for the dying. I had an adult man in each arm and they were so emaciated. I took them to the crematorium to wash them. I asked her, 'Mother, how do you do this and watch them die every day?'

"She said, 'Father, just think when you go home to heaven, all of those faces will be waiting to greet you. Yours was the last face they saw.'

"People live in fear of death. To be a comfort to them in preparing for the other side is a tremendous blessing and very powerful. Mother Teresa also said to me, 'I better do it right because God's watching me.'

"Administering the sacrament is a gift to me. I have known large families who invoke the laying on of hands through the Holy Spirit, and I have anointed my cousin with AIDS when he thought that he would be judged and condemned. I ask the Father to work through me to help others.

"My first parish was in the small town of Belle Rose, Louisiana. There was a seventy-year-old woman named Loyola there whom people called the village idiot. She'd had an abusive husband and her children were all gone. She picked up cans from the ditch to be able to tithe. She was scared of everyone. I would welcome her by name at church and went to visit her at home. You would have thought that the Pope was arriving. She was so proud that I'd come and wanted me to see all of her trinkets. We became good friends.

"One Sunday someone told me that an ambulance had taken Miss Loyola to the hospital, so I went to see her. She was all ragamuffin-looking, scared, disoriented, and didn't recognize anyone. She was like a caged animal.

"When she realized that I was there, a peace came over her. I put her glasses on her and explained that she was in the hospital. I gave her last rites and told her that God was watching over her. She relaxed and she died three hours later. There was an overwhelming sense of God's presence in the sacrament.

"I was really good friends with a Jewish couple, Judy and Irving. The wife had cancer. I visited and prayed with them and would go to this rabbinical teacher's celebrations, and he would come to my masses. When Judy died, Irving told me, 'I'm jealous of you. All I have is a dead body. You have hope.'"

Scriptural References for the Sacraments

Baptism

Romans 6:4

1 Peter 3:21

Matthew 3:10-12

Matthew 3:16

Acts 22:16

Galatians 3:27

Reconciliation

Leviticus 5:5

Acts 2:37-39

Numbers 5:7

Psalm 32:5

Proverbs 28:13

Matthew 5:24

Acts 19:18

2 Corinthians 5:18

Hebrews 3:1

James 5:16

Eucharist

John 6:41-42

John 6:51-56

Matthew 16:5-12

John 6:64-66

1 Corinthians 10:16

1Corinthians 11:27, 29

Confirmation

Hebrews 6:1-2

Acts 8:14

Holy Orders

1 Timothy 5:17

James 5:14-15

Titus 1:5

2 Corinthians 3:6 and 6:4

Ephesians 3:7

Matrimony

Romans 7:2-3

Luke 16:18

Romans 7:2-3

Mark 10:11-12

Jeremiah 29:6

Hebrews 13:4

1 Corinthians 7:28, 39

Anointing of the Sick

Mark 6:13

James 5::14-15

Leviticus 2:4

Mark 8:22-26

Father Jeff's Holy Land Hummus

Inhaling the wonderful and varied aromas of the Lebanese restaurant where we met for lunch, Father Jeff shared one of his favorite mouth-watering recipes. Although the measurements are not exact, the padre says that, as in all things, with practice and prayer, you will perfect it to your own taste.

- Drain and wash a can of chickpeas. Some specialty markets may carry better brands.

- Into a food processor add the chickpeas, one heaping tea spoon of salt, a dribble of olive oil, lemon juice to taste, and plenty of garlic.

- Padre adds tahini, which you can get from a specialty store or favorite Greek/Lebanese restaurant. The hummus should be smooth and creamy. Excellent dip for pita bread!

P.S. (Precious Sacramentals)

As Catholics, we are blessed with many extra "weapons" in our fight to replace our own human-ness with the more spiritual or Christ-driven attitudes and thinking patterns. Some people think of our use of sacramentals as "worshipping idols" and such, but that is because their true purpose is misunderstood. Simply, sacramentals are used as a prayer enhancer.

Sacred objects, art, pictures, and even jewelry are not used to replace the normal means of praying, but are used as an enhancement to those types of prayers. The rosary is loved by many Christians-not just Catholics-for its power to keep our minds honed in on Jesus and his life and the virtues of his Mother, Mary. The Rosary Prayer, which is based heavily in Scripture, reminds us of the life Jesus chose as our model and shows us how we can also best benefit spiritually from taking up our own crosses in life. The repeating of the Lord's Prayer, Hail Mary, and Gloria (Glory Be) prayers take dedication and concentration as we ponder the mysteries held therein. They are anything but an idle chanting of rote prayers.

Having beautiful religious pictures, crucifixes, and/or art objects displayed in our homes, offices, and vehicles is akin to the photos and artistic gifts made or given to us by our loved ones. We look at them and are reminded to reach for higher Christian ideals. Just as we are not worshipping our family and friends' photographs in our wallets or hanging on our walls, we are likewise not worshipping religious items we keep around. Both are simply reminders to give thanks, praise, and prayer for the blessings they bestow upon us daily.

Blessed oil, candles, salt, and oil also add to the spiritual nature of our routines and serve as key reminders that the Lord has blessed many common objects for us in his bounty, as do holy water and statues of the Blessed Mother and other holy men and women who've lived saintly lives. There is also a huge array of jewelry and medals that we can use as remembrances to walk with Jesus. All of these give us opportunities to say, "Hello and I love you" to God.

THE SEVEN SACRAMENTS SUCCULENT SMORGASBORD

BAPTISMAL DIP:

1/4 LB.	UNSALTED BUTTER
1	ONION, CHOPPED FINE
1/2 CUP	FLOUR
2	CLOVES GARLIC, MINCED
5	GREEN ONIONS, MINCED
1 PINT	HEAVY CREAM OR HALF AND HALF
1 LB.	LUMP CRABMEAT
	(OR DELI "KRABMEAT" SUBSTITUTE)
1	LARGE CAN ARTICHOKE HEARTS,
	DRAINED AND CHOPPED SMALL
1/4 CUP	WHITE WINE
	SALT, PEPPER, AND SPICES TO TASTE

- Melt the butter in a heavy saucepan, add onions and garlic and sauté for about five minutes. Gradually stir in the flour. Cook over low heat for about five more minutes. Add in green onions. Cook for two minutes more, stirring well. Add in heavy cream and stir until it thickens nicely. Add crabmeat, artichokes, wine, and spices. Cook for about ten minutes. Serve while hot with any type of cracker or scoop-type chips. Warning-addictive!

NOTE: You may substitute shrimp, crawfish, or other seafood for the crab.

Sin-No-More Antipasto Salad (Low Fat)

Dressing:

1/3 cup	high quality olive oil
3 tbs	white wine vinegar
1/8 tsp	pepper (I prefer white pepper)
1/4 tsp	dry mustard
	Dash of salt and garlic powder
	Dash of oregano (if you like)

SALAD:

Lettuce (torn to bite-size pieces) of your choice
Thinly sliced sweet red onion rings
Black and green olives, whole pitted
Artichoke hearts, halved and drained
Fresh garden tomatoes, quartered
Cucumbers, sliced thin
Avocados, sliced small
Eggs, hard-boiled and quartered
Low-fat summer meats (salami, ham, turkey or chicken breasts, etc.)
Low-fat white cheeses (provolone, swiss, parmesan, mozzarella, etc.)

- Mix all salad dressing ingredients together and refrigerate in a dressing bottle or cruet. Arrange vegetables in a large salad bowl. Pour dressing over and toss. Enjoy!

YUMMY EUCHARISTIC BEIGNETS

Beignet is the French word for fritters. They are a favorite food served for generations in Louisiana and are always appreciated at special occasions.

1 CUP	BOILING WATER
1 CUP	EVAPORATED MILK
1/4 CUP	VEGETABLE OIL
1 TBS	YEAST
2 TBS	WARM WATER (110 DEGREES)
1/2 CUP	SUGAR
2	EGGS
1 TSP	SALT
7 1/2 CUPS	ALL-PURPOSE FLOUR
	PEANUT OIL FOR DEEP FRYING
	POWDERED SUGAR

- Combine sugar, oil, and salt in a large bowl, and pour the boiling water over the mixture. Set aside and let cool. Add milk. Combine the yeast with the warm water and let foam for about ten to fifteen minutes. Combine yeast mixture with the milk mixture, add the eggs and mix together. Add half of the flour to the yeast mixture and beat until smooth. Add the remaining flour. Turn into a covered bowl. Refrigerate overnight.

- Punch down dough and roll out onto a floured surface. Roll into a rectangle about one-fourth inch thick. Work fast in order to keep dough from rising before frying! Cut beignets into 3 x 1 1/2-inch rectangles. Deep fry in peanut oil until golden brown on both sides. Beignets will float to top when cooked. Drain on paper towels and dust with a thick layer of powdered sugar. Serve with dark chicory coffee. Makes about sixty.

Peppy's "Go Get 'Em" Chicken Salad

6	BOILED CHICKEN BREASTS, CHOPPED INTO SMALL CHUNKS
1	BUNCH GREEN SEEDLESS GRAPES
1 CUP	SLICED, TOASTED ALMONDS, WALNUTS OR PECANS
1	CONTAINER COOL WHIP

- Combine ingredients together in a decorative bowl. Set platter beneath bowl and fill with fancy crackers. Once you taste this, it will become a favorite recipe to serve as it is-quick, easy, and deliciously light summer fare.

PASTOR'S SHRIMP AND CORN SOUP

This is a great recipe to make and share with church workers as it keeps well and gets more delicious as it is reheated over and over again.

1/4 CUP	FLOUR
1/4 CUP	OIL
1/2 CUP	FINELY CHOPPED ONION
1 1/2 CUPS	PEELED AND DEVEINED SHRIMP
1	CLOVE GARLIC, MINCED
1	10-OUNCE CAN RO-TEL TOMATOES (MASH WITH THE LIQUID)
1 TBS	MINCED PARSLEY OR DRIED
2	17-OUNCE CANS CREAM CORN
2	14-OUNCE CANS CHICKEN BROTH
	SALT AND PEPPER TO TASTE

- In a heavy pot, make a light roux using oil and flour. Add onion and shrimp and sauté lightly. Add garlic and stir well. Add tomatoes and cook over a medium-low heat. Add in broth and corn. Cook for ten minutes, stirring constantly. Season. Cook slowly for twenty or thirty minutes. During last five minutes of cooking, add parsley.

Serves eight.

Matrimonial Magic Lemon Pie

This is a favorite recipe of my grandmother's. Bigmama says that this pie is always requested for anniversary parties. She likes it because it is tart, sweet, easy, and quick to make!

1	CAN CONDENSED MILK
1	SMALL CAN FROZEN PINK LEMONADE
1	GRAHAM CRACKER PIE CRUST (READY-MADE)

- Mix together the lemonade and condensed milk until it is a smooth and creamy consistency. Spoon into the pie crust and spread evenly. Garnish with mint leaves or lemon zest.

Good for What Ails Ya Tater Casserole

This is also known as Mother's Famous Potatoes Divine and is brought to every family gathering and shared with friends who have lost a loved one. It is a great comfort food.

6	whole Irish potatoes
1	small bunch green onions, chopped
1	small container sour cream
3/4 cup	butter or margarine, softened
1 1/2 cups	cheese (any type), grated
	Salt and pepper to taste

- Boil potatoes with skins on. Remove just before they are tender and refrigerate overnight in a dry bowl.

- The next day, peel and finely grate the potatoes. Do NOT use a food processor, as you will end up with mush. Add to the potatoes green onions, sour cream, butter or margarine, and cheese. Salt and pepper to taste.

- Bake uncovered at 325 degrees for thirty-five to forty-five minutes until the top bubbles. Delicious!

At One with My Soul

~ Deb Anne Flynt ~

So softly he beckons to me,
Whispers to me with feathered voice
Come my love, and quietly
I will show your heart such joy!

Upon my hand, his touch a breeze,
A gentle wisp-gossamer kiss
I cannot escape, he leads my soul
In a dance through rainbow light

He speaks wisdom to me then bids me kneel
My heart would not, could she refuse
I breathlessly await him, my only desire
Our moment approaching, I close my eyes

His flesh is ever sweet to taste
He is delicate and pleasing to me
I close my eyes as my soul takes flight
The moment stays with me, though not our last
He is there, waiting-Holy Eucharist, my delight

ABOUT *the* AUTHORS

~ *Alaine Benard* ~

Alaine Benard is a freelance writer, author, and columnist from Baton Rouge, Louisiana. She is a regular editorial and feature writer for the website ADHD.com. Her column, ADHD: Soaring Above the Storms, has appeared in a variety of weekly papers, psychiatric newsletters, and parenting magazines. Her monthly newsletter, StormWatch (www.ADHDStormWatch.com), is gaining national attention and awards. Benard and her twin sister, Angie Ledbetter, write a weekly advice column, Pair O' Dice. Benard works with special needs children at St. Gerard Majella's dyslexic lab.

Benard has been published in Southern Renaissance, several Catholic and inspirational periodicals, Biker Lifestyles, and in numerous newspapers and websites. Her prose and award-winning poetry have been featured in the Literary Lion. Many of her stories can be seen in popular anthologies, including the Chicken Soup for the Soul series, Travelers' Prayers, 9/11: The Day America Cried, and Nudges from God. Her contributions have also been carried online in the National Association of Women Writers' newsletter and quarterly publications.

Benard is an artist and calligraphist, designing limited-edition prints and book cover graphics. She is currently shopping for a publisher for her ADHD anthology-a unique, positive look at these multi-gifted children.

She and husband Pete have a 12-year old son. "Turbo" is an honor roll student who enjoys reading, friends, pizza, wrestling, three-wheelers, and his rat terrier, Jinx. He is also a published author.

~ Deb Anne Flynt ~

Deb Anne Flynt is a freelance writer in Mississippi. Originally from New Albany, she lived in several towns and cities all over the state before finally settling near Columbia.

Flynt is the owner and moderator of several online groups, including, among others, a Christian writers' group and its affiliate for young Christian writers, and a prayer group. She is a moderator of Angie's Cajun Connection and a member of a few other groups.

During the course of four and a half years, Flynt studied at two small colleges and the University of Southern Mississippi before leaving with a degree in none of her twenty or so majors. She eventually decided on a career in writing after pursuing it as a hobby since childhood.

Flynt's work has been published in several newspapers and publications, and her columns have been carried in a western weekly and in monthly e-zines and weekly newspapers. She has also been published in several online publications. Flynt and her husband Gary have two children who are both avid readers and talented writers and artists.

~ Angie Ledbetter ~

Angie Ledbetter is the mother of three youngsters, stepmother of two grown kids, and grandmother ("Nana") of three. She has been married to her husband Dennis for seventeen years and resides in Baton Rouge, Louisiana. She owns a residential and commercial cleaning service. When not working or engaged in activities with her kids, Angie does ministry work in her church and community and is an involved Scouter.

Ledbetter holds a degree in journalism from Louisiana State University and has always loved the written word, reading, photography, and word games of all kinds. She is a member of several e-groups and is the founder of a faith-based online community called Cajun Connection. The website can be found at: www.geocities.com/thecajunconnection/index.html She is a moderator of Deb's WordWorkers, a Christian writers e-group, and the owner of the prayer warrior group Kids Krusade.

Ledbetter wrote and edited an inspirational column for an Idaho weekly newspaper and website as well as an inspirational/religious column for Christian Roads Online and Ascension Citizen Newspaper. She also writes a monthly column titled "Under the Umbrella" for the e-zine, ADHD: Soaring Above the Storms.

Ledbetter also authors Pair O' Dice, a joint venture advice and humor column, with twin sister, Alaine Benard. She is also the owner of Mustard Seeds, an inspirational/slice of life column.

Ledbetter is a member of the Louisiana Press Women, the National Federation of Press Women, and MomWriters.com and is a regional representative for the National Association of Women Writers (NAWW).

She has been published in newspapers, online publications, magazines and reviews books. Her work samples, awards, and writing information can be viewed at www.writersgumbo.com. Ledbetter is currently working on an inspirational book and a Christian romance and fiction novella.

~ Carol Schwartz ~

Carol Schwartz lives in Boise, Idaho. She writes contracts for the U.S. Department of Agriculture, serving Idaho National Forests of Boise, Sawtooth, Payette, and Humboldt-Toiyabe in Nevada and eastern California. A certified accountant, she designed, wrote, and taught a financial class for setting up small businesses at a California university, where she also taught several financial courses for nearly twenty years while concurrently writing contracts for the Navy.

Her work has been published in an Idaho weekly. Schwartz is a member of the Writing-World.com e-group, the National Association of Women Writers, the Idaho Press Women (an affiliate of the National Federation of Press Women), Catholic Writer's Association, and the WordWorkers e-group.

Schwartz moved to California in January 2003 from New Orleans, Louisiana, where she authorized construction contracts for the Army. She has a bachelor of science in business administration with dual majors in accounting and organizational behavior/change from the University of New Hampshire. She has a master's degree in public administration from California State University Bakersfield.

Schwartz has two sons and five grandchildren.

Printed in the United States
23452LVS00004B/1-39

9 780972 380669